CW01659102

FIELD WORK

Selected Essays

BY THE SAME AUTHOR

A Treasonable Growth
Immediate Possession
The Age of Illusion
William Hazlitt: Selected Writings
Akenfield
The View in Winter
Writing in a War
From the Headlands
The Stories of Ronald Blythe
Divine Landscapes
Private Words
Aldeburgh Anthology
Word From Wormingford
First Friends
Going to Meet George
Talking About John Clare
Out of the Valley
The Circling Year
Talking to the Neighbours
The Assassin
Borderland
A Writer's Day Book

FIELD WORK

Selected Essays

RONALD BLYTHE

Illustrations by
JOHN NASH

BLACK DOG BOOKS

First published in 2007
Black Dog Books,
104 Trinity Street, Norwich, Norfolk, NR2 2BJ.
www.blackdogbooks.co.uk

© Ronald Blythe
Illustrations © The Estate of John Nash

All rights reserved. No part of this publication may be reproduced, stored in a retrieval system,or transmitted in any form or by any means, electronic, mechanical, photocopying, recording or otherwise, without the prior permission of the copyright holders.

A CIP record of this book is available from the British Library.

ISBN 978-0-9549286-6-7

Typeset in Times.

Printed in Great Britain
by Biddles Ltd., *www.biddles.co.uk*.

In Memoriam

IMOGEN HOLST

ACKNOWLEDGEMENTS

I am most grateful to the following for their kind permission to publish essays in this collection:

Allen Lane:Viking, Penguin Books, Chatto & Windus:Random House, Aurum Press, The Boydell Press, Cresset Library, EP Publishing, Hamish Hamilton, The Hogarth Press, Long Barn Books, Oxford University Press, Trent Books, Harcourt Brace, Jovanovich:Canterbury Press, Horizon, The Independent on Sunday, The Sunday Times, The Times Literary Supplement, The Listener, The New York Times, The New Statesman, The Countryman, Church Times, Snape Foundation, Faber and Faber, Country Life, The Observer, The John Clare Society, The Thomas Hardy Society, The Kilvert Society, The Ivor Gurney Society, The Royal Society of Literature.

Ronald Blythe

CONTENTS

OUTPOSTS

CONFESSORS

INTRODUCTION

I see these essays as a lingering comment on my life as a writer. They form a continuous response to what has been important to me, East Anglia, literature, Anglicanism, and my artist and writer friends. They grew from the usual disciplined solitude which is the fate of most writers, although fate is rather an ungrateful word for what is more properly called a gift or even a trade. Not that I had any choice in the matter. Looking, listening, storytelling, dreaming – and toiling in the inescapable Suffolk manner, this is what happened – is happening. I am writing this just after somebody on the radio was mentioning the death of the essay as a literary form, which is strange as the air is filled with wonderful spoken essays every day. Vide Clive James. How else could I have dealt with the many subjects in this collection other than via 'the essay?' Long ago I remember being overwhelmed when I was asked to edit *William Hazlitt: Selected Writings* for Penguin Classics. An essay is something – some idea, some notion – which a writer tosses into the air and adds to as his fantasies and philosophies spin around it until it expands and becomes as complete in its way as a poem or a novel. Hazlitt was a pro at the Fives Court in St Martin's Lane, a master at keeping a ball in the air.

Re-reading these pieces which stretch across my lifetime, I recognise a little altered hand. I noted that I am rather un-decadal, rarely putting things into Sixties or Seventies slots, but seeing life as the old countrymen saw it, seasonally for the most part. Also having lived through the tail-end of the great agricultural depression and through the second agricultural revolution, and having been with people who were born in the nineteenth century as well as with those who were born during the 1980s onwards, I have never felt set in my ways but, as a writer, have shifted about interestedly in both the old and new times.

Similarly, friends and neighbours have been parochial – some with a vengeance – and outsiders. Those close to me when I was young included the artists John and Christine Nash, Sir Cedric Morris, Lett Haines and the writers James Turner, W. R. Rodgers and R. N. Currey. Those close to me now are James Hamilton-Paterson, Richard Mabey and Ian Collins.

For the most part travels were done on the hoof, and looking at what my friend Peter Tolhurst has chosen to put in this collection, I am amazed to discover so much walking. It may be a defensive apology for not being able to drive. But it has certainly contributed to what might be called the art of the essay. That's for certain. Walking also produces spaciousness and an eye for the wonders of minutiae, contemplation and surprises.

A wiry healthiness has made me think little about old age although I laid down the law about it when I was fifty in a book called *The View in Winter*. Having put old age in its place then, I haven't much thought about it since. Writers and artists have the inestimable blessing of not having to retire. Thus I continue to get up at six, winter and summer, read and read, write, walk, listen, watch and toil. Mostly by myself, continuing the process of what has occurred all through these pages.

Ronald Blythe
Bottengoms
August 2007

REMEDIAL SCENES

(From *Second Nature*, Jonathan Cape, 1984)

Does any doctor prescribe landscape nowadays? Until recently, for certain ailments of body and mind, tuberculosis or depression, it was all that could be prescribed. There are, wrote Richard Jefferies, 'three potent medicines of nature', the sea, the air and the sun. And he might have added the scenes which these elements both created and contain, for if anyone set out for a thorough, self-prescribed landscape cure, he did. A long time ago I read an essay of his called 'The Breeze on Beachy Head' and at once recognised in it a correct phrasing of what must be a common experience of perfect well-being. I am walking, climbing, or lying on grass, and not necessarily high up and filled with a great view, and suddenly all that I can see, hear and smell amalgamates and becomes a kind of landscape laser which passes right through me, healing me totally. Never having been ill, I must ask myself, of what? I suppose, in my case, of dullness, of that reduction of my senses brought on by not getting out. For Jefferies and all literary consumptives it was a very different matter, of course. They *had* to get out – doctor's orders! For a while the three potent medicines of sea, sun and air worked wonders, as a remarkable collection of poems and prose reveals. And then the healing had to stop. Some became reconciled to this fact; Jefferies did not. He turned on 'Nature' and said he hated it. Its indifference to whether he lived or died appalled him. Although what was really appalling him was that never again would there be such a fully alive day as that, for instance, which he spent on Beachy Head. 'Discover some excuse to be up there always ... go without any pretext ... it is the land of health.'

My initiatory heights of what we called 'High Suffolk' were little more than half a dozen steps upward in comparison with Beachy Head, but there the countryside would unroll, and any such tensions which I might be feeling with it. This release and revitalisation were not just the products of my native view, as I soon found out when I began to cycle further afield, or make long train journeys to Cornwall and Scotland. Or even, recently, when I walked the hilly outskirts of Sheffield. The landscape cure, originally discovered as a child in Suffolk, usually when I was sulkily in flight from the incessant tasks of goat-milking, brother-keeping, wood-chopping, errands to far-distant shops, etc. which hanging around the house entailed, worked anywhere. 'Where have you been?' they would ask, and I would give the classic answer, 'Out'. In the long run, perhaps, this could be the only answer to 'why does scenery do you good?' Because it takes you out of yourself into its out-ness. It can be a heady business, as Jefferies was to learn, but one which does not necessarily require a numinous vocabulary to describe it. Very much the reverse, in fact. I am transported by 'The Breeze on Beachy Head' because it is so brilliantly down to earth, and with not a yard of its natural geography smudged. Spray, jackdaws, brambles, plough-teams, the immense cliff, the liner *Orient*, Australia-bound, flaking chalk, bees on the furze are seen with intense clarity. It is an accurately recorded view which always reminds me of an incident in the life of the Victorian photographer P. H. Emerson, when the poverty-stricken Norfolk labourers saw their wetlands landscape miniaturised in a camera lens for the first time and were amazed that this beautiful place was just their poor old marsh!

High Suffolk was often similarly perplexing. Distant flint towers gave nothing away about the villages which they marked and the widely stretching scene was, for a boy, too broad to be local. And so the curative properties of landscape must have something to do with travel, and thus exertion. But I would personally put these things low on the list, for what toned me up all those years ago ('You need toning up,' my aunts would advise), tones me up still, and I need only to stare from the window to the steep Stour-side fields to set this desirable process in motion. Never having needed to test the healing quality of these familiar East Anglian scenes against disease, I can only say what they have done for me in terms of stimulus, hedonism and imagination, and while it isn't everything, it is a great deal. As landscape is the source of poetry's main imagery, as well as the limits of an individual's private association with a place, and a perpetual scientific delight, not to mention a larder, it is hardly surprising that it should frequently drug us – always, so far as I am concerned, for the best.

I realise now that my first scenery-seekings were deliberate excursions to find the drug. What I liked, and still like, is the way in which the panorama dominates me. The land is all view and I am all viewer, and soon the ecological patterns and colours not only spread before me but permeate me, and I become part of what I am seeing. I can see patches of medieval forest here and there among the corn, and although I know that 'the woods decay and fall', I also know that in comparison with human flesh they take ages to do so. Thus its ancientness must be one of the healing factors of landscape. High Suffolk tells me that the foundations of my view were laid in the Ice Age, and the shape of almost everything which covers its surface was fashioned centuries ago. But simultaneously with its antiquity it presents its very latest seasonal crop of flowers, birds, insects and sounds. And so I too, wandering on to Monks Eleigh, always have a nice sense of just being born and everything before me. Landscape certainly provides most of us with a lift and although I know it won't keep me buoyant for ever, or maybe for very much longer, I shall go on absorbing all I can of it. When you think of the world's literature, what other cure-all (or at least make it possible to endure-all) medicine has received such thankful testimonials?

Once landscape had to be 'taken' quite literally as medicine. Both doctor and patient accepted that it was a gamble to go off in search of beneficial air or a change of surroundings, and it was a poignant moment when the sick in body or mind set off for the prescribed spring or climate: Naaman testily to a foreign holy river, the medieval hordes to their shrines and John Keats to the Mediterranean. And then there were those like the exiles in Robert Frost's poem 'New Hampshire' who knew that they would never get better until they got home –

I met a Californian who would
Talk California – a state so blessed
He said, in climate, none had ever died there
A natural death.

From Eden on we have been convinced that our Earth has a stratum of health running right through it, and that there are salubrious geographical spots where this healthiness can be tapped. Or so it was until yesterday and the dawn of antibiotics. One consulted the physician and he consulted the map. It did not necessarily mean going off into the wilds. Illness often demands good company, and the lady in Henry James's novel was right – 'She was all for scenery – yes, but she wanted it human and personal, and all she could say was that there would be more in London – wouldn't there? More of that kind than anywhere else?'

The history of the use of landscape and its elements as a cure is a mainly social history. One gets the recluses and the solitary searchers for healing, but the main pattern is of those in trouble following where those in trouble went before. Medicine, even landscape-medicine, has always been the practice of fairly rigid rules. Thus a scattering of attested health centres developed and were called 'resorts' because the sick and old and worried resorted to them, either for curative air or water, or for the re-creational activities which they offered. Anne Bronte resorted to Scarborough, not in any expectation of a cure but in all probability to save her poor father from seeing his third child in less than a year die in the house. Her illness, tuberculosis, right up until the last war, involved more people in landscape as a regime than any other, and her almost hour by hour account of her own illness gives an exact description of what must have happened to countless other men and women — and children – for whom the resort was the last resort.

Branwell, 't' Vicar's Pat', had died in September 1848. Three years before he had written a curious landscape poem entitled 'The Emigrant' in which he compares waking up on an Australia-bound ship, which is still in sight of the blue hills of England of which he has taken sad leave, to a loved one's voice distracting the journey which a dying man needs to make from time to eternity. Branwell signed his poem 'Northangerland'. No sooner was he in his grave, which was just a few yards from the parsonage, than the health of Emily and Anne began to decline with devastating speed. Emily, typically, refused to do a thing about it and, three months later, died lying on the downstairs sofa, sewing, and dressed as for an ordinary day. It was dreadfully cold and the moor winds filled the house the moment a door was opened. She had what was then called 'galloping consumption', a disease which made it pointless for her to take any notice of what was passing. Charlotte attempted to slow down the pace with books and love and flowers from the hillside, but it was all no use. Emily's last words were, 'No, no!' to attempts to get her to bed. A fortnight later, Dr Teale, a Leeds specialist, examined Anne, who immediately dealt with her shock in a poem, 'A dreadful darkness closes in/On my bewildered mind', although, unlike her sister, she had no intention of letting the consumption gallop off with her if she could prevent it. She did everything the doctor told her to, and this, of course, included seeking sea air. She also had a private reason for going to Scarborough, which was to spare Haworth a further association with death. Hers might be said to have been the classic death via landscape route, and one taken, in particular, by countless T. B. sufferers, before the advent of modern medicine. Anne Bronte decided to die in a boarding house, rather than a lodging house, because it would be livelier. She left home on 24 May, 1849 and died four days later. It was glorious spring weather and she behaved as though she were on holiday, sightseeing in York en route, buying clothes, hungrily taking in all the scenery she could on the hour's train journey from York to Scarborough, driving herself up and down the sands in a donkey-cart when she arrived there, appearing to be very happy, insisting on her companions, Charlotte and Ellen Nussey, seeing the elegant new spa saloon. On Monday morning Charlotte found her standing uncertainly at the top of the boarding house stairs, unable to descend them, and drew her back into their shared bedroom. Anne sat in the window while the doctor told her that she was about to die. After they had buried her within full view of the sea, Charlotte did not hurry back home to Haworth but drifted slowly through the countryside for a month, taking in Filey and Bridlington – and the enormity of her position. When at last she did reach the parsonage, she closed its doors on all that lay outside and used the writing of *Shirley*, the novel which three deaths had interrupted, as a therapy to help her come to terms with what had happened.

As the nineteenth century wore on, and indeed right up unto the 1930s, the custom of prescribing places for various illnesses intensified. The tubercular rich thronged the Mediterranean and the Alps, and the tubercular poor East Anglian sanitoria, where I often saw them lying outside in pram-beds in all weathers, sometimes with snow covering the mackintosh aprons which kept the blankets dry. Sea trips were also recommended and by the 1920s no great liner set sail without its quota of convalescents and the spiritually low. Much of the action in the novels and drama of the period is geared to the convention of people having to go somewhere special to get better, and much of the mood of this literature is created by a writer being able to invent a sick man's view of the world. But there were, of course, non-invented sick men's views of a natural scene dearly loved, and all the more so because it was fleeting. Bruce Cummings ('Barbellion'), a brilliant young naturalist who died in 1917 when he was in his late twenties, from disseminated sclerosis, wanted to 'swallow landscapes and swill down sunsets, or grapple the whole earth to me with ropes of steel', and in his *Journal of a Disappointed Man* the reader is made to watch the landscape of southern England being prised from him. Talking of London, he said, 'I live in a bigger, dirtier city – ill-health', and it was because of this that he constantly plunged himself into a cleansing countryside.

It was fine to walk over the elastic turf with the wind bellowing into each ear and swirling all around me in a mighty sea of air until I was as clean-blown and resonant as a sea-shell. I moved along as easily as a disembodied spirit and felt free, almost transparent. The old earth seemed to have soaked me up into itself, I became dissolved into it, my separate body was melted away from me, and Nature received me into her deepest communion – until, UNTIL I got back on the lee side of the hedge where the calm brought me back my gaol of clay.'

That we should not resort to the earth's scenes for comfort, if not a cure, when our own clay begins to crack or warp is foolish, for as Wallace Stevens says, 'Our nature is her nature,' a concept he must have got from Pope, who was acknowledging holism as long ago as the 1730s when, in his *Essay on Man*, he states, 'All are but parts of one stupendous whole,/Whose body Nature is'. But it is easier to be poetic than scientific about what exactly takes place. The actual exercise of a long walk will be beneficial and yet, frequently we know for certain that it is more than just this which has revived us, killed a pain, healed us without a fuss. The land itself seems to have laid its hand on us. Dr Johnson, that very sick man, to whom Hawkstone had offered 'a kind of turbulent pleasure, between fright and admiration', was so put to rights by his long trek through the Highlands that no sooner had he got home to London than he had to set out straight for Wales, saying, 'The longer I walk, the less I feel its inconvenience – as I grow warm, my breath mends, and I think my limbs grow pliable.' Goldsmith told young Boswell (aged 33) that the Doctor (aged 64) would be a dead weight for him to carry all the way to the Hebrides, and when Voltaire heard of the plan, Boswell said, 'He looked at me as if I talked of going to the North Pole,' but go they did and that great travel book is nothing less than a learned testimonial to the curative properties of a superb landscape. Johnson was indifferent to weather. He refused to believe that it was the sun which made one of Boswell's friends reluctant to return from Spain to England and insisted that it must be a woman.

For centuries healing was most sought after in water, spasmodically recognised as emanating from the sun, and vaguely discovered in a change of air. But those in search of health rarely attempted to find it by some kind of deliberate intake of scenery alone. When the latter did improve the spirits, and subsequently the flesh, as the sick travelled to distant wells and better climates, few seemed to realise it. Yet the beneficial effect of a variety of landscapes on pilgrim and patient alike must have been enormous, and often those who thankfully attributed their cures to certain springs and wells would have been on the road to recovery long before they drank from or bathed in them. Exercise and that most exquisite (and taken for granted) of pleasures, of having a rich sequence of near and distant hills, fields, woods, skies, buildings and landscape features of every hue and form fed through one's heart and mind, as it were, day after day as the journey progressed, had performed the miracle.

But holy water is not to be dismissed. To our ancestors, local water had something of the same reputation and distinction as local wines have for us. Among the countless sources of domestic water all over Britain there were found to be a great many springs and wells containing waters which did wonders for aches and pains and skin diseases: chalybeate (iron), sulphurous, lime, thermal, soda- and other mineral-filled special waters, most of which had long been placed under the protection of saints. Seeking cures from sun and air was altogether more problematical, and their recent elevation, really from the late eighteenth century onwards, as health-givers owes as much to romanticism as to science. When the Shah of Persia was visiting Edinburgh during the mid-eighteenth century, a Presbyterian lady accused him of worshipping the sun. 'So would you, Madam,' he said, 'if you had ever seen it.'

What we appear to demand of landscape in health-giving terms is something to soothe us at home and to stimulate us abroad. Take the remarks of two explorers, Fridtjof Nansen and Quentin Crewe, one on his way to an ice barrenness, the other on his return from a sand barrenness. Nansen, leaving his beloved Norway for the polar regions, wrote in his journal, 'You may shrug your shoulders as much as you like at the beauties of nature, but it is a fine thing for a people to have a fair land.' And Crewe, returning to England after crossing the Sahara, and asked what the huge desert had done to him, replied, 'It refreshed me.'

The word once most used medicinally about landscape was 'salubrious', or favourable to health, and it was generally affixed to some resort. Doctors need no longer pack us off to these watering-places but it wouldn't at all be a bad idea if they recommended more of us to sit on Pendle, walk along the Suffolk coast for a week, or give ourselves up to the Dee Valley for a fortnight, etc. Not for a holiday, but for a cure.

The Writer At Home

A JOURNEY ROUND MY FARMHOUSE

(*The Tablet*, 17th September, 1994)

Looking back on my life, I recognise that I am a long stayer, 20 years here, 20 years there. And never more than 30 miles or so between places. These have been unconsciously annexed to form a single personal world which, again retrospectively, has been created as much by the actual task of writing as by what my books contain.

My most influential long-stay landscape was that which made a triangle between the little Suffolk towns of Woodbridge, Wickham Market and Framlingham, each roughly equidistant from the others. I was contained rather like a villager from the past within these few miles because I did not drive. They were as far as I could walk or bicycle and in two decades there seemed to be nothing which they contained which I had not absorbed. I felt I knew them from the green surface down to their neolithic roots.

Their limitations were for me their limitlessness. The little farmhouse in which I lived itself challenged the imagination to let rip, at least from the front, where it stared into a great hedge with massive absence of charm. In the winter, when the solid clay which stretched narrowly between the house and the still straight-as-a-die Roman road could not take further rain, a shallow lake appeared between my walls and what was left of the camber.

But the rear of the house – this was another story. There was a cattle-moat, half a dozen neglected pastures of superlative beauty, tall elms and blackberry mountains, and one of those rides in which Mr Knightley or Mr Rochester, or at least Mr de Winter, should have been seen. These lovely rough meadows and enormous trees were the way to Dallinghoo Weald, an infertile region which in those days produced meagre corn and sugar beet, and all kinds of treasures such as clay pipes, fossils, Victorian buttons, fragments of pottery, glass and iron, and sometimes an old penny or two. It was only explained to me much later how town refuse was carted to the fields and spread as manure, hence these artefacts. Arthur Young, the Suffolk agricultural historian, mentions bones from London's bursting churchyards being carted to Hertfordshire farms and ground-up to make a nice calcium dressing.

My house was rented from an old brother and sister who had come to farm in Suffolk just after the First World War when farms were given away. They had struggled through the lean years and had emerged into affluence, the government having compensated them for using their acres as a bomber base. I delighted in walking the vast runways. Old aerodromes are lark-ridden, their wide skies all song. Cautious scraps of wartime goings-on would be doled out to me by the neighbours as though I was far too fresh on the scene to deserve the whole story.

I did hear that at that time half my ancient house was ruinous and lived in by a donkey, and that the other half made a tumbledown shelter for Americans and girls. My landlord had spent some of his compensation doing it up. Making a kitchen garden, I began to unearth rusty instruments and thin sheets of metal covered with letters and figures. How could the neighbours explain these? They glanced at each other with a 'shall we tell him?' A Spitfire had crashed in the elms, killing the pilot. And now for the real horror. He was only wearing pyjamas under his flying-suit. Well, the madness of war. The runways petered-out to where the Romans had built a bastion, and where the Christians had turned it into a church. The scene was intensely clear yet for me secretive and full of stories.

My farmer-landlord and his ancient sister were caught between the stinginess of a lifetime and their new money. They bought race-horses and waited anxiously for my small rent cheque. I lent them 'something to read' but should it contain the least impropriety I was in for trouble. I once saw them on a September afternoon steering their Jaguar across the peerless pastures at two miles an hour, and stopping here and there to gather blackberries, the whole thing like a dream. They were kind to me and I was ill at ease with them. They were frightened of thunderstorms and would telephone me at midnight to ask if I was all right – meaning that they were not, and could I come across? Bicycling back from Framlingham one black evening I saw lightning strike an oak and the entire tree reach heavenwards in a streak of flame. But I was careful not to tell them.

Framlingham was where Mary Tudor heard that Jane Grey had usurped her throne. On the way there I would sometimes call on the direct descendant of Lady Jane's brother. She was Lady Jane Turnbull, a clergyman's widow. We shared a below-the-surface-of-things knowledge of Suffolk. She and her little house were faded to a delicate colourlessness, into aquatints. The house smelled of beeswax and austerity. George Herbert would have found himself comfortable in it.

Also en route to Framlingham was Hoo, a calm plateau of a village where there was a church of such rough simplicity that it might have been put together by medieval peasants during the slack days between harvests and Christmases. As a Reader in the Church of England, I sometimes took Evensong in it, helped by the octagenarian farmworker ravished by Scripture, and who would pause during the lesson with a, 'That was very foine; I'll read that again'. He was giving God, not himself, an encore. Like so many dear friends from that scrap of Suffolk, he lies under the cow-mumble. His wife used to say, 'Come again, but not too soon', and pass me new-laid eggs over the hedge.

Hoo stares across at Framlingham and its curtain-walled castle. Just beyond it lies Dennington, Chaucer's ancestral home. What continues to enchant me about the whole area is its reticence. By being so much on my own there during the Sixties I was vulnerable to its simplicity. A cats-cradle of tracks and lanes provided that adventurous element which true travel has to have, and which rarely failed to lead to a story or a poem. On the debit side harsh and violent mistakes were being made to some of the agriculture in the pursuit of broad, clean wheat belts, errors since then recognised and to some degree rectified. When an ancient farm at Monewden was protected from chemicals and other modern techniques because of its undisturbed ecology, I joined forces with those who spoke out against this kind of 'museum' solution to 'progress'. We did not accept that patches of the countryside could be preserved in this way while elsewhere spraying was given full rein.

Each of the roads leading to the three towns had something powerful and haunting to show me. In a copse on the way to Wickham Market stood the Georgian gibbet on which a young man had been hanged for murder. A rusty rail and a host of conifers protected it. On the road banks nearby there was a handsome parade of mullein and now and then gypsies. The spiky yellow plants and the dark people could have shared the patch for generations, could have been there during the uproar of a rural execution. The spot would come to mind when I was working on the New Wessex edition of Hardy.

But it was the road to Woodbridge which offered my favourite diversion, for there under a line from the *Jubilate* ('It is He that hath made us, and not we Ourselves') and a rose from the tomb of Omar lay Edward FitzGerald in Boulge churchyard. The rose-seed had been brought back from Persia during the 1890s, when FitzGerald's rendering into English verse of *The Rubáiyát of Omar Khayyam* was all the rage, and propagated at Kew, and the bush planted on Fitz's grave by the jolly Omar Khayyam Society. There it was constantly nipped in the bud by souvenir seekers, and it certainly failed to 'blow'. The late Shah, hearing of this, sent a dozen new rose trees from Iran and the rector, Mr Braybrook, was informed that the ambassador himself would drive to us to plant them. It was a gloomy day with a power cut and we waited all the afternoon in the famously gloomy church for our distinguished visitor whilst Mr Borrett the organist ran out of Introits. The Shah's emissary had been tempted to have a good lunch at Newmarket, and when at last he appeared, to find that we ourselves had heeled in the roses, he was amazed. Only two hours late, he expostulated – 'You English are so punctual!'

FitzGerald had walked everywhere I was then walking, and countless times. As well as the Shah's roses, there were marguerites and quaking-grass surrounding his grave. He used to protest at the 'petty squires' who destroyed trees. So nothing is new. And nothing at all in this old country which I seem to have dreamed and worked over, yard by yard.

ROADS TO DEBACH

(*From the Headlands*, Chatto & Windus, 1982)

Living at the conjunction of the Suffolk light and heavy lands gives everything an extra edge. To the north-west stretches 'the old clay' itself life-providing and death-reminding. To the south-east lie the sandlings and the sea. The soils do not mix to form some kind of moderate intermediate territory but remain sharply defined. It is one land or the other. You know where you are. What you can do is to journey to what is virtually another country in thirty minutes. In this brief time every ecological thing changes, oak to pine, hawthorn to broom, arable to marsh, hills to flats. The sandlings are a subtle shading-off of all that is emphatic in landscape, a series of earth and water abstractions which, just beyond those walled villages which border The Wash, reach some ultimate of geographical indefinition.

The old clay, on the other hand, never ceases to shout its hard-line reality. It is the ancient forest bed over whose bumpy surface the first ploughs rode after the defeat of the trees. The farms were once locked in scrubby woods or approached through glades; now they lie exposed for miles. To confound matters further, since the 1920s the Forestry Commission has roofed in huge tracts of the old open country with conifers, so that acres of the sandlings have lost their wild candour and have grown dark and secretive.

Mercifully the Suffolk and Norfolk heaths are still such a complex mixture of social and physical forces that the larch and pine regiments will never be able to march all over them. So one can relax in the sand gardens of Snape and feel comparatively safe. And even pit-props must hesitate when they come up against the peach orchards of Iken. But the marvellous Breckland can never be the same again, and it is moving to recall that East Anglia's unique moor survived unchanged and unchecked from prehistoric days to just after the First World War. An order nominating a similarly ancient landscape all along the Suffolk coast arrived just in time a decade or so ago to save the sandlings from such a fate. Science farming, block afforestation, NATO installations and now a proposed second nuclear reactor at lonely Sizewell, like the hosts of Gideon, are on the prowl all the same.

Winter reveals vivid contrasts between the water patterns of the two lands. On the sandlings they are anarchic, spilling over for miles beyond the estuarial limits and flooding the shallow valleys of the Stour, Orwell, Deben, Alde and Blyth. Thin bright lakes spread themselves with colourless deliberation round the traditional defences. On the heavy land the water is disciplined by medieval utility measures. Few in these days of mains could guess at the number of splendid moats, wells and ponds which still exist in fine working order the county over. There is not a hamlet which cannot boast something extraordinary by way of catchment. Such a variety of quiet, trapped waters, few of them to be seen until one has almost tumbled into them, has multiplied the mallard population. The field ditches alone still remain workaday, churning incredible amounts of Tiber-yellow liquid along icy cuts a few feet below the corn. The sound of all this half-hidden water is the voice of our arable winter. No babbling brook but 'a cry of Absence, Absence, in the heart, and in the wood the furious winter blowing...' Except that in East Anglia the blowing tends to arrive with the spring. It is no wonder that the oldest man-made structure in Suffolk – according to M. R. James – is a wind shelter near Ipswich. Who could argue this?

One road from my house near Woodbridge begins with surprisingly Persian references. It is the land which Edward FitzGerald walked every time he went to sea, which was as often as he could. It drifts along pleasantly past his family's Home Farm, their park, their coverts and past the poet's grave, which is lush in summer with quaking grass, ox-eyed daisies and the roses which the late Shah sent all the way from Omar's tomb. Past too, on the left, the rectory once inhabited by George Crabbe's son and the path which Fitz took many an evening to smoke a pipe with him. And so, in a matter of four miles, one encompasses Suffolk: the Plain Facts and Suffolk: the Transcendental. Then comes the Deben and a quite different climate.

Sparseness, freedom, the view running away to the palest of land markings and then into the illimitable. To the south a few small humps can be seen. These are Sutton Hoo, the graveyard of the Anglo-Saxon kings. This is where they pulled their funeral ships out of the river and buried them shallowly among the faint evidence of an Iron Age settlement. Domestic hearths and princely ashes. The hole left by that tremendous haul of gold and garnets, harp, mystic standard and banqueting silver is now the merest ghost of a boat and could be taken for a gravel scratching. But for years after it had been archeologically looted it held the full imprint of sand prow, sand ribs, sand keel and a profound impression of its sandy destination.

Arrow-straight roads lead to the sea from here. In summer the unhedged fields dry to dust and drift across the lanes. In January their sheer featurelessness establishes a great calm. Here is a country which specialises in renewal; there is space in it for action. Anyway, it is far too cold to sit about. Old Suffolk people say 'I fare to be all right if I keep on the goo.' Soon the North Sea strikes across our consciousness from just below a natural flint barrier called Shingle Street. It is intriguing to come to Shingle Street in the hot weather and to find it apparently deserted, and then to plunge along this huge shifting stone wall and stare down on the holiday-makers, each bare shape fitted into its flint matrix and each face turned to the horizon and the precise departures of the Harwich-Hook line.

Stones in such quantities and diversity are mesmerising. The sea-pea which so curiously thrives on them is said to have saved the local people from starvation during a famine long ago. They pay it respect. Apart from the beautiful grey-stemmed sea-poppy, the most delightful flower on this spartan coast is the rare *Vicia lutea*, the vetch whose pale yellow petals light the beach just where it begins to gather soil. Bracken and wild mignonette spread along the sea path. Marsh harriers and gulls swoop across military litter left over from old scares, Martello towers and concrete machine-gun nests. FitzGerald liked to hug his boat, the *Scandal*, along the shore here and was certainly happier than he has since been imagined. But another poet, Alun Lewis, stationed here during the last war, found its bleakness more than he could bear:

> From Orford Ness to Shingle Street
> The grey disturbance lifts its head
> And one by one, reluctantly,
> The living come back slowly from the dead.

There is another subtly indefinite area of Suffolk which I sporadically attempt to explore, and this is the one which lurks among the more comprehensible wonders of the famous local architecture. Not perp and dec but the all but rubbed from history creatures, human and divine which they housed. A holy romance world, in its way, in which Felix, Gobban, Dicuil, Fursey, Foillan, Mindred (whose well at Newmarket is now in the possession of the Jockey Club), the Pied, White, Grey and Black friars, Tobias, Sir John Shorne (a medieval Dr Scholl who conjured the devil from a boot), Edmund, of course, Apollonia, cherubyn, sarafyn, potestate, principatus, Michael Arkeangelus *et al*, still faintly crowd. And a prevalence of painted St Christophers on north walls, with carp and pike gliding around their naked legs, could indicate that wateriness was a common feature met with by generations of travellers crossing England's driest county.

GUMA'S VALLEY

(*Places: An Anthology of Britain,* O.U.P., 1981)

I was about to begin, 'I remember my first sight of this remote old house', only to realize that I do not. It is a wholly unexpected realization. Does it mean that, from now on, I must assume some loss of recall of what happened at the beginning of things, and that I could be one of those people who fail to stock up naturally with initial impressions, whether of places or people? The notion that my brain doesn't start its docketing processes until the importance and necessity of someone or something in my life has been confirmed by subsequent encounters, is a novel one. But a few tests prove the opposite, and so it is just this farmhouse. There was a day when I first saw it, but the day has got lost and since diary-keeping has always been a stop-go affair with me, and those who lived here then had no reason at that time to put me in their journals, no words exist to jog my memory. It would have been summer, certainly, which may be why, even in bare and open January, the site for me retains an all-the-year-round seclusion and density. I never so much as come back from a walk without feeling that I have to break my way into it, although winding grassy paths give access in all directions.

My old friends John and Christine Nash bought it for a few hundred pounds in the middle of the last war. It was quite in character that although he was busy in the Marines and she working endless hours at different ports, there should run parallel the dominant peace-time obsessions of a home from which one need never walk more than half a mile to find plenty to draw and paint, and a garden in which there was a soil for all seasons. They'd actually had their eye on it for a decade or more before they took the plunge and took it off Mr Lewis's hands, as they said. He must have given one of those great heartfelt sighs of agricultural relief, for it had been empty for years and was rapidly becoming, in the way of ancient dwellings of its kind, all of a hummocky, bosky piece with its grounds. Nettles (which always grow at their mightiest best where men have lived for generations) grew all around it by the acre, and fruit trees had impacted themselves with the architecture, so that here and there one could reach up in a room and pick Blenheim Oranges or elderberries. And just as there were boughs trying to get indoors, so there were writhing hanks of convolvulus doing their best to get out. After all these years one still finds a few inches of it curling from the crevasses in the scrubbed floor where the patterns created by moist clay set out to dry on Stuart or Georgian grass show up vividly after a dose of Flash. Brick-floor scrubbing is, of course, a lost art – and a well-lost art at that, most will say. But the colour it brought to the interiors of all sorts of buildings, churches, inns, farms, and cottages, used to be an important element in their aesthetic. The brick floors in this house don't stay wet and brightly coloured for more than an hour or two. One has hardly had time to put the rugs back before the little flattened shapes of plants of centuries ago vanish from their fast-drying surfaces and they take on their parched, anhydrous look, clinking silverly where they are loose. When John and Christine took the house on (I use this phrase judiciously, for its ownership involves one in a running battle of wills between occupier and half a millennium of local building materials) the stream actually ran straight through it, like the stream in Wordsworth's Dove Cottage. It is a few yards to the north of the garden now, I'm relieved to say, but still part of the watery network which culminates in the slow-flowing Stour, Gainshorough's and Constable's river only a mile or two off. At certain moments when the light is caught, this famous river, one of whose little arteries enticed a Saxon farmer to chance his luck in this spot, glitters and winks against the windows, and the sound of the stream running to it never ceases. Neither ice nor drought has ever silenced it.

Although the house had suffered some of the typical vicissitudes of the agricultural depression, having its hundred or so acres annexed by a neighbouring farm, coming down in the world from yeoman independence to squire's tenantry and even to becoming a double-dweller for farm-workers, and ultimately to years of emptiness, it had never been entirely abandoned, for I recently discovered the following pencilled on the inside of a 'Tenner' cigarette-box which had been carefully placed on a ledge under the stairs: 'Feb 19th 1937 painted outside of this House and Distempered inside. H. W. Spooner and H. Welford. NAYLAND & Boxted.' The box also contained a nail and a hazel-nut. But the abandonment of its ancient roadway, barns, piggery and stackyard was another matter. There had been no attempt to keep these in some ticking-over order, and from being the means of access and operation of the place, they had, with astonishing swiftness, reversed their roles and become the chief threat to its future habitation. There is almost no more daunting ruin than a ruined farm, or a more unappealing one. The merciful thing was that neither John nor Christine would have seen the place in such terms. Its past and future laid lightly on their conscience and imagination. They simply had an exciting hunch of the uses it could be put to *now*, even in the middle of a war, and in this respect they were like that great seventeenth-century gardener John Tradescant who, while fighting in a battle, was observed botanizing during the carnage, bending down among the swords and blood and digging up interesting specimens. And so they spent the latter part of their work-filled lives here, and myself the first part of mine. These years running away from and towards the centre have passed slowly and thoroughly, leaving parallel but differing impressions. For quite a long time after their deaths I felt it a compulsion and a duty to let things run on in the way they always had, and which they could have done, because strong personalities and well-regulated lives leave behind them rhythms and patterns which have learnt how to repeat themselves long after those who originally set them in motion have departed, but one morning this need simply wasn't there. It had evaporated, had been overcome like the hoar-frost hanging around in the frost-pocket by the bay-tree when the sun burst in on it.

It is always a problem to know what to do in a landscape where others have done so much. Do nothing, could be the answer. It is finished, so contemplate on what is. But gardens and antiquated water supplies, and banks and medieval tracks, not to mention the view itself, partly exist to keep one on the go, physically and intellectually, and the mere maintenance of what 'is' subtly turns it into what you would like it to be. I doubt if one could so much as weed a bed without leaving one's own creative mark. Not that such minimal activity would have done for Bottengoms, or Guma's Valley, where I have an increasing sense of its inhabitants being kept well on the go for centuries. A closer stare at its situation tells me that the farm crouches sideways in a valley which is in a valley, that ages ago the people who worked here dug out a shallow recess in the western hill so that they could dwell in a high-rimmed saucer lowered into the natural declivity. And more digging on an heroic scale must have gone on between the front garden and the first of the front fields, where one side of the ditch is as steep as a defensive earthwork. The up-hill, down-dale of it all makes it laborious still. Nowhere can one see everything at once; it is all vistas within vistas and, from less than a mile off, even these interlocking definitions vanish and last winter, plunging back from the village along the field ridges where the snow was thinnest, I found to my amazement that Guma's half-dug, half-natural valley had utterly disappeared in a white-out and that a compass wouldn't have come amiss. On that icy day I understood an important aspect of the farm's siting where John was concerned, how its landscape was both domestic ('Back to the old homestead!' he would say as his little car, crammed with drawing-boards, bottles of milk, fishing-tackle, plants, and plenty of rubbish, jogged down the track) and dramatic. How its solid 'peace', as the visitors invariably describe its atmosphere, is for its residents shot through and fractured by sharp little threatenings which you can't actually put your finger on but which keep you on your toes. Low-lying places are supposed to be soporific but this sunken house isn't. Cunningly masked by an extravagant display of calm, it has its own uneasy system of alerts to raise the adrenalin.

It could be the valley's objection to the hubris which has unconsciously beset its most recent occupancy. All this painting and writing, it is saying, what does it amount to in my time-scale? Forty years of art as against possibly fourteen hundred years of ploughing, of centuries of feeding off those slopes which provide only your views. Even in your present house, the valley insists, men and women have been looking out of the windows since the Tudors, and seeing much the same folds and clefts in the soil, and their accompanying skies, and it is likely that not a fraction of what you say you see so much as crossed their minds. Rooms, grounds, the stream, the track, how can they be expected to run without protest to these come-lately rhythms after running for such ages in time with the great drudge of the seasons.

There scarcely exists so much as a pencil scrawl of the house itself by John. Every kind of oil, water-colour, drawing, and woodcut of everything spread out around it, of course, but not of the building itself. Its purpose for him was to be able to work away inside it at what he could see from it. Like the subjects people never mention, there is a special eloquence about this deliberate omission. What was it about the house that forbade him putting it into the picture? The barns, yes (the last tumbledown skeleton of which is being battered into the earth by tractors as I write), the basic lines of Guma's land certainly, for such patterns provided him with a kind of ultimate poetry; every tree, every cutting and, if he could have had his way, every flower, but not the old homestead, a phrase often said in a tone of cagey mockery.

It is a beautiful house, powerful, confident. It is a typical East Anglian long house which likes you to think that it is younger than it is and no more than three or four hundred, but tucked away under its artful bodging lurks its true antiquity. But it follows the traditional style of a huge rectangular oaken frame set on brick sills, and with the interstices of its half-timbering (halved or cut wood, as opposed to unshaped logs) stuffed tight with wattle screens plastered with earth. The roof is its crowning glory without a doubt. Originally thatched and dizzily steep, it has since the eighteenth century boasted one of the most generous tile slopes in the neighbourhood, for after the addition of the Georgian dairy and store-rooms its descent was carried to within four feet of the garden. These lovely hand-made tiles in their many thousands, and some still pinned to the battens with delicately whittled hawthorn pegs, do not descend with a sheer, hard linear force, but with a slightly dipping, skirt-spreading concavity which is so gentle that one doesn't notice at first that there is such a lovely tilting check in their rush towards the grass. The rooms ramble into each other with a not so much as 'by your leave' and have never heard of anything as discreet as a corridor. Here and there are fragments of generations of partitioning, shoved up and pulled down as many now unknowable births and deaths required. In the roof itself, and quite windowless, but still white- and blue-washed, are a lot of little rooms which can only be reached by ladders, and which could have been the bothy, or the unmarried labourers' quarters. Straw pallets, snow on their faces, and mouse fidgetings. Downstairs the vast open hearths still hide behind a Victorian grate and an oil-fired Rayburn respectively. The latter is very near to being the house-god, so comfort-and pleasure-giving is it. William Barnes once wrote a furious and despairing poem about the usurpation of the ancient hearths by the Rayburn's nineteenth-century ancestors.

The garden surges urgently against the walls and has to be beaten back. In summer the south wall completely vanishes behind a thirty-foot vine in which birds sleep in their scores. One hears their weary flittering and cheeping just behind the bedhead, and when there is a strong wind, the scrunch of vine boughs on the brickwork. The vine is so high that I've never managed to get at the topmost grapes and they swing just below the apex of the roof until November, when they tumble, soft and rotten, in to the huge euphorbias which flourish here. Dioscorides, who was physician to Antony and Cleopatra, and who also wrote one of the first herbals, is said to have named this great spurge after Euphorbus, physician to King Juba of Mauritania. John considered it 'very handsome', an accolade he bestowed on women as well as favoured plants. Along the dairy wall and recessed between fat brick buttresses are fuchsias and, in late summer, a forest of balsam whose seed-pods explode at the merest finger-touch, communicating their own urgency to the human nervous system. *Impatiens*, the botanists call it. The saucer-shaped ground tips sharply upwards here and the garden John made loses itself in the Old Orchard, a tangled, fruitless place which is a rabbit and pheasant kingdom, and from which one bursts on the far side upon a soaring view that encompasses Bures and the land-sweep towards Arger Fen. This is East Angle – East Saxon border country where King Edmund was crowned in 855. He was fifteen and he reigned for fifteen years before the manner of his death turned him into England's St. Sebastian. I can see Cuckoo Hill, the site of his coronation, from the garden-edge, as well as the smudge of brown which is Bottengom's Farm from the spot where Edmund, Offa's adopted son, received the Saxon diadem. The Stour divides these tribal lands. Its name means 'powerful' or maybe 'worshipful stream' and perhaps there is a mystic connection between this lovely Suffolk-Essex river and the River Stura in Cisalpina Gallia which flowed near the Rubicon and into Italy to join the Po. These classical thoughts are allowable to someone living in an old valley only six miles from Colchester, the birthplace of St. Helena, mother of Constantine, the shrine of the deified Claudius – and the capital of Cymbeline. Our church tower is partly built of Roman bricks, and as children we searched for arrow heads on the hillside below Edmund's chapel as this particular field was said to be where Boadicea skirmished, although we never found one. The harvests from Bottengom's would have floated slowly past it on the river barges which collected up produce from Harwich to Sudbury. My neighbour who has farmed the Bottengom's fields for fifty years tells me that deep in the chalk of those which rise so spectacularly to meet one's gaze as one clambers from the Old Orchard, there are seven springs. One of them has 'watered' this place ever since it was inhabited, man and creatures. The others break surface further along in ponds, a small lake, ever-running ditches, and cuts.

John loved a pond as much as anything. 'Never pass up a good pond', was his motto. The four in his garden are tiny but crammed with fish and plants. In the summer you need a machete to find them. The boggy ground near them produces an heroic vegetation, partly exotic, partly native, which totally conceals them. In the old days there would be pond-cleaning forays when the weather was hot so that we could work in them stripped except for a thin, silky covering of mud, and with the perch darting between our knees. 'It's clean mud', we told each other as we dragged up the weed. He often painted these ponds in their catholic thickets of bamboo, crab-apple, giant dock, guelders, willow, and hemlocks. Nightingales would sing there as he drew, though these have gone now.

To the east the garden is bordered by the track, the bastion-like entrenchment, and the pastures – now in the process of being ploughed for corn. Above this hill are the Horkesleys, the 'hurks' or Saxon lamb shelters, and a mysterious fortification called Pitchbury Ramparts, and below the hill on the other side lies the little wool town of Nayland whose bells and church clock can be heard in the farmhouse when the wind is right. A huge palette-shaped bed crammed to the edges with pink and yellow peonies, carpets of cyclamen, tea-roses and a lifetime's amassing of flowers of every kind is spread out here. I have sometimes seen friends or visitors attempting to formulate or diagnose what taste or impulse lay behind the creation of this garden, and I myself found it hard to say what judgement and rules made it and governed it. Until, after John's death, I began to read Dean Hole. Although in his enchanting *Book About Roses* – which I commend to anyone who is interested in pure pleasure – S. Reynolds Hole deals only with this supreme flower, I recognize both in accent and attitude a concept of gardening lust and philosophy, aesthetic and preferment which was John's to a T. It was an entirely unselfconscious, really wholly unaware Victorian standard of intellectual gardening that he introduced to Guma's midden and cabbage-patch, and maintained. Guma's garden, if such an unlikely thing existed, would certainly have been succeeded by a long list of country gardens with their matter-of-fact mixing of blooms and food, all different, all gone, save in remnants such as the great Portugal quince with its regular hundredweight of furry-skinned fruit and its not-quite-nice scent. Village folk used to add quince to an apple-pie to make it 'brisk', and they set it among their pear-trees to make them extra fruitful. It is very acid and maybe the pectin called quin is named after it. Fragments of old walls, too, circumscribe earlier garden patterns. And there is a stout holly hedge, half veiled in bryony, which was planted as a barrier against something or other long ago-though what? Lightly digging in the early spring, I now and then exhume a yard or two of the cinders and flints of Victorian paths. There remain, too, inconclusive stumps in the blond aftermath of rough scythings where fine old trees once stood, and which seem to petrify and remain, rather than rot away. John drew out the present garden above or around all this, as well as in terms which owed nothing to mid-twentieth-century taste in such matters.

He himself illustrated many excellent gardening essays by some of the best garden-makers of his time but the emotion or spirit of his own garden derives from the immediately preceding taste. And where is this taste most confidently and unaffectedly displayed – but in Dean Hole's *A Book About Roses*. Once, wandering about Falmouth, I stumbled across, as they say, the Dean's autobiography, *Then and Now*, which I triumphantly presented to John. He received it with the caution which one would show at being offered a key to what one has always privately known, and I was reduced to reading my own gift, though allowed to 'call bits out' (which he rather liked).

'Call a bit out', he'd say.

The bits I'd call out now would not be from the Dean's life, sensible and kind though it was, but from his little masterpiece, for if the essence of what occurred during the 1940s and '50s in Guma's Valley can be found on any printed page, it lies in this Victorian rosarium. John's pencil ticks against his favourite blooms in the appendix – *Charles Lefebure, Mrs John Laing* ('a continuous bloomer'), *Prince Camille de Rohan* ('the freest flowering of all the dark roses' – he had a passion for dark roses), *Cristata, White* (Provence roses), *De Meaux* (miniature Provence or pompon), *Red Damask, Rosa Mundi*, and *Tuscany* (adored), *Boule de Neige* (dazzling white clusters), *Dundee Rambler* (Ayreshire), the creamy *Felicite Perpetue*, which is an evergreen, the *Old Blush* and *Cramoisie Superieure* china roses, the great tea-roses *Bouquet d'Or* and, of course, *Gloire de Dijon* (his favourite flower) and the pretty little Japanese picotee-edged rose *Fimbriata*, all beloved roses of the Nineties, and most could have been found in Benjamin Cant's celebrated nursery at Colchester at this time – reveal his determination to collect those necessary for his existence, but it is the actual style and philosophy of the Dean's outlook on gardening generally which is echoed at Bottengoms. How amazed the previous owner, Mr Lewis, and indeed all those centuries of farmers and their wives who 'like to see a bit of a show, like, near the house' would have been by what John Nash liked. Winding, irregular paths, particularly with plants flopping over the edges, secret dank corners, walks mown between tall grass in which a sequence of flowers appeared from February to November, everything from precious things such as fritillaries and martagon or Turk's cap lilies, to lords and ladies, and especially handsome stands of sheep's parsley, and dead trees clothed in climbers. Wildness and cultivation were lured into hob-nobbing.

The only way in which this early and this belated Victorian gardener differed entirely was in their botany. John called himself an artist-plantsman, not a gardener, the Dean a rosarian – and 'a true gardener'. John was also a brilliant botanist but the Dean, because he could not master the subject himself, doubted if one could find 'a scientific botanist and a successful florist [i.e. grower of flowers] under the same hat'. The Dean said he was like the undergraduate who, told off by a farmer for riding over his wheat, answered, 'I am no botanist'. So that while the Bottengoms garden is, in summer, knee-deep in those delights recommended by Dean Hole, it also contains a certain intellectual force which is not exactly relaxing. Except for eating his meals in it during good weather, I never saw John lying about on the grass, as I do. It kept him very much on his toes. The Dean, I fancy, would have been neither learned nor idle but would have walked about from shrub to shrub, joyful and exclaiming. Guma, should he catch sight of either one of us from his forgotten barrow on some stony hoo by the river, would be bewildered by the elaboration of it all. He who had the sheltered corn slopes, the beasts in the hurk, the running water, and the wooden hall to live in.

A SUFFOLK WOOD

(*Britain: A World by Itself*, Aurum Press, 1984)

Childhood is, among so much else, a matter of attainable destinations. That early getting about on one's own two feet is a thrilling business. Woods of all shapes and sizes were high up on my desirable destinations list. There were plenty to choose from, although none of them actually spectacular. According to books, woods were where the action was and my heart used to race and thump when I reached them. A few steps into a wood altered all this, switched my expectancy. Its silence, which was really the amalgamated sound of its murmurings and snappings, instantly transformed me from adventurer to contemplative. Except that to prop one's bike against a roadside tree and walk in and in and in needed quite a bit of physical daring as well as that state of mind which, at home, was referred to as 'his mooning'. Serve them right if, poignantly, there were banner headlines shouting, 'LOST BOY'S BICYCLE FOUND AGAINST OAK, WOOD CLAIMS ANOTHER VICTIM.'

When ones comes to think about it, the sole purpose of woods in children's literature is as places to get lost in. It was both a relief and a disappointment to the nine-year-old me to wander half a mile through a Suffolk wood and suddenly step out into a land of non-wood and familiar bearings. Also, it now occurs to me, our local woods were apt to get rather crowded at certain times of the year, bluebell time, blackberry time and just 'wooding' time, when people of all ages could be seen lugging home the spoils. These were always hauled off in quite immoderate quantities: bluebells in such arm-loads that they slipped steadily for miles, blackberries heaped into fishbags until they soaked through the straw, mutilated fungus (it is strange how so many people are compelled to break a fungus) and a good log which someone couldn't carry another yard. Woods were universal providers of nuts, fruit, fuel, flowers, holly, mistletoe, birds' eggs and so on, and were not then noticeably infested with gamekeepers. Lovers, of course. Woods made girls uneasy and boys brave. 'Going bluebelling' would usually raise a laugh. A gypsy or two might be encamped on the verges. 'My mother said, that I never should/Play with the gypsies in the wood.' Chance would have been a fine thing. They were so exclusive, so unreachable. Their dogs barked but they themselves never said a word.

The wood I liked best was six miles away and was variously referred to as Assington Wood, Assington Thicks, Arger Fen and Tiger Hill, the latter because the tooth of a tiger had been found there. It covered a deep little valley and had a lane running through the middle of it. There was never the least doubt when you reached it that you had come to somewhere very special. A swift, gravelly stream hurried through this ever-fascinating wood on its way to the Stour, and ran bridge-less across the road itself so that everybody had to splash through it. There were also nightingales, 'thick on the ground', as an old woman strangely said, although we knew what she meant.

Almost a lifetime later I find myself within sight of this beloved childhood wood from a house on the south bank of the Stour. Seen from such a distance of time and cornfields, it looks formidable. But when I walk to it, it gradually dissolves from being a dark massif into its old pleasant self. More than ever it constitutes an important destination. It is amazingly unchanged, and because visiting it is less like going back than just going on, I suddenly felt the need to take some kind of stock. It was warm mid-October and a good moment to make an inventory. No nightingales but a yaffle among the diseased elms whose crowns had snapped off, so that they looked like the shelled trees of the Western Front. No blackberries still fit to eat but plenty of sloes and cerise spindleberries. Leaves everywhere were thinning but not yet down, and made their special fleshless autumn sounds, the poplars most of all. There were token remnants of summer flowers, red campion particularly. Nettles which only a month ago would have barred the way lay vertical to the earth but were raising soft, fresh branches from their tumbled old stems, and there was woody nightshade in abundance. Startling even amongst so much turning foliage were the intense crimson leaves of the wild cherry, a tree which John Evelyn called 'mazzards'. The wood was warm, even snug. 'One impulse from a vernal wood', wrote Wordsworth (had he in mind that profoundly wooded impulse at Alfoxden?) could teach one more than 'all the sages can', and the impulse which Assington generates, if that is the word, is, I now recognise, intellectual. Here is every grade of existence from soaring bird to mulch. This is a lightly managed wood which is wayward and a mite rough. It is the kind of woodland which travellers to almost anywhere once had to blunder through, a thriving mile or two of an earlier England, a woodland like that painted by Gainsborough in the 1740s at Cornard, which is just up the road.

Assington Wood has always been and continues to be genuine woodlanders' territory. A few families, hidden from each other but whose voices sometimes carry through the trees, have lived in it for centuries. Its modest architecture manages to survive the general dampness and verdour and remains solid enough. The buildings consist of a little farmhouse with pointed windows, its tall cart-shed gaping trustingly on to the lane and crammed with retired implements, and two or three labourers' cottages. The wood in fact is a tye, or a minute centre of population far from the main village. It must have bred a distinctive people who lived well on rabbits, fruit and pure water. Their warrening, draining, lopping pursuits still mark every foot of the area. It is due to their efforts that Assington offers its intriguing mixture of total wildness and ancient hand-marks. The small, flinty fields cultivated all round the wood have now been pulled into one or two vast fields, still very stony, and the bracken warned off for good. But the occasional sarsen lies by the field-edge, just as it did long ago. And the wood itself juts in and out of the corn in such a way that some of the fields are like three-sided rooms with huge green and brown walls. The adjoining pastures have remained as they were and cap each other in a series of succulent humps like the cheerful meadows in a child's picture-book. John Nash, who painted all round here, referred to this landscape as the Suffolk-Essex Highlands. These woods never look better than they do in late October, when the penultimate moments of their summer density is scored across this border countryside of new wheat and drillings, sharp distances and vivid skies.

It is usual to be badly let down when one returns to the scenes of youthful excitement, but not so at Assington. These woods do not lure me even one single step towards mind-weakening nostalgia – which is what I expected when I returned to them. I think it is because they have so much going on in them at the moment that they divert one from the past. Even more than the fields – which in any case now seen to have acquired a computerized motion – old, personal-to-one's-self woodlands like Assington-Arger Fen-Tiger Hill possess that powerful cyclic movement which gives a kind of reflective zest to the present. 'Enter these enchanted woods, you who dare,' wrote Meredith in his poem 'The Woods of Westermain', and that is it: the daring to enter what is in effect the jurisdiction of the forest. This modest wood of, perhaps, some fifty acres has always suggested to me a sampling of the forest proper in many of its varieties. It *was* the forest proper when I was a boy. Now it is a sequence of glades, sluices, stands of ash, oak and beech, gardens, flowery banks, scrub, conifers, rabbit runs, tracks – anything a visiting woodlander can ask for.

LETTER FROM EAST ANGLIA

(*European Travel and Life*, September, 1987)

I am up 'betimes,' as they say around here. Very early. Warm rain and a promise of sun. The dawn chorus roars away in the orchard, the wind voluptuously backing the noisy birdsong. But no other sound as usual. Except for a passing plane or tractor, the ancient house hears few of the contemporary rackets. It listens to what it has heard since Shakespeare and before, a stream trickling along to the river, turbulent or sibilant weather, distant bells, and its own beams settling and cracking. It stares east across a valley where each year the ground plan of a long-vanished farm that nobody knows anything about is perfectly visible in the young corn. On the hill, my neighbour, originally from Scotland, flies St. Andrew's flag from the apex of his barn. On Saturday we shall attend his daughter's wedding breakfast – at four in the afternoon – in the barn. The lanes are at their most opulent, dense with lilac, Queen Anne's lace, and apple blossom.

I walk to see my aunt in a village farther along the valley. She is almost eighty and is preoccupied with secret giving to her parish church. Like Proust's Aunt Leonie, she has always enjoyed poor health, especially 'my poor heart.' She believes that she is the last of the old people and despises the village's current population of commuters. 'I don't know one of them to talk to,' she says with pride. The road past her house is the one that Gainsborough walked. Opposite aunt's tiny garden rises the height from which he painted 'Cornard Wood.' 'I won't move now' she announces unnecessarily, having scarcely shifted out of sight of this famous view since her marriage in 1928. She plans her grave as absorbedly as she once planned her flower bed.

I take stock of our agriculture. At this midyear moment there is little to indicate that it is once more in crisis. The classic patchwork of valley fields contains scattered acres of oil-seed rape, heavily scented and gaudy. Some find these harsh Van Gogh-yellow crops alien to the English scene, but I love their dramatic colour. They are part of the new diversification that is hitting farming. Last year there were acres of borage, an exquisite soft blue crop of starry flowers and cucumber-tasting leaves. However, the farmers are in no mood to dwell on these visual pleasures. Their forty years of postwar prosperity is at an end with the cutting down of the subsidies that guaranteed the butter and grain mountains: hundreds of thousands of tons of food that was surplus to our needs – enough to feed starving Africa were it possible to get it there. But, on the whole, it is not possible, so it rots in storage. And now, finis to the crazy success of the grain growers.

I think back to my childhood East Anglia of the great farming slump, the abandoned fields and the stagnation that turned the countryside into a paradise of flowering wildernesses for a small boy. It won't be as bad, or as beautiful, as that again, but also it won't be as we all have taken it for granted for most of our lives. Thus diversification, the new buzzword throughout rural Britain. Turn your farmhouse into a holiday home for tourists, make folksy goods, plant sunflowers. Farmers need only to glance at history to see that it is one of notorious ups and downs, a decade or two of golden years alternating with longer stretches of slog. They will never again be as ruined as they were, but also never be as rich through surpluses. Having lived right through an ups-and-downs cycle of historic magnitude makes me feel as old as my aunt. I think of the farmers who woke up in my room in the late spring of 1687, say, to birdsong and streamsound, and to anxiety.

It is festival time. Aldeburgh, King's Lynn. Colchester, Cambridge, Chelmsford, and scores of local centres compete for audiences. The mantelpiece is laden with invitations to concerts, talks, exhibitions, and plays. My contribution has lasted nearly as long as my awareness of agricultural change. The invitations remind me of my beginnings as a writer, living in Aldeburgh and working for Benjamin Britten while starting my first book, a novel. Walking with Britten by the North Sea and by myself on the Suffolk marshes, young and lost. When his festival was a quarter of a century old, I wrote its history. I shall go to Aldeburgh and listen to music, sit in the lee of its shore breeze and have lunch on the shingle, and, later, walk to the little house where I wrote my novel.

Minor roads late at night. The car is pressed well down below the corn level and twists and turns obediently to directions that were originally given flocks and herds as they wandered to ponds and pastures. The banks are high and impacted with oak and ash roots. Most of these meandering arteries that a millennium of carts, cattle, and humans have stamped into the land are those along which the East Anglians journeyed to Massachusetts in the 1630s, Winthrop and his chosen people. As children we walked through the Waldingfields to Groton, passing all that they left behind, their homes and stony churches, which were now ours. All that is left of John Winthrop's manor are some bumps in a rough meadow and a mulberry tree – *Morus nigra*. Mulberry trees were all the rage when this Suffolk lawyer sailed away to found Boston.

Frustration. The entire district has been fighting tooth and nail to stop the government from building a second power station at Sizewell, a once beautiful fishing hamlet whose previous claim to fame, for us country lads at any rate, was as a spot for swimming naked. Then drinking pints in the pub. Then cycling home. Now it gives off a constant nuclear humming, like an immense and threatening hive. At night, all lit up, it shines like a docked liner. I gave evidence for the Suffolk Preservation Society against a second such threat, but to no avail. Even Chernobyl fallout in our rivers failed to persuade the government. I stood before the tribunal, talking about poetry, music, and botany, the Suffolk coast's influence on Britten's operas and the glories of this scrap of England, and felt eccentric and irrelevant.

Rogation, which means to ask. Just before summer comes the asking time. At Charsfield (the better part of Akenfield) we always ask in the old manner, the Anglican and Nonconformist congregations processing together from crops to water, from holy places to the village school, from cottage to grave. We make a stop at each of these key sites of our moral existence and say prayers and sing hymns. Mr. Laurie, the vicar, a farmer's son, strides ahead of a garlanded trailer on which sits our organist at a roped-down harmonium. There are no sightseers. It is not that kind of custom. *Rogare* – we ask for food, although you would have to be pretty old to know what it was like to go hungry. At night, after huge Sunday dinners, we shall eye skeletal Mozambicans on the television news and attempt to rationalize a puzzling world. What right, or need, have we for this medieval food-asking rite? For its potent symbolism, I tell myself, wheat, water, the environment, learning, new life, old life, death. And love, if you happen to notice some crushed grass by the brook.

My farmhouse at midyear. Fat bees trapped in the larder and furiously perishing if I don't carry them back into the garden one by one. The rooms smell of resin paper, and flowers, damp scrubbed bricks and old furniture. I am a three or four books at a go reader, and the current choices lie strategically around: *Little Dorrit* in the kitchen, with the cat asleep on it, *The Englishman's Flora* waiting to be reviewed on my desk, Geoffrey Hill's poems on the bed, Michael Ignatieff's *The Needs of Strangers* on the doorstep. I write from early morning until lunch, then garden. Tea at four, then a kind of reading-writing, notes, notions. The cat, who likes to sit on paper, has to be shifted around. The best days are those with blank pages in the diary. No appointments. Just long runs of silence and selfishness, hard labour and sloth. Well out of sight and earshot throbs the hyper-industry of today's village-based leisure pursuits, games, barbeques, restaurants, flower arranging, rustic pop groups, sailing, fancy dress, dances, archaeology, classes for every subject under the sun, choirs, charities, and, of course, festivals, all these things booming. The energy of those involved is beyond calculation. East Anglia proper, as it were, with its Puritan credentials, at the moment is a little uncertain where it stands regarding all this.

Fêtes, those Victorian sprees, remain tremendously popular. I drive to open one at Alphamstone in Lord Abinger's garden, and am amazed all over again, hardened as I should be to tents and pennants, snowy table-cloths and magnificent lawns, by their 'rightness' and brilliance. Not to mention the presence in the solid flesh of English fiction's most splendid prototypes, all still with us. And I myself am stared at, being typical of the bookish creature occasionally thrown up in this old community. It is nice to have one around – the indigenous voice. Or at least I like to think so.

Where They Toiled

THE LITERARY SHRINE

The writer, anywhere, is a basically solitary animal who needs bouts of gregariousness on his own terms, and his house, even when it contains a young family, usually reflects this. On the whole today's successful British writer tends not to set himself up in anything like the domestic style adopted by his equivalent during the first half of the century. The British revere literary shrines and they approved the well-staffed country-houses of great living novelists in particular. A favourite county was Sussex, where Henry James lived in an exquisite Georgian house in Rye, Virginia Woolf in an ancient home filled with 'Bloomsbury' art at Rodmell and Rudyard Kipling in a mansion in a park at Burwash. Joseph Conrad during his later years, Somerset Maugham (the last of the old literary tycoons), Arnold Bennett and a host of lesser talents who were the gods and goddesses of the circulating libraries before television, lived in great style. They worked in handsome studies, usually with a secretary as all their books were handwritten and had to be typed, and surrounded themselves with lovely gardens. Royalties bought privacy and solid comfort or, in the case of Maugham, luxury.

But there were other writers whose living conditions were an uncompromising display of their moral values, most notably George Bernard Shaw. He was fifty when he bought a newly-built rectory in the Hertfordshire village of Ayot St Lawrence and called it 'Shaw's Corner'. A tomb in the local churchyard to a seventy year-old woman inscribed 'Her time was short' convinced him that it was a very healthy spot, which is why he chose his nice dull villa. It remains exactly as he left it when he died in 1950 aged ninety-four. There is a witty Spartan charm about the very clean uncosy rooms, the exercise bicycle fixed to the hall floor, his Oscar for *Pygmalion* on the drawing-room chimneypiece, the bronzes by Prince Troubetskoy and Rodin oddly at ease among the chintzes, the framed photographs of Lenin and Gandhi and, like the watch given him by William Randolph Hearst and his mistress Marion Davies still ticking away in the dining-room, the mementoes of an era lying so casually and unpretentiously around. Just below the main lawn is the little hut in which he wrote on warm days:

> In shattering sunlight here's the shelter
> Where I write dramas helter skelter.

Thomas Hardy's house Max Gate, built about the same time is, in contrast, withdrawn and even rather forbidding. Paid for out of the royalties from the novels and planted around with hundreds of conifers for seclusion, its stiff red-brick and slate architecture has as much the bastion about it as the home. Hardy insisted on quiet servants. His semi-estranged wife lived partly in the attics. Now and then he changed his dark, polished study so that he could face a different view. Max Gate, because of what was created in its walls, awes one. It was never intended to be welcoming.

Between the 1920s and 1950s, much influenced by the grandeur of the Sitwells and other artists and literary figures from upper-class backgrounds, a number of novelists in particular set themselves up in aristocratic style, most notably Evelyn Waugh and Anthony Powell. Waugh lived in a classic 18th century small mansion according to the manners and outlook of the classic English gentleman of the 'old faith' – i.e. pre-Reformation Catholicism, considered at that period very chic. Such country houses played a large part in fiction and plays, and their furnishings, gardens, staff and guests were the popular ingredients of innumerable stories.

But there were other writers, and some of the best, who cannot be placed in the 'address' sense. T.S. Eliot, for instance. Eliot's work is, among so much else, a brilliant evocation of modern London, but there would be very few who could say where his rooms were in the city and what they were like inside. Everybody knows Keats's house, although he inhabited it so briefly; nobody has a picture of Eliot's flat, although he wrote in it for decades. Such comparative anonymity is common among certain authors and people are often surprised by how little their homes reflect their genius, fame – and sometimes wealth. Sir James Barrie, who made a fortune from his plays, lived in a notoriously dreary apartment not far from Charing Cross Station.

Now, as ever, the British writer is instinctively drawn either to 'town' or country. These remain the great alternatives. Town always means London and the country can mean provincial towns, and even cities, as well as the rural wilds. The primary consideration remains one of privacy. The English (less so the Welsh and the Scots) worship it. It is far more easily obtainable in London, where it is quite in order to do no more than nod to your neighbours, than in a village, where it is virtually impossible to hide oneself or not join in. Writers have to put up with being watched in the countryside, which can at first (they get used to it) be disconcerting, as their own role is that of observer and recorder of human behaviour.

Then there is the often much-admired 'local' or indigenous writer who never leaves the area in which he was born and who is its voice and soul, and of which Jane Austen is the exemplar. Their cottages, halls and castles, parsonages and birthplaces nearly always become literary shrines, whilst large areas of land become identified as their 'country' for ever more. If a general picture not only constitutes the provincial writer's home base, but today's 'literary workroom' anywhere in Britain, it would reveal masses of books and papers, some strongly individual taste in the matter of furnishings, a minimum of office gadgetry, and that rather out of date, dogs and cats and plenty of plants, and, most noticeably, the particular writer's own brand of trapped quietness.

Once he or she has found a suitable corner the writer tends to cling to it. The novelist Angus Wilson still lives in the Suffolk woodman's cottage which he bought in the 1950s. Made of flint, the traditional stone of the area, it can be reached only by a rough track. During the summer the little building is almost submerged in its celebrated 'wild garden'. Felsham Woodside is in effect the literary beginner's dream of a rural retreat, which could be why Wilson, now one of the major English novelists and biographers of the post-war years, still retains all the exuberance of a man with an unexplored universe sprawling ahead of him. Unlike Graham Greene, the doyen of British novelists who lives in fairly unapproachable seclusion in Nice, Wilson's cottage always seems to be in a permanent state of welcome while, at the same time, never shedding its feeling of protectiveness where each day's work is concerned. Coping with interruptions whilst not losing the thread or mood is something the average home-based writer has to learn to do. The discipline of writing books in an atmosphere which has to be both domestic and creative is one which every author has to discover for himself. The most intriguing aspect of any writer's home is not its décor but the essential work conditions which he demands from it. A sternly locked door, or a trickle of visitors to cheer-up the lonely day; these are the chiefly desired alternatives.

Then there are the difficulties resulting from fame – something which novelists as long ago as the Bronte sisters and Dickens found it hard to contend with. The filming of a successful book can place a writer's house in a great glare of interest and publicity. John Fowles (*The French Lieutenant's Woman*) lives on the outskirts of Lyme Regis, the beautiful seaside town made famous by Jane Austen, where between novel-writing he runs the local history museum, and he feels particularly grateful for the way in which his neighbours respect his privacy. He is a shy, diffident man when it comes to journalists and sightseers, and he recognises how vulnerable he is to the kind of celebrity which could have made it hard for him to go on working in a place where he is so well known. It is not unusual for a community to subtly guard and respect the conditions which the famous writer in its midst needs for his art. Writers accept that, although sometimes loved, they are really outsiders. One of Britain's finest novelists, James Hanley, who has always acknowledged this, recently stated, 'I once said that the writer's real home was on the fringe of society and that is where I spend my writing life. I have never mixed in literary society, belong to no clubs, attend no popular lunches ... I have spent most of life locked away in a Welsh fastness, and there I went on and on, in my own way, following no fashion.'

The Nobel Prize-winning writer William Golding, whose novels criticise British moral values, is a good example of an author who has stayed-put and had his imagination developed by things he saw as a child, such as the powerful symbol suggested by the spire of Salisbury Cathedral, and the type of society which he has seen growing up not far from his quiet comfortable house overlooking chalky Salisbury Plain. Penelope Mortimer too, a severe critic of tradition, especially where it seeks to control middle-class women who are no longer young, surveys a familiar world from a pretty stone cottage set in the deep Cotswolds countryside. Once the village's post office, she has planted a lovely garden at its rear and extended her own working universe, as it were. Although she has the expected book-lined study, she does a lot of her writing on the kitchen table with the minimum of fuss. Many writers take their work round the house. The doorstep, the bed, but most often the lawn on a sunny day.

The people who make the biggest fortunes these days, as ever, are the popular storytellers whose light romance, thrillers, spy-tales, historical yarns and adventure fiction dominate the paperback market. Writers such as Jean Plaidy, Catherine Cookson, John le Carré, Jeffrey Archer, Jack Higgins and Barbara Cartland. Also Dick Francis whose brilliant racetrack novels it is said the Queen enjoys because of her passion for horses. Such writers are rich and can live as they please, grandly or simply. Dick Francis chooses a bit of both life-styles. 'We have two homes, one in Oxfordshire and one in Fort Lauderdale, Florida, and my wife and I love them both. I write equally well, I think, in either place. I seem to spend a lot of time travelling back and forth over the Atlantic Ocean. In England I mix more with the racing world, and in Florida I proudly do more of my writing than in England. Otherwise both places are equally congenial.' Catherine Cookson's enormous popularity stems from the fact that she writes very much from the heart, having herself, when young, endured many of the hardships which she so accurately describes in stories based upon poverty and struggle. The colourful opulence and comfort of her northern house reflects an unashamed pleasure in bright furnishings, even luxury of a quite unpretentious kind. A semi-invalid and married to a schoolteacher, she dictates some of her chapters into a tape recorder by her bedside. Jeffrey Archer represents the opposite end of the sophisticated scale. He writes heavily politicised thrillers in well-documented present-day settings, and has a vast following. A rich businessman who once lost a million, writing was originally for him a means of recouping, but his first book brought him such huge success that there just had to be more. His royalties have installed him in one of England's most evocative addresses, the Old Vicarage, Grantchester, immortalised by the poet Rupert Brooke and close to Byron's Pool and Chaucer's mill. The house has that sunken-into-the-garden feeling which so many ancient parsonages possess and gives no hint of the bestselling industry taking place inside it. Such a reticence is typical of many of today's literary addresses; they give very little away.

John le Carré, master of the espionage novel, (the British are obsessed by the dramatics of political treachery) favours an uncluttered eyrie on the wild Cornish coast in which to work, whilst Barbara Cartland, the now octogenarian queen of the mass romance market, resides appropriately in a Victorian mansion surrounded by secretaries and servants.

The poets appear to make the least domestic demands. They live in university flats, old farmhouses, quiet London streets, tucked away terraces and, customarily, nowhere particularly poetic. Ted Hughes, the newly-elected Poet Laureate and once the husband of the American poet Sylvia Plath, lives deep in the rural West Country.

Money and fame do not always go together, and many of the best writers are comparatively poor and, if they don't have money from a regular job, live in great insecurity. Some novelists prefer a certain austerity and their rooms remain very simple even when they have arrived at celebrity, and the remarkable West Indian writer V. S. Naipaul lives like this. Others, including Iris Murdoch, Muriel Spark, Harold Pinter and his historian wife Lady Antonia Fraser, live elegantly. The old deliberate and exciting bohemia no longer exists, alas, indeed has long vanished, for few writers need to challenge the bourgeoisie as they once did. The chief contrast now, house-wise, seems to be between a certain traditionally British interior elegance or rusticity (the latter can be very elegant!) and what might be called the student-pad of the 'Sixties' carried forward into early middle-age, with its posters and coffee-mugs. The actual workroom, its arrangement, warmth, peace, privacy and view, is of tremendous aesthetic and emotional importance, and the remainder of a writer's house can be not much more than a conventional afterthought in comparison.

COLERIDGE AT NETHER STOWEY

(*Writers at Home*, The National Trust, 1985)

The frantic circumstances which brought Coleridge to Nether Stowey, and which have long since made his cottage in Lime Street one of English literature's most potent addresses, were crammed with that worry and despair which is special to moving house, and which, even now, is instantly recognisable. Unbeknown to him, as he, his wife and baby son took possession of its cramped quarters on the last day of 1796, the year which was to follow would be his *annus mirabilis*. Never again would he write as he did then, never again, or so he later affirmed, would he be so happy. For in these small rooms, in the garden and in the Quantock countryside all around he was to write a dazzling succession of poems, which would include 'The Rime of the Ancient Mariner', the first part of 'Christabel', 'Frost at Midnight' and 'Kubla Khan'. When William and Dorothy Wordsworth were to rent Alfoxden, a country house some three miles distant in order to be near him, he was also to assist in launching from this spot the little book which was to redirect the course of English poetry, *Lyrical Ballads*. It is this cottage and the web of lanes between it and Alfoxden, rather than the Lakes, which is the birthplace of the Romantic Movement. To it came not only the Wordsworths, but William Hazlitt, Robert Southey, Thomas De Quincey and Charles Lamb; all of them, like Coleridge, young and made even more 'new men' by the ecstatic hopefulness released by the French Revolution.

The cottage was called Gilbards when Coleridge became Mrs Rendle's sub-tenant at £8 a year. It comprised two rooms downstairs and three up, a kitchen without an oven, a thatched roof and a huge garden, most of which has disappeared under subsequent buildings.

After he left it became a manse and then a pub – 'Coleridge Cottage Inn' – but in 1892 a local clergyman saved it from the hazards of further development and possible extinction, and in the autumn of 1909 it became the property of the National Trust. Simple though it is, its profound associations give it an importance equal to anything which the Trust takes care of. Coleridge tumbled into it during a housing crisis, attained the peak of his genius while living in it, and was soon to find it unbearable. From Germany, where he was on a walking tour, he wrote to Tom Poole, the new friend whom he had wildly persuaded (against the latter's better judgment) to bring him and his family from Bristol to Nether Stowey: 'I must not disguise from you that to live *in* Stowey, and in that house ... is to me an exceedingly unpleasant thought.' But more had happened at this time between the move and the flight than either Coleridge or Poole (or the Wordsworths) could possibly have anticipated. Coleridge came to the Lime Street cottage because marriage had tipped him into responsibilities with which he had little ability to cope, and he left it, partly because he and Sara's life together did not improve, and partly because, quite unwittingly, he and the Wordsworths stirred up a local hornets' nest.

He was 24 when he arrived, Wordsworth and his sister Dorothy a little older. All three were at the zenith of their literary powers, and astounding intruders they must have appeared to the native eye. Moreover, the Coleridges were accompanied by an epileptic young man and the Wordsworths by a little boy. Both families walked about the countryside at all hours of the day and night. What was going on?

Troubles came thick and fast. Yet the intensity of everything which Coleridge experienced here, his domestic confusion notwithstanding, remained enviable to the last. Later, the Stowey Coleridge was to become for him his real but now unreachable self. As for the brave politics which made him and the Wordsworths so unwelcome here, they soon guttered out. Near to his death, he recalled this halcyon time, 'We [John Thelwall the reformer and himself] were once sitting in a beautiful recess in the Quantocks, when I said to him, "Citizen John, this is a fine place to talk treason in!" – "Nay, Citizen Samuel," replied he, "it is rather a place to make a man forget that there is any necessity for treason!"' Thelwall had touched on the double motive which had brought the poet to Nether Stowey. Its lovely neighbourhood and the enlightened mind of his dear protector Tom Poole had become the fused ideal which had lured him to this spot. Shortly after he had settled in Lime Street, Poole had written him a reassuring note: 'By you, Coleridge, I will always stand, in sickness and health, prosperity and misfortunes.' This comradely version of the marriage vows Poole was to observe to the letter, and the support which followed is reminiscent of that which John Fisher poured out to John Constable. Both benefactors had no doubt that they were duty-bound to protect genius.

Samuel Coleridge was the last of the ten children born to the Reverend John Coleridge, vicar of Ottery St Mary, Devonshire, and master of its grammar school, and his second wife Anne Bowdon. Before he was five the poet had headed off into a private realm of reading and dreaming which was to take precedence over the formal pattern of education provided by Christ's Hospital and Jesus College, Cambridge. Where books were concerned, he called himself a 'cormorant'. They, above anything, helped to carry him through the horrors of Christ's Hospital, with its bad food and violence. Southey, his future brother-in-law, had been sacked from Westminster School for daring to protest against the flogging there, but Coleridge, already lost in the reality of his imagination, came through the rough vicissitudes of his youth with impaired health but no great grudge. Much later, learning of the death of their brutal headmaster, he told Charles Lamb, 'PoorJ.B. – may all his faults be forgiven; and may he be wafted to bliss by little cherub boys; all heads and wings, with no bottoms ...' He was still at school when he fell in love with Mary Evans, sister of one of the pupils. At Cambridge he continued on his wayward path, having long since devoured everything in the way of reading matter which the university required. He also ran into political trouble, being what he called 'an extreme democrat', into debt, and into deeper and deeper feelings for Mary Evans. In 1793, unable to cope with all this, he ran away and enlisted in the 15th Dragoons as 'Silas Tomkyn Comberbacke', an absurd name he had seen written up in the Inns of Court. As he was hopeless on a horse and nearly as hopeless on the parade ground, Coleridge's four-month military career was mainly taken up with writing letters home for his illiterate comrades and nursing them when they were ill. In the spring of 1794 his brothers bought him out and he returned to Cambridge.

A few weeks later, while visiting an old Christ's Hospital friend at Oxford, he was introduced to Robert Southey, whose father kept a draper's shop in Bristol and whose grandfather farmed in the Quantocks. The road to Nether Stowey, and to the shore of 'The Ancient Mariner', and the dreamland of 'Kubla Khan', begins here. During these Oxford days Coleridge, matchlessly eloquent, turned Southey into a Unitarian, and Southey, equally persuasive with another idea, began the process of setting up a utopian society in New England. Twelve young men and their wives were to live as a 'pantisocracy' on the banks of the Susquehanna River, Pennsylvania, a site chosen because of its pretty name. Here again we see Coleridge being drawn into youthful half-baked commitments which would soon have a profound effect on his art and future happiness. Much of the Susquehanna adventure was planned while he and Southey were on a walking tour of Wales that summer (1794). Southey then took him to Bath to meet a girl named Mary Fricker who was engaged to one of the Susquehanna River boys, Robert Lovell. Mary had four sisters and her mother was the widow of a bankrupt tradesman from Bristol. Soon these ladies were back in Bristol and so were the Susquehanna men, who were all sharing a house in College Street and saving up to emigrate.

Just before this Coleridge and Southey went on another of their great hikes, on this occasion tramping from Cheddar and the Mendips, and eventually to see Nether Stowey for the first time. Each had an undergraduate friend in this beautiful countryside, Southey's being George Burnett and Coleridge's, Henry Poole. This latter introduced the poets to Stowey's most distinguished resident, his remarkable, self-educated and highly 'democratic' (a designation as suspect in late eighteenth century England as 'Marxist' is in the late twentieth) cousin, Tom Poole. The Pooles were the sons of the local tanner who had put one of his children through the local university and kept the other, Tom, at home to run the family business. This seemingly unfair treatment was to have astonishing results, for Tom Poole used the family money for the welfare of the whole town, set himself up in fine houses with an extensive library, and became host to some of the greatest writers of his age.

It was through Tom Poole that Coleridge, after weeks of panic over housing, recovered his footing after a series of upsets which included his enlistment, his Cambridge failure, losing Mary Evans, marrying Sara Fricker, having the Pantisocracy plan quashed by Southey, running out of money and becoming very ill through anxiety. Poole gave in to Coleridge's implorings, brought him to Nether Stowey and steadied him. If he did so reluctantly at first, it was not because of any lack of love on his part or because of not wanting to have a young hot-head whom his family detested on his doorstep, but because the practical side of him told him that Coleridge simply would not be able to live the kind of life he had planned here. Tiny country towns do not support idylls. Coleridge's popular reputation in the West Country at this juncture was less that of a writer, although he had published a collection of poems and edited a magazine, *The Watchman*, than of a thrilling lecturer and preacher who made the Unitarian chapels ring with the new politics. But even where his writing was concerned, it was no gentle literary figure who was coming to dwell in Mrs Rendle's uncomfortable cottage, but a poet on the threshold of an unimaginable power. He arrived modestly, determined to make the best of his situation, 'I shall have six companions; my Sara, my babe, my own shaping and inquisitive mind, my books, my beloved friend Tom Poole, and lastly, Nature looking at me with a thousand looks of beauty', and he left having completed everything necessary for him to be seen as one of poetry's most extraordinary masters.

No sooner had he settled his family and arranged their meagre belongings, and then begun his self-imposed regime of early morning gardening, reviewing, and preaching on Sundays at Bridgwater (he was still thinking about becoming a Unitarian minister as a way out of the precariousness of his existence), than his entire being caught fire.

Never before and never later was he to know such joy. He filled the house with guests who could not but notice the drudgery to which Sara was reduced. Charles Lloyd, Coleridge's disciple-pupil, and son of one of the founders of the bank of that name, had a bed-sitting-room, and Nanny the maid also slept in, so these months could not have been anything but a crush. There was also Hartley, the adored baby son 'Like the moon among the clouds,' wrote Coleridge, 'he moves in a circle of light of his own making. He alone is a light of his own. Of all human beings I never saw one so utterly naked of self.' Hartley was cradled by his table as he worked, sometimes finding his way into the poetry.

The cottage contains an indelible imprint of the first years of this 'strange, strange boy', as his father described him, and even of the short-lived Berkeley, his second son. For a sleeping child usually accompanied him in the room on the right where he worked when everybody else had gone to bed. One February at midnight in 1798 he shared the room thus:

> The Frost performs its secret ministry,
> Unhelped by any wind. The owlet's cry
> Came loud – and hark, again! loud as before.
> The inmates of my cottage, all at rest,
> Have left me to that solitude, which suits
> Abstruser musings: save that at my side
> My cradled infant slumbers peacefully...
> 'Dear babe'... all seasons shall be sweet to thee,
> Whether the summer clothe the general earth
> With greeness, or the redbreast sit and sing
> Betwixt the tufts of snow on the bare branch
> Of mossy apple-tree, while the nigh thatch
> Smokes in the sun-thaw; whether the eave-drops fall
> Heard only in the trances of the blast,
> Or if the secret ministry of frost
> Shall hang them up in silent icicles,
> Quietly shining to the quiet Moon.

An amazing literary toil had been taking place, not only in the small hours in this parlour with its cot and writing-table side by side, but seemingly everywhere within walking distance from the cottage, during Coleridge's every waking moment. The event which carried him to such heights of creativity was the arrival of the Wordsworths at Alfoxden in the summer of 1797, where, as Coleridge was to put it in his *Biographia Literaria*, they were to re-direct the mind from the lethargy of custom 'to the loveliness and the wonders of the world before us'. To the young poets this meant both life in the ordinary village world and life which was 'romantic' and supernatural. Wordsworth was to deal with nature and Coleridge with what lay beyond it. 'With this in view I wrote The Ancient Mariner' – and in this low room. This terrifying ballad for which he hoped to get £5 and thus begin to pay the bills which, in spite of Poole's generosity, were themselves a nightmare, was in fact to mark a lasting turn in his fortunes, for no sooner had he completed it and gone off to preach at Shrewsbury (where the 20-year-old William Hazlitt walked ten miles to hear him), than he heard that the rich Wedgwood brothers were to offer him an unconditional £150 a year for life. It would be wrong to omit from the various factors which made 1798 such a matchless time for Coleridge, his inspiration, his friendship with the Wordsworths, his discovery not only of where he should go but where he could go, his new and modest financial security.

Hazlitt encountered the headiness of this brief moment as soon as he arrived in Lime Street that spring. So sublime was it to be invited there that he had prepared himself for the Quantocks, now made paradisal by the presence of 'my first poets', by tramping all the way to Llangollen. 'In the outset of life our imagination has a body to it. We are in a state between sleeping and waking, and have indistinct but glorious glimpses of strange shapes, and there is always something to come better than what we see.' Hazlitt hints at the theme of Alain-Fournier's *Le Grand Meaulnes*. He crossed the threshold of the cottage, believing himself to be at this stage an artist, but already taking notes which were to make him Britain's finest essayist. Two days later Wordsworth arrived, gaunt and looking like his own Peter Bell. After wreaking havoc with the cheese, he looked through the window and said 'How beautifully the sun sets on that yellow bank'. The next day the poets told their guest how they wrote. 'Coleridge has told me that he himself liked to compose in walking over uneven ground, or breaking through the straggling branches of copse-wood; whereas Wordsworth always wrote walking up and down a straight gravel-walk, or in the same spot where the continuity of his verse met with no collateral interruption... Thus I passed three weeks at Nether Stowey and in the neighbourhood, generally devoting the afternoons to a delightful chat in an arbour made of bark by the poet's friend Tom Poole, sitting under two fine elm-trees, and listening to the bees humming around us, while we quaffed our *flip*.' Coleridge took him 'for miles and miles on dark brown heaths' through Minehead and on to Linton, the seascape of 'The Ancient Mariner', and told him that in *Lyrical Ballads* he and Wordsworth were going to 'use only such words as had probably been common in the most ordinary language since the days of Henry II'. It was a language which neither critic nor ordinary reader associated with poetry and the book was a failure. Besides 'The Ancient Mariner' and other great poems, it also contained Wordsworth's 'Tintern Abbey'.

The starry conjunction of Coleridge and Wordsworth in the Quantock Hills occurred because each young man had drifted into Somerset about the same time. Some might call it destiny, others accident. After searing political experiences in revolutionary France and a love affair with Annette Vallon which resulted in the birth of their child, Wordsworth had returned to the demands of his family to enter either the church or the law, and settle down. He was then suddenly freed from either of these unwelcome occupations by a legacy of £900, and on top of this good fortune, invited to tutor the son of a widowed friend in exchange for £50 a year and a rent-free farmhouse near Crewkerne. Coleridge had already read some of Wordsworth's early poetry, and Wordsworth had heard of Coleridge's glorious republican oratory when they met in Bristol. Each immediately recognised in the other a personification of all that they longed for and the power to achieve it. Visits to Stowey and Racedown, Dorothy and William's village, were made and a thrilling new language for their mutual beliefs and emotions discovered. All three were intoxicated by what could happen – by what must happen – and during the hot summer of 1797 the Wordsworths decided that they must join Coleridge and went house-hunting around Nether Stowey. They found Alfoxden, a country house standing in a picturesque park near the sea, and below which lay a glen with a roaring waterfall. With Tom Poole as reference, they were able to rent it for a year. This move inaugurated for each of them, and for Coleridge especially, a season of fulfilment and pleasure such as would never be repeated. They had scarcely decided on how they would use the extraordinary freedom which Alfoxden promised them, with its many rooms and spacious grounds, when the three-mile journey between it and Coleridge's home in Stowey began to establish a regular pattern of daily walking and talking in their lives. But although they constantly immersed themselves in the same scenery of 'that dear and beautiful place', as Dorothy was to refer to it when she and her brother were driven from it by busybodies, they viewed it in three separate and distinctive ways. For Wordsworth, fresh from France, it was a paradise where simple labouring people, orphans and common soldiers half-starved; for Dorothy, it was a paradise of plants, creatures and geographical colours and shapes; for Coleridge it was both a paradise and an earthly territory for the limitless thrust of his imagination.

This walking and talking had hardly begun when an interruption far more grotesque (although less damaging in the long run) than that of the 'person from Porlock' occurred. A combination of local tittle-tattle, genuine mystification and 'patriotism' reached the ears of the Home Office, which sent a government spy down to Nether Stowey to see what was going on. With rumours of French invasion and even of a possible French-revolution by the 'people' of Britain, Pitt's administration was taking no chances. Here was an unorthodox group in a key position by the Bristol Channel made up of a man who prevented his countrymen from burning Tom Paine's *The Rights of Man* (Poole), a Unitarian minister preaching democracy and other heresies (Coleridge), and a man (who had come from France) and a woman who called themselves brother and sister, who, although they had rented a mansion, spent all their time wandering about having conversations with peasants. Walsh, the government spy, put up at the Globe Inn in Castle Street, almost next door to Tom Poole's house where the poets met, and watched them. The result was that the Wordsworths had not been at Alfoxden for more than a month or two when they were given notice to leave after their year's lease had run out. If they were upset and disturbed by all this suspicion, there is little evidence of it in either Dorothy's *Journal* or in *Lyrical Ballads*, or, indeed, in all that we know about the way in which they continued to live, roofless for the most part, whether it shone or poured, whether it was morning or midnight. Dorothy and Coleridge, especially, were during these months ceaselessly exploring the combes and woods, she quietly in love with him, he, experiencing for the first time the companionable glories of a mind such as hers, and now bitterly convinced of his wife's inadequacies.

There was one famous walk which Coleridge took on his own. It was from Porlock to Culbone where, just above the church, he found an old house, Ash Farm, where he hid himself away after a row with his difficult lodger, Charles Lloyd, had made him both physically and emotionally ill. He had brought with him some opium and an old book called *Purchas his Pilgrimage* which contained 'a history of the world in sea voyages and land travell by Englishmen and others'. Seated downstairs in the farmhouse he took two grains of opium and, while he waited for it to take effect, read the following:

> In Xamdu did Cublai Can build a stately Palace, encompassing sixteene miles of plaine ground with a wall, wherein are fertile Meddowes, pleasant Springs, delightful Streames, and all sorts of beasts of chase and game, and in the middest thereof a sumptuous house of pleasure.

Coleridge then slept for three hours, had what he called a vision, woke up with a complete recollection of it and was in the act of putting it all down on paper when the most notorious interruption in English literature occurred when 'a person on business from Porlock' called, stayed for an hour, and caused the poet's marvellously remembered dream to vanish. Only fifty of what he believed would have been a poem of some two to three hundred lines had been caught on the page. He returned to Lime Street with them in his pocket, the peerless fragment 'Kubla Khan'. It was only published many years later at Byron's insistence.

An equally propitious ramble, and one taken in far happier circumstances, had occurred a few months earlier than this, when Coleridge and the Wordsworths had suddenly taken it into their heads to walk to Watchet and back. They started late on a dreary November afternoon and so it was nearly dark when they descended West Quantoxhead and looked for beds in the seaside town. For some time Coleridge had been visiting the shore north of Nether Stowey to stare at a ship just as it came into sight on the open sea. It seemed to him an immense moment. The landfall of a ship manned by ghosts was a scary notion with which seafaring people had long frightened themselves, and a friend of Tom Poole's had told Coleridge such a tale. Coleridge was engrossed at this period in a book called *A Voyage Round the World, by the Way of the Great South Sea* by George Shelvocke, a rascally sea adventurer who, in 1719, while steering a ship named the *Speedwell* round Cape Horn, was driven as far south as latitude 61°30' by appalling weather until 'We all observed that we had not had the sight of one fish of any kind since we were come to the southward of the Straights of Le Maire, nor one sea-bird, except a disconsolate black albatross, who accompanied us for several days; hovering about us as if he had lost himself, till Hartley, my second captain... imagining that from his colour it might be some ill-omen, after some fruitless attempts, at length shot the albatross, not doubting, perhaps, that we should have fairwind after it.' After the death of the albatross, the *Speedwell* suffered dreadful gales for six weeks until at last it sighted the coast of Chile. It was Wordsworth who had first read this story and who drew his friend's attention to it. Between the walk to Watchet in November and his journey to Shrewsbury in January (and his meeting with Hazlitt), Coleridge had embodied in 'The Rime of the Ancient Mariner' Shelvocke's anecdote and everything which Nether Stowey's vicinity to the sea had taught his imagination. This became his chief contribution to *Lyrical Ballads* which was to be published, but not understood or much bought, in 1798.

The months of collaborative genius at Nether Stowey came to an end when the Wordsworths were obliged to return the keys of their beloved Alfoxden. They left, as they had arrived, after a short stay with the Coleridges in Lime Street. Coleridge found life without them intolerable and caused concern by temporarily abandoning Sara for a tour of Germany with John Chester, a young neighbour, Dorothy and William. While they were away, poor Sara and the children went back to Bristol to live with her mother. When Coleridge returned from Germany he had no intention of resuming life in a Wordsworth-less Nether Stowey, and in June 1800 he followed them to Grasmere, there to become estranged from one Sara and to begin a hopeless love for another, Sara Hutchinson, Wordsworth's sister-in-law. Soon the Quantock Hills and the cottage in Lime Street were to be recognised by Coleridge as the landscape and home of his most splendid achievements. For the remainder of his life he waited for the lost lines of 'Kubla Khan' to come to him, but they never did. Similarly lost for ever was that spontaneous mastery which, through all the hardships, accompanied him everywhere at Nether Stowey. The place itself remains essentially as he and his friends saw it; scores of the buildings which line its streets, its brook and, of course, its views are those which he and the Wordsworths knew. One does not have to be over-fanciful to see Coleridge hurrying through Castle Street and Lime Street with his zig-zag gait, a thin, dark-haired man in his mid-twenties with clear grey eyes and wide mouth with bad teeth. A confession written by his son Hartley when he was seven might almost apply to the poet himself.

I see it – and I saw it, and tomorrow I shall see it again when I shut my eyes, and when my eyes are open, and when I am looking at other things. But... it is a sad pity, but it cannot be helped, you know, but I am always being a bad boy when I am thinking my thoughts.

MISS MITFORD AND THE CRICKETERS

(*A Writer's Day Book*, Trent Editions, 2006)

With Mary Russell Mitford it is hard to know what to praise most, her style or her spirit. Both rise to heights rarely found either in the women's journalism of her day or in a woman who by every law of the time should have been crushed by adversity. Yet the most obvious aspect of her life and her writing is a kind of thrusting joy, a lack of complaint, a particular type of female sturdiness which pushed on, and against the odds. The odds should have been her own plain, dumpling person and one of the worst fathers in English literature, financial, and thus social ruin, old maidism when she had such an eye for beautiful men, and many other handicaps. Instead she soared and left us, almost by default, one of the best of all village histories. Had she not come down in the world money-wise, had she not been obliged to leave the Big House for the cottage in the street, had not the deplorable Dr Mitford her father needed every penny she could earn for his gambling (whist), she would no doubt have continued to write plays or finish her novel. But having run through two fortunes he needed even the small sums paid by the *Ladies' Magazine*, and so the wonderful little essays about Three Mile Cross near Reading had to be written, eventually five volumes of them. Far from blaming Dr Mitford for being the most selfish parent alive, his daughter dedicated *Our Village* to:

Her only surviving relative and most cherished friend, her beloved and venerable Father, these volumes full of endearing recollections of the beautiful scenery where they have so often wandered, and of the village home where for so many years they have dwelt together in weal or in woe, are affectionately inscribed by the Author.

Nor is she being polite according to the traditions of her day. She adored George Mitford just as her mother had done and she wrote her fingers to the bone to supply him with funds for the card-table and hare-coursing. Youthful and very good-looking Dr Mitford had arrived from Hexham, Northumberland in Alresford, Hampshire about 1785 and by October that year he had courted and married an heiress ten years his senior. It has since been disputed that he had the right to call himself a doctor at all, although he was indisputedly a member of the distinguished north country family, although not a close one. He was attractive, good natured, idle and the complete Georgian wastrel. Mary Russell his wife brought him a splendid town-house with grounds, plus a fortune of £28,000, an enormous sum then. Their only child, born 16 December 1787, inherited her mother's squat body, beetling brow and prominent eyes, and none of her father's beauty, yet her enchanting voice, her warmth and dazzling intelligence, courage and absence of vanity, at once dismissed all that was unprepossessing about her. Unfortunately, Alresford was far too close to Reading for a man with Dr Mitford's weakness. Due to raffish French *emigrés* and their followers, and the stationing in the borough of dashing regiments such as the 15th Light Dragoons (in which in 1793 the poet Samuel Taylor Coleridge hid under the pseudonym of Trooper Silas Tomkyn Comberback), Reading was full of gaming-tables. And thither drifted George Mitford with his wife's capital where, and in London, he lost it all. The family fled penniless to Lyme Regis and from thence to Blackfriars where, on 16 December 1797, the most amazing luck befell it. Dr Mitford had taken his daughter Mary, aged ten, to the Irish Lottery office and told her to pick a number. She picked number 2224 and won £20,000. So the Mitfords returned to Reading, in funds and in triumph. Dr Mitford then bought a nice old farmhouse three miles out of town, demolished it, and erected on the site a handsome Georgian residence, laid our a park, acquired servants, horses and hounds, and launched himself into Hampshire and Berkshire society. And there his loving, though presumably uncritical wife, for they never seemed to quarrel, watched the lottery money dwindle and run out. After some years of financial muddle to which only a Charles Dickens could do justice, total ruin repeated itself.

Between these two disasters Mary received what for her would be the perfect education at M. de St Quintin's girls' school, 22 Hans Place, Chelsea. Dr Mitford had made friends with this aristocratic schoolmaster when he was teaching in Reading and it was at his establishment that Mary was taught English literature, taken to the London theatre and introduced to European culture. At seventeen she returned to live with her reckless father and complacent mother in their debt-ridden mansion. In April 1820, broke once again, they moved to a small, rented cottage only a mile down the road. There George and his wife lived until they died, and from there Mary gradually assembled, month by month, her rural masterpiece *Our Village*. Grand recluses such as the Ladies of Llangollen and other refuges from the hurly-burly of life had made 'retirement' fashionable. The genuineness and simplicity of Mary Mitford which was such a dominant factor in her work, plus her robust personality, soon turned the poor cottage on the side of the Basingstoke-Reading highway into a famous address. To be accurate the cottage was as the ever-truthful Mary wrote, 'a miniature house, with many additions, little odds and ends of places, pantries and what not; all angles, and of a charming in-and-outness; a little bricked court before one half, and a little flower-garden before the other; the walls, old and weather-stained, covered with hollyhocks, roses, honeysuckles, and a great apricot-tree; the casements full of geraniums, the closets full of contrivances and corner cupboards; and the little garden behind full of common flowers, tulips, pinks, larkspurs, pionies, stocks and carnations, with an arbour of privet, not unlike a sentry-box, where one lives in a delicious green light ...' It was in fact a house not all that dissimilar to that lived in by Jane Austen until only three years previously, and Mary Mitford's mother belonged to that same rural gentry which Jane described. Mary's special genius was for accurately and affectionately describing an English village which, on the whole, Jane Austen avoids. There is no need for blame. Both women were artists, not social historians, and artists are selective. Though what they choose to write, and because of their unique vision and literary power, becomes a form of social history in its own right.

Had Mary Mitford stayed on in Bertram House (Dr Mitford could scarcely have invented a more Austenesque name for his mansion), she could never have come close enough to the ordinary folk of Three Mile Cross to know and admire them so intimately. But then, had not her father lost every penny he had for the second time she would never have tried her hand at writing little articles for the magazines. She would have pressed on as a not unsuccessful dramatist, and as a hopeful novelist. At no time was 'Miss Mitford' the lady-amateur scribbling away; she was a serious professional writer whose career was both jeopardised and eventually assisted, though no thanks to him, by her father's ceaseless cry for cash. It was not easy for her. She wrote her eyes out, often late at night when the crowded little home was quiet. A barrier of silence was put up, and great care was taken not to allow the Doctor's weaknesses to become the talk of the town. People were puzzled to hear his daughter speak of him with such love and respect, that is until they realised she meant it. Now and then the facade cracked, as when she wrote to her friend Elizabeth Barrett, another father-burdened writer:

> I may truly say that ever since I was a very young girl I have never, although for some years living apparently in affluence, been without pecuniary care-a care that pressed upon my thoughts the last thing at night, and woke in the morning with a dreary, heavy sense of pain and pressure of something which weighed me to the earth – which I would fain cast off, but could not.

Dr Mitford would even go to London sometimes to collect small sums like £19 from the magazines that published the pieces – which would eventually make up the classic *Our Village* – and lose them at cards. He took to seeing Mary as provider, and she herself harboured the notion that, like the winning of the Irish lottery, her plays would bring a windfall of royalties which would restore the family fortunes. These plays were originally inspired by her seeing William Macready in a popular history-drama entitled *Wallace*. Due to twenty years of war, history-drama and history-painting and poetry were all the rage, and money and reputation was to be made out of all three. John Constable's rural masterpieces stood no chance against Sir Thomas Lawrence's heroic portraits, and failed to sell. At Christmas Mary Mitford wrote in her diary, 'Began *Fiesco*. God grant we may make money of it.' She did not. Two years later, however, the irritable Macready was playing the lead in her play *Julian*, and the royalties from this and other work has been estimated to have been bringing her some £500 a year. These were solid professional earnings for a woman writer and they should have brought comfort to the small house at Three Mile Cross but the appalling Dr Mitford gambled them away. Mary's nickname for him was 'Drum'. Filial declarations in her letters are scarcely credible – 'It is not fame or praise that I want, but the power of assisting my dearest and kindest father.'

It was while she was making her first attempts to conquer the London stage that she began to write the modest sketches which, all unknowingly. would make her immortal. The early nineteenth century saw the birth of women's magazines, pocket-books and annuals. On 37 March 1821 Mary wrote in her diary, 'Went violeting. Worked at my sketch.' Was this *Wild Flowers*, the first of the many and inimitable contents of *Our Village*? If it was, she could never have guessed it. At this moment she had no idea that she had begun one of the greatest country-books. All that she was conscious of was that a magazine was accepting her work and that its decidedly unheroic subject was conveniently near – just outside her front door. Not even when, due to her sketches, the circulation of the *Ladies' Magazine* soared from 250 to 2,000 copies a month did it occur to her that she was engaged on something unusual, an affectionate yet authoritative account of the common people such as no woman of her position had written before. She sent the sketches off one or two a month for the next ten years and gradually accounts of her neighbours, and those of other nearby villages, and occasionally folk from Reading, made her readers see rural England in a new light. She was neither radical nor particularly questioning but she was warm-hearted and because of this social difference gave way to ordinary human closeness in her view of things. No park, no crested gates held back the farming populace, it toiled and played within her hearing. Her habit seems to have been to walk around for copy and to shape her impressions – in her execrable hand – by candle-light. Though each essay is short it reveals the most careful construction and art in the writing.

Another remarkable village chronicle was being created at the time, the 1820s, John Clare's marvellous *The Shepherd's Calendar*, in which village England speaks with its own voice. To read Clare in tandem with Mary Mitford is a startling experience, the one illuminating the other. The first of the five volumes of *Our Village* was published in 1824 and swiftly went into three editions, and soon the astonished author found herself, not only the favourite contributor to an undistinguished periodical but admired by Harriet Martineau, who regarded her 'as the founder of a new style'; Felicia Hemans, who placed *Our Village* among her 'green books'; and Elizabeth Barrett Browning who, although declaring that her old friend tended to see the world in stripes of black and white, recognised that her prose was like the interiors painted by the Dutch masters, accurate, pure, satisfying. There was then nothing like it.

Our Village is introduced to the reader as 'a little world of our own, close-packed and insulated like ants in an ant-hill, or bees in a hive, or sheep in a fold, or nuns in a convent, or sailors in a ship; where we know every one, are known to every one, interested in every one, and authorized to hope that every one feels an interest in us ... Even in books I like a confined locality.' Mary Russell Mitford then proceeds to do the honours of Three Mile Cross, walking the reader from cottage to cottage, garden to garden. occupant to occupant, to make sure that he knows his way around before she begins on the full story. She warns from the start that her preferences will be for plants, cricket and handsome country boys so that one is not to expect a genteel point of view. The effect of her observation is frequently like being able to glimpse village scenes photographically before the camera was invented. People are caught at work, at play, or just coming out of a gate or up a lane, and it is indescribably moving. *Our Village* is a kind of antidote to the tragic anonymity to be found in the 'annals of the poor' school of total literature. It allows the sun to shine through the rural economy of a decade which contained particularly difficult hardships for country people. They are there in the background, the workhouse, the monotonous toil, and especially the physical handicaps for which there was no cure, and which bred a philosophy of life which is now quite gone. It drew the peasantry and the upper classes together in a common plight. Mary Russell Mitford needed to look closely at the village street for the sake of her art, and in looking she came closer to its inhabitants than any woman writer of her time. She was absolutely at ease and her drastically altered circumstances never for one moment gave her the feeling of having come down in the world. It was this ease which allowed everyone around her to be true friends and intimates if they so wished. Although now and then she strikes a note of caution in what she can write about her neighbours – her readers sometimes wondered how she got away with some of the things she said – the keynote of *Our Village* is that of open affection, a keen ear and an honest gaze. The sights and sounds of Georgian England could nor be clearer.

Mary Russell Mitford had a gift for forgiving. She could forgive anything, or almost. Her tolerance must have reached epic proportions in Three Mile Cross, for boys and young men, usually the most intolerantly observed section of any community, found to their astonishment that she liked them as they were, and not as most people wanted them to be, subdued, respectful, quiet. 'I pique myself on knowing by sight, and by name, almost every man and boy in our parish, from eight years old to eighty – I cannot say quite so much for the women.' And in another frank passage she admits to being guilty 'to a strong partiality towards that unpopular class of beings, country boys. I have a large acquaintance among them.' These lads rollick through her pages, Joe Kirby who works from five in the morning until seven at night, and then plays cricket, 'batting, bowling, and fielding, as if for life'; Jem aged thirteen, 'ugly and stunted' who rushes from school into the field, 'fresh, untired, and ripe for action'; George Coper the ploughboy 'singing "Home, sweet Home" at the top of his voice', and most of all the incomparable Jack Hatch who is like an early version of Alain-Fournier's mysterious hero Meaulnes:

I seemed beset by his name, and his presence, invisibly as it were ... He haunts one in dark places. The fiddler, whose merry tones come ringing across the orchard in a winter's night from Farmer White's barn, setting the whole village dancing, is Jack Hatch. The whistler, who trudges homeward at dusk ... is Jack Hatch ... the indefatigable learner of the bassoon ... is Jack Hatch. The name meets me all manner of ways. I have seen it in the newspaper for a prize of pinks; and on the back of a warrant on a charge of poaching ... Everywhere that name meets me ... Can Jack Hatch die? Yes! there is the coffin and the pall – all that I shall ever see of him is there!

Just as Mary Russell Mitford understood village men with a completeness which would have made most women authors of her day blush, so her 'A Country Cricket Match' reveals a totally unfeminine knowledge of the game. This is cricket's first great essay and it deserves to stand alongside those of Neville Cardus and the famous chapter on the cricket-match in L. P. Hartley's *The Go-Between*. Its zest and expertise also reminds us of Hazlitt's sporting essays which Miss Mitford could have seen in the newspapers and journals. Should there still linger in the mind of today's reader the notion that she is a lady-like commentator on life in Three Mile Cross, this marvellous piece of writing will drive it away for good.

She is severe and comical in turn when it comes to her own sex. It irritates her that girls should waste time making samplers or be forced to play musical instruments when they clearly could not. She believed that 'poverty and finery were the twin pests of the age' and throughout *Our Village* there are pleas and demands for women from every background to exert their intelligence and to brush aside the convention of fripperies and tedious accomplishments', and to get out into the countryside to breath the woodland air and walk through the meadows. To be like her. The female fault of compulsive chatter receives a devastating blow in 'The Talking Lady' which must rank as one of the most cruelly accurate accounts of a woman who never draws breath ever written. Jane Austen was more charitable with Miss Bates – 'I am a talker, you know' in *Emma*. Mary Russell Mitford never trivialises any of her characters but presents each one as biography.

She foregoes politeness where certain things must be said but is on the whole good-natured, even if it occasionally gets the better of her. Her outspokenness is that of the eighteenth century and although she was to live until 1855, there would never be anything Victorian about her, the Queen herself was not 'Victorian' and the slow pace of the nineteenth century countryside carried along with it all kinds of rough Georgian values which contrasted greatly with 'progress'. There is little sense of progress in *Our Village*. The seasons and the hours of the day follow each other. The harvests come and go, as do the feastings. The church is no more than a pretty building. The field-work is back-breaking as it always was and always will be. Now and then a coach rattles through. People are young and play a lot, then old and do as best they can. Beauty is concentrated in flowers, children – and dogs. Miss Mitford immortalises her greyhound Mayflower and gives her friend a cocker spaniel. Elizabeth Barrett Browning adores Miss Mitford's present and calls him Flush. Later on, Virginia Woolf will write his biography. In this and other ways, *Our Village* can be seen as the foundation of all kinds of later books, especially, of course, the ever-popular genre of rural life, nature and customs.

It is not possible for a writer to work over so many years in such a small space without revealing almost as much about herself as those about her. Except where her father's disreputable affairs are concerned, Mary Russell Mitford is lacking in caution and goes about the world knowing her own feelings. Her history of Three Mile Cross is also very much her own history – her autobiography. We see a deeply affectionate, clever and rather isolated woman who pays little attention to appearance, who is grossly over-worked by having to look after her invalid parents and at the same time run a professional career, and who seems to have gained the love and respect of her intellectual equals, plus – which was enchanting for her – every young villager in sight. Having an entire population to write about allowed her to vent her private emotions. Residing in the street and not in the park, created intimacies which held exciting ambiguities for a writer, and she was very conscious of them. All these years later we can still detect her liberated spirit and feel the fresh air which she breathed, and, what is as important, shared. Her countryside was a commonwealth.

Nothing is ignored or neglected, even if her distance from large parts of the common experience can only make her take stock of it from afar:

> Jem and Mabel have been parted: they are now at opposite sides of the field – he looking very angry, working rapidly and violently, and doing more harm than good – she looking tolerably sulky, and just moving her hoe, but evidently doing nothing at all. Farmer Thorpe, on his part, is standing in the middle of the field, observing, but pretending not to observe, the little humours of the separated lovers.

This is what Thomas Hardy would see, and what few village watchers will ever see again, courtship among the crops.

JOHN CLARE AND FOOTPATH WALKING

(*John Clare Society Journal*, 14, 1995)

None of us now realise what walking was like to the people who lived in villages like Helpston, all over Britain, for centuries. In her interesting study *The English Path* (1979) Kim Taplin wonders why this, one of the main routes to our literature, particularly our poetry, has received so little social investigation. There are plenty of books on roads, but few explanations of paths. We do of course have a whole library on roads, rambling, and walking these days. But the study of paths themselves is as fugitive as these tracks, which have to be traced through our own rural world and rural writers alike, for us to have any real knowledge of them. One of Kim Taplin's chapters is called *Solvitur Ambulando*. She describes this as an 'old Latin tag [which] means something like "you can sort it out by walking"'. She continues:

> Working out, finding out, unknotting and freeing are all possible connotations of the word *solvitur*, and in this chapter I want to look at the claims of certain writers for the benefits of footpath walking to the spirit. Andrew Young used the words in his poem *A Traveller in Time:*
>
> > Where was I? What was I about to see?
> > *Solvitur ambulando.*
> > A path offered its company.
>
> A companionable path was more apt for a curative release than a road, since solitude, peace, and close contact with nature, as well as the action of walking, are all important ingredients. Problems unravel as the feet cover the miles, but through the body's surroundings, as well as the body's action. (p. 103)

My own existence is as controlled by footpaths as those of my farming ancestors in Suffolk. Friends have often told me that my life would be transformed if I drove a car, forgetting how transformed it has been because I don't. And so I walk a mile of flinty track to fetch the milk, and two miles to the village post office, church or pub, and more miles too when I get stuck with my writing, and wander off to the river path for a little *solvitur ambulando*. So I have done since a boy, in these more or less same scenes. And so of course did most of our forebears, including quite recent ones. And did we but comprehend it, a great amount of our best poetry, novels and essays smell, not of the lamp, but of dust, mud, grit, pollen, and, I expect, sweat. Even the clergy took to the inspiring tramp via something called a 'sermon walk'. There was one at Little Easton rectory, where I used to stay a long time ago. It was a long lawn between discreet hedges and borders, where the Rector could stroll up and down, spinning thoughts around his text for Sunday.

John Clare is the genius of the footpath. So poignant is his statement on the road that it tends to overlay his many and various statements on the footpaths. That wretched road journey, in July 1841, just after his forty-sixth birthday, when he was alone, weakening and penniless, and when he had to, as he said, 'lay down with my head towards the north to show myself the steering point in the morning', was a walk entirely isolated from every other walk he had made, or would ever make. But it is these other walks I would like to dwell upon here.

But first of all I should add that during the nineteenth century – or any century other than our own – to tramp eighty miles along one of Britain's main highways in daily stages was commonplace. Enormous distances were covered by Dorothy and William Wordsworth, and by Coleridge and the Hazlitts – especially Mrs Hazlitt, who was the kind of initial modern woman. She hiked to and fro from Edinburgh to Glasgow during her divorce proceedings, which was a great nuisance to the people carrying them out. Gustav Holst would sometimes walk home to Cheltenham from St Paul's Girls School, in order to compose. William Langland composed much of *Piers Plowman* whilst on the hoof from Cornhill in London to the Malvern Hills where he was born. Had John Clare been the man he was before disasters of all kinds struck at him, being an inspired walker he would not have been either spiritually daunted or physically wounded by the Great North Road trek: but then he would not have needed to have made it.

His true way, though, was the village footpath. Clare's misfortune was to have some of his favourite paths either ploughed up or straightened out. What we have to appreciate is that part of his personality was as concealment-seeking as the nightingale, as hopefully-hidden as that of certain tucked-away plants on the limestone. The other part was, during his youth at least, like that of any other young man: gregarious, fond of company, of drink and of girls. It was the Clare of the footpaths, and their fugitive destinations, and their hidden bends where he could 'drop down' as he described it to write, to daydream, to have his soul fed by what surrounded him, which produced the poetry. Clare was clearly unaware of how often he mentions footpaths, and his essentially secret wanderings, often just within a stone's throw of the little toiling or playing groups of Helpston itself. Some of his finest footpath writing appears in his essay 'The Woodman, or the Beauties of a Winter Forest'. Here Clare reveals his closest observation, not of birds, but of his footpath-walking neighbours, who are exposed by winter, when all the growth is stripped. There was no cover in winter in the countryside. So he wrote:

... the shepherd cuts his journeys short and now only visits his flock on necessity ... Croodling with his hands in his pockets and his crook under his arm he tramples the frosty plain with dithering haste; glad and eager to return to the warm corner of his cottage fire ... The milk-boy too in his morning rambles no longer saunters to the pasture as he had used to do in summer (pausing on every pathway flower and swanking idly along, often staring with open mouth thoughtlessly musing on the heavens as if he could wish for something in the passing clouds; leaning his lazy sides 'gainst every stile he come[s] to, and can never get his heavy clouted shoon over the lowest without resting sighing as he retires with the deepest regret to leave such easy chairs) – But now in hasty claumping tread finding nothing but cold and snow to pause on... he wishes for nothing but his journeys end (*Natural History*, pp. 4-5)

In March that same year, 1825, Clare's footpath presents, where he is concerned, sights more vigorous and fascinating, although he is still not entirely alone. We cannot comprehend – I can just remember it as a child – how peopled the countryside was. I went for a walk not long ago, about six miles, and never met a single person in the fields or gardens, and hardly any cars in the narrow lane. But had I walked in my grandfather's time there would be groups of people – hedging, ditching, doing things, children playing, hundreds of people going for walks, courting couples, etc., because the fields really *were* where everybody met. On 25 March, Clare writes:

I took a walk today to botanize & found that the spring had taken up her dwelling in good earnest she has covered the woods with the white anemonie which the childern call Lady smocks & the hare bells are just venturing to unfold their blue drooping bells the green is covered with daisies & the little Celandine the hedge bottoms are crowded with the green leaves of the arurn w[h]ere the boy is peeping for pootys with eager anticipations & delight (*Natural History*, p. 59)

Well, *our* footpaths are either deserted, or protected, or threatened, or deliberately walked on by self-conscious ramblers and others, and many still exist for their original purpose, which was to make bee-lines across the farmland to moors, or along coasts, or to work. And vast numbers exist on local maps, but not in real local knowledge. Many have grown into lanes, and the lanes themselves have grown into roads. A lane is defined as a narrow way between hedges and banks. A footpath is the narrowest way, trodden between crops or wild plants. John Clare mourned the loss of many of them after Helpston was enclosed. Indeed he raged and ranted about it justly, at what for him was the sacrilege of destroying one of the holiest places in any village: that way along which his people had walked for centuries, a sanctified route to work, a sanctified route to love, a sanctified route to companionship, and to things which were infinitely precious to a man, a woman, or a child.

Some years ago I was taken to Bunyan's footpaths by a friend, and I saw that the site of the great writer's family house was just a rough little cot by the side of a rivulet, which had supplied water for the Bunyans for centuries: nothing there except a few tiles amongst the weeds. The total disappearance of his house excepted, Bunyan's home fields at Elstow must be among the least changed surroundings of any major British author. But they still can only be reached by the footpaths which he used, one of which follows the stream from Harroden, and the other of which leads to the centre of his village. And – shades of John Clare – the vicar of a neighbouring parish had written that in Anno 1625 (this is when Bunyan was three years old) 'one Bunyan of Elstow, climbing of rook's nests in the Berry Wood, found three rooks in a nest, all as white as milk, and not a black feather in them'.

Footpaths did not guarantee solitude; we make a mistake sometimes to think that Clare by simply walking away from the middle of his village found solitude. There was always somebody up a tree, or under a bush, or just riffling about, as they used to say, with a scythe, or hiding away with a sweetheart or a book, or usually just routinely travelling to the workplace. Bunyan was a whitesmith who had to carry a heavy anvil on his back to the houses which needed their pewter mended, and he would sensibly have always chosen the narrow way. But it was not a lonely way.

Footpaths may have had to be used by everybody, but they often could only be walked in single file, and should you meet someone coming from the opposite direction you would step into the undergrowth to let them pass. The constant narrow walking seemed to stimulate the wild flowers which separated just far enough to allow human feet to progress. And similarly there were ground nests perilously close to where one walked. I used to know the writer Adrian Bell, who wrote his trilogy in an old farmhouse, just below mine. During the snowy Christmas of 1928, Adrian Bell noted how, due to the lanes being blocked by drifts, the people were seen plodding straight to their objects across the fields, whether it is to the church spire, snow-encrusted cottages, or the chimneys. 'And who are they?', he asks, 'not travellers from afar, for they would not venture out today at all. No, these are the parish workers, who when times are normal, take serpentine routes by by-roads on bicycles'.

'Take the gentle path', advises George Herbert in his plea, 'Discipline'. Bunyan maintained that a simple way to become a heavenly footman – he means a walker in paradise, not a servant – was to walk the earth. Until recently, few had any alternative. Just before this century, everyone walked. Clare's constant walking in his landscape was the norm; except that sometimes he walked, where his Helpston neighbours were concerned, to what was recognisably work – gardening, ploughing, hedging, erranding, and sometimes to what to them was clearly not work – reading and writing, in dips and hollows – a very strange thing to do; and sometimes he walked just to look. And so he became what most village people dread being, odd, strange, different. With so many of the hereditary footpaths over-exposed by enclosure, Clare walked on, until he himself was mercifully enclosed by the woods and the wilds, and by the useless waste at Barnack, where the plough could not go in. These remote and, in summertime especially, overgrown footpaths became his dreamlines.

He often writes of dropping down, a kind of birdlike movement, when some thought strikes him, in order to make a note of it. When he was working as a lime-burner, he had to walk between two kilns which were about three miles apart, one at Pickworth and one at Ryhall. At Pickworth, he worked with another man; at Ryhall, by himself, and he wrote:

> I often went there to work by myself w[h]ere I had leisure to study over such things on my journeys of going and returning to and fro; and on these walks morning and night I have dropd down 5 or 6 times, to [write] (*By Himself*, p. 22)

There was no dropping down when he was ploughing, which is a very public thing to do. What came to him in the fields he had to hold tight in his head, after a day's toiling on the farm, until he got to his bedroom, then he would write. In his autobiography, Clare uses the walk metaphor to describe his early sense of being both different and isolated. His mother had talked of his going into service, at which he winced, and had given him a box for his things when he left home. All servants left home with a box. But he filled his box with books, and his first poems, and he wrote:

I always looked sullen when my mother talkd of Service ... I now began to value my abilitys as superiour to my companions and exulted over it in secret ... I considerd walking in the track of others ... had as little merit in it as a child walking in leading strings ere it can walk by itself when I happend with them [i.e. his companions] in my sunday Walks I often try'd their taste by pointing out some striking beauty in a wild flower or object in the surrounding s[c]enery to which they woud seldom make an answer and if they did twas such as 'they coud see nothing worth looking at' ... I often wondered that, while I was peeping about and finding such quantitys of pleasing things to stop and pause over, another shoud pass me as carless as if he was blind I thought somtimes that I surely had a taste peculialy by myself and that nobody else thought or saw things as I did (*By Himself* pp. 16-17)

They didn't, of course – until Clare had turned these observations into poems, and then they did. But 'peeping', 'secrets', 'seeing', 'finding': this is the language of the footpath walker. Clare's first poem was called 'The Morning Walk' and it was composed while walking to Glinton, two miles. Years later, when he was working on the great book that never was, his Helpston version of White's *Natural History of Selborne*, he remembered a marvellous sight from a footpath, and wrote:

once when I was young man on staying late at a feast I cross[ed] a meadow about midnight & saw to my supprise quantitys of small nimble things emigrating across it a long way from any water I thought at first that they were snakes but I found on a closer observation that the[y] were young eels making for a large pond called the Islet pool which they journeyd to with as much knowledge as if they were acquainted with the way I thought this a wonderfull discovery (*Natural History*, pp. 69-70)

Clare was more than acquainted with the *way*, that simplest, purest, most eloquent of ways, the footpath. And life only went wrong when he was diverted from it. He knew where he stood. He knew where he should walk. He knew when he should drop down. He knew what no other English writer knew or knows, which is what the English countryman's eyes saw, or sees, in its purity. Clare was hard on the 'downs', as he called them, but we know that countless people, whilst on the way to work, or at work itself, are unwittingly visionary, and that they do not pass through these scenes on earth without taking them in, and wondering at them sometimes. What they – or few of us do, is to drop down in our tracks to write because the need to write is overwhelming, as it is with writers. There were days when Clare could not follow the footpaths. On Thursday 23 September 1824 he writes:

A wet day did nothing but nurse my illness Coud not have walkd out had it been fine very disturbd in conscience about the troubles of being forcd to endure life & dye by inches & the anguish of leaving my childern & the dark porch of eternity whence none returns to tell the tale of their reception (*Natural History*, p. 181)

But a few weeks later – what a change!

Sunday 31 October 1824
Took a walk got some branches of the spindle tree with its pink colord berys that shine beautifully in the pale sun – found for the first time 'the herb true love' or 'one berry' [*Paris quatrifollia*] in Oxey Wood brought a root home to set in my garden (*Natural History*, p. 197)

The following Spring, we have endless footpath walks: one at three o'clock in the morning, and one that ended up with the comic scene of Clare barking like a dog to see off a vixen (13 May 1825):

> Met with an extrodinary incident to day while Walking in Open wood to hunt a Nightingales nest – I popt unawares on an old Fox & her four young Cubs that were playing about she saw me & instantly approachd towards me growling like an angry dog I had no stick & tryd all I coud to fright her by imitating the bark of a fox hound which only irritated her the more & if I had not retreated a few paces back she woud have seized me when I set up an haloo she started (*Natural History*, p. 239)

He had all the countryman's terror of spooks, of shadows, of following footsteps, of fierce animals:

> The boy returning home at night from toil
> Down lane and close oer footbrig gate and style
> Oft trembles into fear and stands to hark
> The waking fox renew his short gruff bark
> While badgers eccho their dread evening shrieks
> And to his thrilling thoughts in terror speaks
> (*Shepherd's Calendar*, 'March', ll. 170-6)

As Margaret Grainger has pointed out, many of John Clare's walks were systematic. He often wandered, but there were times when he walked to plan. She traces three walks: a walk due east from Northborough, to the River Welland and up the west bank to Deeping Gate; a walk from Nine Bridges, Northborough, along the north bank of the North Drain to Lolham Bridges; and a walk between Waldram Hall and Welland Ford (*Natural History*, p. 328). These were systematic walks for work purposes, such as naturalists walk. She also saw signs on some manuscripts which showed that many natural history notes must have been jotted down as he walked, just as he used to do as a young man, when he says 'I usd to drop down behind a hedge bush or dyke and write down my things upon the crown of my hat' (*By Himself* p. 78).

And this also reminds me of the youthful Thomas Hardy. I had to help edit the new Wessex edition of Hardy in the 1970s, and read a lot about his work methods (writers are always fascinated by other writers' work methods, even down to ink and pens, and where they sat). I went to Bockhampton, the thatched birthplace, near Dorchester, and into the room he shared with his brother. There was a little cupboard where they kept their clothes, and there was the narrow wooden window-seat in a casement, on which Hardy sat to write *Far From the Madding Crowd*. The house had been built by his grandfather, in a woodland – the woodland of *The Woodlanders* in fact – and when Hardy needed to stretch his legs he would dash out of the cottage and go for a walk where the woodlanders were working with axes, not chainsaws. When you cut a tree down two men axe it in alternative strokes and white chippings fly out. Thinking of something new to put in *The Woodlanders* Hardy would pick up the chips and write on them, place them in his pockets, take them home and fit them into the chapter. Clare too was doing this kind of thing when he used his hat as a desk. Both writers shared this urgency to put things down.

References to his footpath walks to both of his kinds of work, on the farms and on the page, are myriad in Clare's poetry. In 'Stray Walks' he says:

> How pleasant are the fields to roam and think
> Whole sabbaths through, unnoticed and alone
> (*Middle Period*, IV, p. 302)

And there is the ever-sacred walk to Mary Joyce, the walk he took when he could no longer walk alone. One of the horrible ironies of Clare's life was that he, the walker, was incarcerated for so long (it is one thing to walk on footpaths, and quite another to walk in the grounds of an asylum, or even to Northampton Church). The sacred walk to Mary Joyce went on many years after the courtship: it went on at Northborough, at Epping, and at Northampton. He wrote:

> I've ran the furlongs to thy door
> And thought the way as miles

> With doubts that I should see thee not
> And scarcely staid for stiles (Summerfield, p. 133)

And he wrote:

> Path stiles on which a steeple we espy
> Peeping and stretching in the distant sky
> ('Pleasant Places', *Selected Poems and Prose*, p. 160)

(That is Glinton of course).

I will conclude with that masterpiece of footpath observation, 'The Pewits Nest'. As we read Clare we recognise the poetry of a walking man. It touches us because we are all descended from the walking men, the walking women, the walking children: and not so very long ago either. Sometimes we forget that it wasn't only the poets, and novelists like Hardy, who had these wonderful ideas as they walked. *Solvitur ambulando* was for all of us, because it stimulates (1 don't know whether jogging does that: I rather doubt it). Certainly, these long walks to work, these long walks to school, these long walks with a friend, these long walks just to get out of the house, etc., were part of the pattern of the life of people right up until the modern age. And whilst it happened, their minds ticked over in an extraordinary way. Because men and women haven't all been able to write, or paint, or make music about certain things, it doesn't mean they haven't experienced them – this is a common mistake. When Crabbe was writing his extremely critical descriptions of *The Village* and *The Borough* he always maintained, and made great care, to sort a few individuals from among the sullen inhabitants who, although ordinary fishermen, fieldworkers, and so on, were also ornithologists, collected butterflies, made gardens, knew about marsh flowers and other things. These were the kind of people Clare used to meet. We call them self-educated, but their true education is not something we can comprehend. It was far deeper than the reading of a few books. It was the landscape being articulated in their heads, via their normal work practices. They had to work long hours. They didn't live as long as we live, but they often saw things as much as poets see things. But they didn't write them down. We cannot possibly sum up what happened long ago, we can only accept and know what artists and writers have taught us. The social historian now travels these paths.

Here is a walking poem, called 'Pewits Nest':

Accross the fallow clods at early morn
I took a random track where scant & spare
The grass & nibbled leaves all closely shorn
Leaves a burnt flat all bleaching brown & bare
Where hungry sheep in freedom range forlorn
And neath the leaning willow & odd thorn
And molehill large that vagrant shade supplies
They batter round to shun the teazing flies
Trampling smooth places hard as cottage floors
Where the time-killing lonely shepherd boys
Whose summer homes are ever out of doors
Their chock holes form & chalk their marble ring
And make their clay taws at the bubbling spring
And in their wrangling sport & gambling joys
They stride their clock like shadows – when it cloys
To guess the hour that slowly runs away
And shorten sultry turmoil with their play
Here did I roam while veering overhead
The pewet whirred in many whewing rings
And 'chewsit' screamed & clapped her flopping wings
To hunt her nest my rambling steps was led
Oer the broad baulk beset with little hills
By moles long formed & pismires tennanted
As likely spots but still I searched in vain
When all at once the noisey birds were still
And on the lands a furrowed ridge between
Chance found four eggs of dingy olive green
Deep blotched with plashy spots of chocolate stain
Their small ends inward turned as ever found
As though some curious hand had laid them round
Yet lying on the ground with nought at all
Of soft grass withered twitch and bleached weed
To keep them from the rain storms frequent fall
And here she broods on her unsavoury bed

FIELD WORK

When bye and bye with little care and heed
Her young with each a shell upon its head
Run after their wild parents restless cry
And from their own fears tiney shadows run
Neath clods and stones to cringe and snugly lie
Hid from all sight but the allseeing sun
Till never ceasing danger seemeth bye
(*Middle Period*, III, p. 472)

THE FIELDS OF HARDY AND CLARE

(Lecture to the 11th Thomas Hardy Conference, Dorchester, 1994)

Every now and then the philosopher-historian stands back from the continual cycle of wars and trade to wonder why, throughout the centuries, it is the warrior who receives the honours, and the man who grows the corn little or no honour at all. The customary reason given for this imbalance is that he who protects the tribe must govern it, and he who feeds it must, well, get on with his work. Both know that springtime and harvest wait for no man, and whoever's task it is to turn with the turning year must abide in his 'condition'. Yet why, persists the philosopher-historian, has this so-called 'condition' to be so low in men's esteem that 'peasant', a word which derives from the Old French for a countryman, and which in consequence should have the ring of beauty about it, has instead a ring of what is ignoble? Peasant, says the *Oxford English Dictionary*, is 'a member of a class of low social status that depends on agricultural labour as a means of subsistence'. Yet who, in a society which devours bread and meat and milk and fruit and wine and beer and fish, does not depend on agricultural labour as a means, not of subsistence, but of existence? So why has Hodge had to stumble his way through history, the living image of all that is considered crude and uncultured, when he himself is the cultivator of everything which sustains life, not to mention the creator of landscapes which inspire poets and painters, and which all of us now venerate?

In the nineteenth century two great English poets spoke for this 'condition' in a language which disturbed their readers. John Clare actually spoke directly from it. Thomas Hardy daringly elevated its so-called simple dramas to what he called 'Sophoclean' heights. John Clare, like Robert Burns, had touched the degrading soil. Thomas Hardy, although closely related to those who ploughed and sowed, had not.

Recent biographers and literary critics have had to face up to both Clare's and Hardy's 'peasant' dilemma in order to make sense of both their genius and their predicament. Robert Gittings reminds us of the large number of labouring folk who were Hardy's relations, and whom he passed by. But I have frequently seen such apparently either snobbish or uncaring attitudes during funerals in our village church. One of the 'old people' dies and, behold, the church is, for half an hour, filled with the indigenous population, many of whom I learn only now belong to the dead person's family. 'Oh, yes, didn't you know, I am his cousin. She is my wife's aunt. That is his nephew, the one who went away...' And I have to tell myself that I have witnessed little or no acknowledgement of such relationships during the lifetime of the deceased. Weddings and funerals apart, closely related village people often have a way of living apart although they share the same few miles. In Clare's and Hardy's day, families were vast and full of secrets regarding blood relationships. They were also rather 'cool' – which was due, maybe, to the unmanageability of sustaining true family feeling on such a scale. And there was, too, that other reason, which I shall come to, for why John Clare and Thomas Hardy behaved as they did towards their roots – that local earth out of which sprang their greatness. To be any kind of writer where one was so deeply rooted could be an awkward business – still can. To be one who needed as much environmental nourishment as the crops themselves could be both a godsend and a disaster. John Clare and Thomas Hardy had everything they required for their inspiration to hand, and they knew it. Yet to translate such common stuff into the finest rural poetry and the finest rural novels in the language carried with it a personal exposure which was hard to bear. As we know to this very day, there is a fugitive aspect to every village. The indigenous writer or artist of any kind blows his own and his neighbours' cover, often injuring both himself and his background in the process. No one will ever know where Hardy and Clare 'got it from'. They are sports: odd, strange individuals who are at one and the same time 'one of us' – and yet clearly not one of us. They see what we refuse to see, or cannot see until it is pointed out to us. They are both reporters or chroniclers, and visionaries.

The conventional nineteenth-century reader was puzzled by what was then called 'peasant poetry'; he allowed for its novelty but nothing more. John Clare's publishers – who had published John Keats – promoted Clare as a second Robert Bloomfield. Bloomfield's long poem *The Farmer's Boy* appeared when Clare was a child – a real farmer's boy, a gardener's boy, pot-boy, a little working lad. It sold 26,000 copies. And Clare himself was always to feel a tender affinity with the Suffolk poet whose origins, single burst of literary success and long years of subsequent neglect pitifully reflected his own background and experience. At the same time Clare, the next generation after Bloomfield, was not like him in any way except in his peasantry. He was more learned, more a naturalist, more a poet and, sadly, more grandly tragic. Robert Bloomfield did not work the soil but was exiled from it. In his famous poem he was a London shoemaker remembering his distant village, and who had become literate by reading the London newspapers. Because of his living in London, his ability to write poetry was less amazing than John Clare's ability to write his. There were no crushing village eyes to dodge. All the same, it was more Bloomfield's novelty value than being a writer in the usual sense which made his work sell. The literary establishment abused Keats for his 'cockney' nerve at daring to invade a classic territory, but it gave Bloomfield a condescending pat on the head. And it did much the same twenty years later when Clare's startling collection *Poems Descriptive of Rural Life and Scenery* appeared in 1820 under the publishers' description of him as 'a Northamptonshire Peasant' – the kind of description which initially crippled Robert Burns.

John Clare was twenty-seven when he met his first and only fame. Not for the next century and a half would his rightful standing as the most direct voice of rural Engiand be acknowledged. 'Where did he get it from?' was the question most asked in his own time. They knew where Mr Wordsworth and Mr Coleridge and Lord Byron got it from – and almost where poor young Keats got it from (not the best source) – but where did this little ploughman get it from? Clare's readers were both genuinely and sensationally interested. His reply to a question which dogged him all his life was, 'I kicked it out of the clods.' The poetry, he meant. The rudeness of the questioning received a rough answer which was no answer at all. It reminds us of Christ's first sermon in his local church, given when he was thirty – late in those days for such a debut. He had unrolled Isaiah and spoken so eloquently that those who had known him all his life were bewildered. 'Where does he get it from? Isn't he the carpenter's son?' They meant that he was not a graduate of the rabbinical schools and that neither until this moment had he shown any gift for language.

Both John Clare and Thomas Hardy were recognised by their mothers as being 'different' or special – or indeed odd. As we know, Hardy's mother (aided by his paternal grandmother) nourished the difference with her stream of dreadful tales about Napoleonic War soldiers, ferocious assize justice, rural melodramas, gossip and scandal. Mrs Clare could neither read nor write and, in her son's words, thought 'that the higher part of learning were the blackest arts of witchcraft'. Inadvertently she fed him with those insecurities which were to haunt the cottages right up to the Second World War. He added, however, that his mother's ambition 'ran high of being able to make me a good scholar as she had experienced enough in her own case to avoid bringing up her children in ignorance'. To make him literate, no more. But not to make him a poet – steer him clear of that, please God. Hardy's mother, on the other hand, was determined to give her son as excellent an education as possible and she offended those who charitably provided what they thought was sufficient learning for such a boy. Mrs Clare – 'God help her', wrote her son – had her 'hopeful and tender kindness crossed with difficulty, for there was often enough to do to "keep cart upon wheels", as the saying is, without incurring an extra expense of pulling me to school, though she never lost the opportunity when she was able to send me? A penny a week could not always be found.' But child-labour could. Jemima Hand, Hardy's grandmother, would have none of this. Hardy seems never to have done anything manual, not even a bit of gardening. John Clare carried sacks of flour from the mill, toiled at The Blue Bell, the pub next to his parents' cottage, gardened for Lord Exeter, planted the quickset hedges around the village after it had been enclosed, and ploughed.

What the two poets did have in common was a physical slightness which could have been due to their difficult births. Clare was the weakest baby of twins – his sister died – and Hardy was thrown into a basket as stillborn until the midwife noticed that there was life in him. Clare was a small handsome man of five foot two – the same height as Keats. Hardy was taller and with the disproportionate head and body which one often sees in Victorian photographs. Both writers possessed a kind of watchfulness of expression which made them unusual, even beautiful at times. Both adored women. Each suffered and yet was made great because he could only 'breathe' his native air. This air was both vital – and tainted.

Although it is fanciful to dwell on possible meetings between writers, in Clare's case he would never have heard of Thomas Hardy, who was twenty-four when Clare died and had published nothing. The poor, everlastingly scribbling old man in the Northampton Asylum would not have known of Hardy's existence. Many years before, when Clare was in the Epping Asylum, young Alfred Tennyson was living next door and they might well have glimpsed each other, Clare toiling in the rascally Dr Allen's garden and Tennyson writing *In Memoriam*. Each would have heard the bells of 'Ring out, wild bells!' for they were those of Waltham Abbey. So, Tennyson in mourning, and Clare digging. Being a peasant, it was the policy of nearly all those who tried to help John Clare to set him to manual work.

But it came in handy. Throughout the splendid *The Shepherd's Calendar* we can see the literary strengths of Clare's agricultural skills and expertise. The hand which wrote 'The Nightingales Nest' stacked the sheaves. If Hardy knew of Clare's poems he never mentioned them. His 'Clare' was, of course, William Barnes. Barnes and Clare once wrote with a marvelously similar emotional quality on the same theme – the being forced to leave the old home. Barnes's poem is the unforgettable 'Woak Hill' of which E. M. Forster once said that 'if one has not tears in one's eyes at the end of "Woak Hill", one has not read it'. John Clare's poem on this subject is 'The Flitting', written after a kind but uncomprehending patron set the poet up in a cottage in a village which was not his own village:

> Strange scenes mere shadows are to me
> Vague unpersonifying things
> I love with my old haunts to be
> By quiet woods and gravel springs
> Where little pebbles wear as smooth
> As hermits beads by gentle floods
> Whose noises doth my spirits sooth
> And warms them into singing moods
>
> Here every tree is strange to me
> All foreign things where ere I go
> Theres none where boyhood made a swee
> Or clambered up to rob a crow
> No hollow tree or woodland bower
> Well known when joy was beating high
> Where beauty ran to shun a shower
> And love took pains to keep her dry...

William Barnes is still accused of inaccessibility because of his use of dialect, which astonished me, as it did E. M. Forster and countless other readers who knew nothing of Dorset's local language. Barnes was born eight years after Clare and outlived him by almost a quarter of a century. In the social terms of their day, Barnes the farmer's son, the schoolmaster and clergyman, would have belonged to a realm that was quite dizzily aloft from that of the country-folk whom he wrote about. And yet he articulates their very souls.

Clare's poetry is the English field given voice. There was no kicking it out of the clods but a profound drawing of it from both the cultivated and uncultivated land of his birthplace. If our farms and wildernesses could utter it would be in his words. His is a uniquely informed utterance. A huge reading as well as a constant contemplation of his native scenery, between them, produced in him a kind of rural scholarship which causes the modern student to alter his or her perception of what it was like to be a farm labourer in late-Georgian Britain. Simply because a shepherd or ploughman could not, or did not, write, we have no reason to believe that he did not feel or see the things which a realistic poet such as John Clare felt and saw. Or indeed, did not share William Barnes's knowledge of the innermost tenderness of humanity. John Clare's gradual collapse of health (exacerbated, as is so often the case, by 'helping hands' and pressures of all kinds) robbed us of what surely would have been one of the most remarkable rural works of all time, a 'peasant' naturalist's version of Gilbert White's classic *The Natural History of Selborne*. Fractions of this wonderful book appear in Margaret Grainger's *The Natural History Prose Writings of John Clare*.

The land and its workers also speak through Thomas Hardy with an authentic but different voice. It is the voice of the trapped, of men and women who are hedged in as much by what we now call the environment as by their parish boundaries. Not by any other writer is an indigenous group so fatally blown about by localised storms. *Far from the Madding Crowd*, published in 1874 when Hardy was 34, heralded his arrival as a great novelist. In this tale he spreads a few fields and pastures, a few houses, a few short travels in that humdrum direction or this, and a few villagers in stances which have been ordained by local tradition or by classical myths. So far, so familiar. But then Hardy does something not seen before. He gives his characters a double dimension, the one which they recognise and the one by which a Greek playwright would have recognised them. They work incessantly, and time for such business as making love or sightseeing or gossiping has to be snatched. Talk takes place during tasks and if you wanted to do something extraordinary in the improving line, you hoped for a little accident or a brief illness. I once read of a nineteenth-century parson who, walking by a cottage about 9.30 p.m., heard a family singing Wesley's hymns and reproached it for not getting enough sleep to do its fieldwork efficiently. It was not uncommon for labourers to be given very small gardens so that all their energies went into their master's farm. ''Twas a bad leg allowed me to read the Pilgrim's Progress', says Joseph

Poorgrass. Cain Ball managed a visit to Bath due to a respite from toil caused by having 'a felon upon his finger'. The plot of *Far from the Madding Crowd* is so firmly tied in to the implacable demands of work that an element of its comedy insists that, by right, there should be neither the strength nor the opportunity to do anything else. In Hardy leisure frequently breeds disaster. In *Far from the Madding Crowd*, and like John Clare, he saturates all the common knowledge of his home place with his reading. Hardy's intention, brilliantly realised, was a stylised actuality, the style being that of the classic pastoral, the actuality that of standard farming practice during the time of his mother's youth. He said that he meant to complete this novel 'within a walk of the district in which the incidents are supposed to occur', and that he found it 'a great advantage to be actually among the people described at the time of describing them'.

An advantage, yes, a comfort, no. They were too close for that. A few years later Hardy was to explain what he believed was the purpose of fiction. It was, he said, 'To give pleasure by gratifying the love of the uncommon in human experience, mental or corporeal', this succeeding most when the reader was made to feel that the characters were 'true and real like himself'. The critics were upset. How could farm-labourers ('peasant' was going out by the 1870s) think and hope and behave, well, like us? Whilst admitting that Mr Hardy had 'hit upon a new vein of rich metal for his fictitious scenes', a contemporary critic viewed Hardy's treatment of farm labourers with some irony: 'Ordinary men's notions of the farm labourer of the Southern counties have all been blurred and confused. It has been the habit of an ignorant and unwisely philanthropic age to look upon him as an untaught, unreflecting, badly paid, and badly fed animal, ground down by hard and avaricious farmers, and very little, if at all, raised by intelligence above the brutes and beasts to whom he ministers.'

Such remarks in a review of *Far from the Madding Crowd*, in the *Saturday Review*, shockingly illuminate the predicament of John Clare half a century earlier. In 1823 he was at the pinnacle of his brief celebrity. Here was a peasant writing books! Here was a peasant who had been to London and who had hobnobbed with men of letters,

Coleridge, Lamb, Hazlitt. Taylor the publisher, still with the once bestselling Robert Bloomfield in mind, exulted in this phenomenon and he worked hard to polish up Clare's grammar in order that ladies and gentlemen would be able to read his work. In vain the poet protested. The miracle – or novelty – was that he could write verse. It need only be made readable. His publisher promoted Clare but wrecked his poetry, and there was little he could do about it. He was a peasant and had to be guided. The restoration of Clare's text during the 1960s onwards (plus our ever-increasing interest in the countryside) has uncovered a Clare as fresh and captivating as a landscape from which the varnish and dirt of ages have been skilfully removed.

Far from the Madding Crowd is set between two long stretches of agricultural depression and in what historians like to dub 'a golden age'. In his later novels, Hardy would be accused of darkening the English countryside for his own melodramatic purposes. The truth of the matter was that towards the close of the nineteenth century, and a whole hundred years after the birth of John Clare, the lives of Britain's farmworkers had become so poverty-stricken and tragic that the Norfolk novelist Mary Mann, herself a farmer's wife, could look at their lot and presume that only some grim purpose known to God could justify it. In Hardy's essay 'The Dorsetshire Labourer', written in 1883, we have a direct piece of rural sociology which reveals how much he knew of what was going on all around him. And yet he could say, quite truthfully in certain respects, 'that happiness will find her last refuge on earth [among those who till the soil], since it is among them that a perfect insight into the conditions of existence will be longest postponed'. Where ignorance is bliss, in other words.

Impertinent questions drew Clare's response that he kicked his poems out of the clods. Does Thomas Hardy celebrate the life of the (human) clod? Never. This slur on village England he refutes from the very beginning. For one thing, it was too near home. Yet the problem of animating what had, until he began to write, been ignored as being below the level of polite interest, or as being simply lumpen, would have been insuperable had he tried to work it out. But he did not. What he did was to write so superbly about his own people that it made it pointless to ask, 'Why these poor toilers?' Behind him lay the harsh facts of Jemima's youth. All around him lay a mass of inherited material of every kind: the best, the worst. In a poem called 'Spectres that Grieve', one of many which are threnodies for the ordinary country folk, Hardy makes the dead who have been denied a proper history by their so-called betters, protest from the grave:

> We are stript of rights; our shames lie unredressed,
> Our deeds in full anatomy are not shown,
> Our words in morsels merely are expressed
> On the scriptured page, our motives blurred, unknown.

Much of Hardy's work defends the dispossessed. But it has to do so from a height. Being what he was, he could not be what he had come from. Similarly John Clare. This is the dilemma of the great writer or artist who stays at home. Hardy's actual touching-the-soil poems are few and far between. One is 'The Farm-Woman's Winter':

> If seasons all were summers,
> And leaves would never fall,
> And hopping casement-comers
> Were foodless not at all,
> And fragile folk might be here
> That white winds bid depart;
> Then one I used to see here
> Would warm my wasted heart!
>
> One frail, who, bravely tilling
> Long hours in gripping gusts,
> Was mastered by their chilling,
> And now his ploughshare rusts.
> So savage winter catches
> The breath of limber things,
> And what I love he snatches,
> And what I love not, brings.

Hardy is unusual as a writer in that he lets characters from his novels have an extra life in his poems. There is 'Tess's Lament', and in 'The Pine Planters' we have Marty South, the heroine of *The Woodlanders*, having to fell trees alongside the lover who refuses to look at her. Their actions are mechanical:

> We work here together
>   In blast and breeze;
> He fills the earth in,
>   I hold the trees.
>
> He does not notice
>   That what I do
> Keeps me from moving
>   And chills me through.
>
> He has seen one fairer
>   I feel by his eye,
> Which skims me as though
>   I were not by.
>
> And since she passed here
>   He scarce has known
> But that the woodland
>   Holds him alone.
>
> I have worked here with him
>   Since morning shine,
> He busy with his thoughts
>   And I with mine...

But it was for Hardy the desolate fields of Flintcomb-Ash which represented the nadir of farm toil. It is where poor Tess ends up when she is reduced, as so many women were, to near-slavery. In 'We Field-Women' Hardy shows this place in varying degrees of weather:

How it rained
When we worked at Flintcomb-Ash,
And could not stand upon the hill
Trimming swedes for the slicing-mill.
The wet washed through us – plash, plash, plash:
How it rained!

How it snowed
When we crossed from Flintcomb-Ash
To the Great Barn for drawing reed,
Since we could nowise chop a swede.
Flakes in each doorway and casement-sash:
How it snowed!

How it shone
When we went from Flintcomb-Ash
To start at dairywork once more
In the laughing meads, with cows three-score,
And pails, and songs, and love – too rash:
How it shone!

But of course it is in his magnificent set pieces of the farming year, such as the famous scene in chapter 22 of *Far from the Madding Crowd* in which shearing is given a sumptuous treatment unlike anything previously seen in literature, that Thomas Hardy reveals the closeness of his eye, if not his hand, to his local earth. Similarly, the description of the patriarchal splendours about dairying in Tess where a Dorset farmer controls a world like that of Abraham. In such scenes Hardy challenges every previous concept of the 'simple task' and directs the reader's vision to a view of labour which holds within it those satisfactions which are usually found in poetry and religion. His story-telling is filled with meditation. One is made aware of his divided intelligence as he sees life as the shearers see it, and then as he himself sees it. Joseph Poorgrass sums up the whole business of farming with his, 'Tis the gospel of the body, without which we perish, so to speak it.'

John Clare would have agreed. But his position was a complex one. When a man ploughs, it is with one foot in the furrow and one on the level. It makes a rough progress, up and down, up and down. He was the peasant; he was the supreme English poet of the countryman's experience. Eventually – one could say inevitably – the unevenness tripped him into Northampton General Lunatic Asylum where, far from insane most of the time, he wrote. With little else to do, the output was enormous – and uneven. This cache of sometimes earthbound, often soaring rural poetry lay mostly buried until the 1920s onwards, when writers such as Edmund Blunden, the Tibbles, Geoffrey Grigson, Geoffrey Summerfield and Eric Robinson brought it into the sunlight.

The progress of agriculture is a kind of Alps, all peaks and plunges. For so natural an activity, it is strangely precarious and easily ruinous. Clare and Hardy sang its heights and charted its depths. Clare lived through the trauma of Enclosure, cursing its evils, and then through the bitter years of Chartism. Hardy was just at the beginning of his career when a biblical spell of rain washed away all the brief farming prosperity of the 1850s and brought in the long years of depression. By the 1890s, when he renounced novel-writing for poetry, there began what they called 'the flight from the land' as the labourers fled from agricultural misery. At this moment another young writer, Henry Rider Haggard, who had made a name with exciting adventure stories about Africa and who in his thirties was now farming in Norfolk, tried to halt the exodus. All this just a century after the birth of Clare and just when Hardy had abandoned fiction.

Clare was in continuous flight from the land as workplace, but only to find his true working place in the little hidden copses and dells and woods where he could write unseen and undisturbed and especially unnoticed. His and Hardy's poetry differed because one touched and the other watched the soil. Each fully understood its majesty and its treachery. Clare's work is alternately a *Te Deum* and a *De profundis* to the cultivated and uncultivated acres of his native Helpston, the place of endless work and endless dreams.

WHERE HARDY DWELT

(From *Writers and Their Houses*, Hamish Hamilton, 1993)

The Higher Bockhampton cottage and the Dorchester villa stand some three miles and eighty-five years apart, although with Thomas Hardy there was never any kind of separation. Both emotionally and imaginatively, his two homes remained interconnected. Between them there had been a number of other addresses in which poems and stories had been written, but all of these were in effect ante-rooms to Bockhampton and Max Gate. His great-grandfather had built the cottage in 1800 on ginger sand and the author and the third Thomas had built Max Gate in the cemetery of Durnonovaria (the Roman Dorchester). Hardy's, as the cottage was known before Hardy was born in 1840, is the Georgian version of the type of cottage in which the countrymen of Dorset had lived for centuries, a snug shelter of cob and boughs. To one side stretched the plantation which supplied its open hearth with limitless fuel; to the rear stretched the powerful heathland he was to call 'haggard' Egdon. Woods and wastes, the Frome valley pastures and stony cornfields provided the ecology and the mystery for both houses. Late in life Hardy continued to walk or bicycle between them, for his mother, Jemima, lived until 1904. She was his original muse: the seeds of much of his finest work, *Tess, The Dynasts* and many of the poems, had been sown by her. Hardy called himself a Victorian, but through Jemima, who died aged ninety, he reached back in his conversations with her to Napoleon and to the horrors of the Georgian countryside, to the implacable nature of the English class system and to the huge old melodrama of human existence as villagers had always witnessed or endured it.

Hardy's fate, like that of so many great writers, was to be caught between two cultures: that into which he had been born and that into which he was led by his genius. Bockhampton and all that it represented was what made him a novelist and poet. But when, eventually, he set up house for himself on the outskirts of the county town, Hardy's went with him. Max Gate has drawn some of the strongest responses ever to a writer's house. Maybe Hardy, when he designed it and got his brother Henry to build it, sharp Broadmayne brick and slate throughout, thought that its sheer conventionality would deflect the remorseless interest in his background which, almost from the start, had become such a worry to him. Or maybe, and this is something which none of his biographers appears to have considered, his wife, Emma, determined what their first real home should be like. In the ten years since their marriage in 1874 her little architect had become a famous novelist who could afford to give her a respectable house with maids and a gardener, something in the line of the new parsonage houses which the Church of England was building everywhere. If Max Gate suggests anything, it is a nineteenth-century rectory, and this would have delighted Emma. But in whatever way this unforgettable and hauntingly strange yet ordinary house came into being, there is no doubt at all about the kind of life which Thomas and Emma lived in it. Literature apart, it was one of severe bourgeois order and respectability. The determination on both their parts was to live, not as artists – and Emma was in her own muddled and sometimes impressive way unorthodox and free-spirited, as well as the 'onlie begetter' of one of the most profound sequences of love-poetry in the language – but as gentry. Max Gate thus confronts everyone who enters it with its never-to-be-solved puzzle. Why such a facade when everything he wrote allowed such open access to the very source of his being, socially and imaginatively? He and Emma were forty-five when they moved into it, there to lead an existence which, for all that has been written about it, remains a mostly untold tale. Hardy often allows vivid glimpses of the hidden life behind what he would have called 'the front elevation' of a house. In his courtship novel *A Pair of Blue Eyes* we have a writer calling out, "'Come in!" from distant penetralia. He and Emma were famously welcoming to their visitors, maintaining the facade of their marriage in the approved Victorian manner. Max Gate retains its formality and its welcome. It is not only the succession of studies used by Hardy which are so overwhelmingly inviting, but every stick and stone. It is a 'calling' house whose unusual voice can be heard above the traffic now rushing past it. Set back among what remain of the hundreds of trees which Hardy planted round it, it is as instantly recognizable to the literary traveller as is the Taj Mahal to the tourist, and its physical reality as surprising.

Thomas Hardy was born in the cottage that his great-grandfather had built at Higher Bockhampton, a hamlet which was part of the parish of Stinsford. His father was a self-employed mason and his mother, Jemima Hand, was a servant girl whose family had suffered crushing poverty. Her mother was a well-read woman who had come down in the world by falling in love with and marrying a servant. Jemima Hand was four months pregnant when Thomas Hardy II married her on 22 December 1839. Their son was born in the middle bedroom of the cottage on 2 June 1840 after a desperate labour, and then cast into a basket as dead. A few minutes later the midwife rescued the boy and exclaimed, 'Stop a minute: he's alive, sure enough!' From then on Hardy's young parents, his handsome father, his pragmatic mother, appeared to have had an understanding of the special nature of this child, filling his early years with the richest kind of rural culture and, before long, daring to offend the lady of the manor by seeing that he received an education which would take him out of village toil and into one of the professions. Hardy remained never anything less than embarrassed by the informality of this education, but it did for him what 'Christminster' could never have done, kept him at the heart of all rural experience whilst giving him a unique language and philosophy in which to describe it. Taught music by his father, story-telling by his mother, poetic form by the Anglican liturgy, the true depths of local speech by William Barnes, architecture by both provincial and London standards, and classical drama by a young friend whose own life was as tragic as anything to be found in Sophocles, Hardy's culture could not have been more perfect for his purpose. Added to which was his minute interest in everything which had happened to him personally, so that the reader enters both the cottage and the villa, as well as Hardy's private life, painfully and brilliantly well-briefed. He is the supreme poet of regret, of what was and what might have been.

The Hardys were 'liviers' or life-holders of a property, rural craftsmen and businessmen whose position had a certain independence from both the local farmers and the gentry. Most of their relatives, however, were less free and worked as labourers and domestic servants. As was common with sprawling Victorian families, Hardy maintained strong links with just a few of those close to him and ignored the rest. Chief among the former were his mother, his sister Mary and his cousin Tryphena. Beautiful Tryphena, later a headmistress, was his first great love. Quiet Mary, also a teacher, occupied a role in his development, it has been suggested, similar to that of Dorothy Wordsworth in the art of her brother William.

Although his family modestly extended the Bockhampton cottage, Hardy's imagination expanded it in various ways, first to accommodate scenes from *Under the Greenwood Tree*, in which it is Tranter Dewy's house, and, towards the end of his life, to accommodate a part-factual, part-dream notion he was anxious to purvey of his ancestry. But now and again the architect speaks, as when Hardy describes the actual making of such a building. He was supporting an appeal by the Royal Society of Arts to correctly understand and preserve England's ancient cottages which at that moment, the 1920s, were being torn down in their thousands as unhygienic and being replaced by brick and slate:

> By merest chance I was able, when a child, to see the building of what was probably the last of these old-fashioned cottages of 'mudwall' and thatch. What was called mudwall was really a composition of chalk, clay and straw – essentially, unbaked brick. This was mixed up into a sort of dough pudding, close

to where the cottage was to be built. The mixing was performed by treading and shovelling – women sometimes being called in to tread – and the straw was added to bind the mass together, a process that had doubtless gone on since the days of Israel in Egypt and earlier.

It was then thrown up by pitchforks on to the wall, where it was trodden down, to a thickness of about two feet till a 'rise' of about three feet had been reached all round the building. This was left to settle for a day or two, and then another rise was effected, till the whole height of the wall-plate was reached, and then that of the gables, unless the cottage was hipped, or had a 'pinion' end, as it was called. When the wall had dried a little the outer face was cut down to a fairly flat surface with a spade, and the wall then plastered outside and in. The thatch projected sufficiently to prevent much rain running down the outer plaster [rain pouring from roofs was a desolating sight to Hardy], and even where it did run down the plaster was so hard as to be unaffected, more lime being used nowadays. The house I speak of is, I believe, still standing, unless replaced by colder brick-and-slate ... I have never heard of any damp coming through these mudwalls ... Yet as everybody, at any rate every builder, knows, even when brick walls are built hollow, it is difficult to keep damp out entirely in exposed situations.

Landowners who have built some of these latter express their wonder that the villagers prefer their dingy old hovels (as they are regarded) with rooms only six feet high, and small dormer windows with little lead squares, to the new residences with nine-feet rooms and wide windows with large panes. The explanation is the simple one that in the stroke of country winds a high room is not required for fresh air, sufficient ventilation entering through the door and window, and that the draught through the hollow brick wall makes the new cottages cold in winter.

I would therefore urge owners to let as many as are left of their old cottages remain where they are, and to repair them instead of replacing them with bricks, since, apart from their warmth and dryness, they have almost always great beauty and charm.

As with virtually everything Hardy wrote, there is no private detachment from this public advice. He had passed from mudwall and thatch to bricks and slate, and had felt the chill. He had loved

Bockhampton, but what he felt for Max Gate could not be put so simply. In the defensive autobiography which he wrote in the third person under his second wife's name, he says that the old homestead is only a fragment of what it was, although the reverse is true. The cottage he knew was nearly twice the size of that built by his great-grandfather. Moreover, the original cob had been bolstered with brick and cement. Up until 1857 there were in effect a pair of cottages, one of which was the home of his widowed grandmother. When she died that year, it is probable that these two little houses were turned into one. Forty years later it was altered once more, and the lean-to was given cavity walls! Country people will always do the domestic best for themselves as their families swell and as what they believe to be improved building materials arrive in the district. Young Hardy ruined St Juliot's church with his 'restoration'; and many a devoted cottage-dweller in the 1990s is ruining some old home with his DIY improvements. Each man kills the thing he loves.

The teenage Hardy celebrated the unity of his birthplace with his first poem, 'Domicilium'. In it the cottage itself barely exists, only its setting. His real home is landscape, not a roof:

> In days bygone –
> Long gone – my father's mother, who is now
> Blest with the blest, would take me out to walk.
> At such a time I once inquired of her
> How looked the spot when first she settled here.
> The answer I remember. 'Fifty years
> Have passed since then, my child, and change has marked
> The face of all things. Yonder garden-plots
> And orchards were uncultivated slopes
> O'ergrown with bramble bushes, furze and thorn:
> That road a narrow path shut in by ferns,
> Which, almost trees, obscured the passer-by.
>
> 'Our house stood quite alone, and those tall firs.

And beeches were not planted. Snakes and efts
Swarmed in the summer days, and nightly bats
Would fly about our bedrooms. Heathcroppers
Lived on the hills, and were our only friends;
So wild it was when first we settled here.'

The poem is full of undercurrents. It would be in his maternal grandmother's bedroom, now connected with his paternal great-grandfather's cottage, that Hardy would write *Under the Greenwood Tree* and *Far from the Madding Crowd* and from which, in 1870, he would set out for 'Lyonnesse' and all its consequences. And those 'ferns, which, almost trees, obscured the passer-by' point to *The Return of the Native* and to Hardy's recognition that people living in certain ecological circumstances are in a trap. And it was also in this small room under the eaves which he shared with his brother Henry that he would define his literary territory and write the name Wessex for the first time. In his eighties he wrote a vivid description of his home hamlet, showing the changes during his lifetime, and including the come-down from cob to brick.

The domiciles were quaint, brass-knockered, and green-shuttered then, some with green garden-doors and white balls on the posts, and mainly occupied by life-holders of substantial footing like the Hardys themselves. In the years of his infancy, or shortly preceding it, the personages tenanting these few houses included two retired military officers, one old navy lieutenant, a small farmer and tranter [carrier], a relieving officer and registrar, and an old militiaman, whose wife was the monthly nurse [and to whom English literature owes an incalculable debt for noticing that the stillborn Thomas was in fact faintly breathing]. These being mostly elderly people, the place was at one time nicknamed 'Veterans' Valley'. It was also dubbed 'Cherry Alley', the lane or street leading through it being planted with an avenue of cherry-trees. The life-holds fell into hand, and the quaint residences with their trees, clipped hedges, orchards, white gatepost-balls, the naval officer's masts and weather-cocks, have now perished every-one, and have been replaced by labourers' brick cottages and other new farm-buildings.

Hardy had an eye for the conditioning of people by what he termed 'meditative solitude', something a poet or a religious would pursue as a necessity, but which was part of the lives of the villagers of his day without their knowing it. The cottage at Bockhampton was filled with it, even when it was full of Hardys. Those seven little rooms with their chestnut floorboards and bumpy whitewashed ceilings, ancient adze-marked doors from another house, fragile stairs and solid flags, exuded it. It was in the porch that his mother had discovered him sleeping with a snake on his chest. Inside, the watching boy would wait for the westering sun to fire the Venetian-red wall of the staircase and then sing Watts's 'And now another day is done'. The Max Gate study would be given this rich colour, which was both vital and elegiac. Both houses were where the living doubled up with the dead:

> Here is the ancient floor
> Footworm and hollowed and thin,
> Here was the former door
> Where the dead feet walked in.

On his forty-fourth birthday – the year before he moved into Max Gate – he had walked from the cottage to what would be the setting of *The Woodlanders*, his own favourite among the novels, and into what as children he and Henry had called 'the birds' bedroom', and written:

> Alone in the plantation, at 9 o'clock. A weird hour: strange faces and figures formed by dying lights. Holly leaves shine like human eyes, and the sky glimpses between the trunks are like white phantoms and cloven tongues. It is so silent and still that a footstep on the dead leaves could be heard a quarter of a mile off

Soon it would be:

The change to a high new house,
He, she, all of them – aye,
Clocks and carpets and chairs
On the lawn all day ...

Hardy had published nine novels by the time he moved to Max Gate and the tenth, *The Mayor of Casterbridge*, was completed just a few weeks before the wagons carried his furniture up the newly made drive. An earthwork called Conquer Barrow had been flattened to make this drive, during which operation a row of skeletons had been decapitated. Two of them lay clasped together like lovers. They were Romano-British but he placed them in pre-history:

So long, beyond chronology,
Lovers in death as 'twere,
So long in placid dignity
Have you lain here!

Years later, taking a spade from the shed to bury one of his beloved cats – they sometimes came to grief on the nearby railway line – he wondered if some passer-by might think he was doing a bit of archaeology. Instead, was he not laying to rest 'a little white furred thing' whose existence had meant more to him than the whole of the Roman empire? Interring among the legions' dust Comfy, Snowdove, Tippety, Marky and all the others when their time came spoke to him, as every other thing did, of human vanity.

When Hardy and Emma came to Max Gate, they had been married for eleven years and had lived in a succession of rented houses, both in London and in the country. Max Gate set the seal on Hardy's becoming a popular novelist with an assured income. His stories were serialized in the best magazines and he was being accepted as a distinguished figure in the literary world. Also, that interest of his readership in his background as well as his books, and which caused him so much anxiety, was running high. Max Gate stood at the very centre of what he was and what he knew. An early visitor found it stark and reported, 'The place is as lonely as it is elevated.' At first Hardy himself seemed to shrink from what he had created on an acre and a half of Duchy of Cornwall wasteland just outside Dorchester, and complained:

> The house is bleak and cold
> Built so new for me!

Its name derived from Mack's toll-gate, which had stood on this spot. One of Hardy's first tasks was to create a windbreak to protect his property from the coastal gales roaring across Egdon. He built a garden wall and planted a forest of Austrian pines, between two and three hundreds in all. Their function would be not only to protect him from the weather, but to hide him away from ever more inquisitive eyes. Also they could be a birds' bedroom for Emma, a great bird-watcher. Soon after moving in, he began work on *The Woodlanders*, which acted as a bridge between his seedling pines and the soaring plantation at Bockhampton, crowded with 'figures formed by dying lights'. Hardy uses trees as a haven against the 'he'th', as the Dorset people called their pitiless moor, although his pine shelter round Max Gate was to prove excessive:

> I set every tree in my June time,
> And now they obscure the sky.

The house remains tree-ringed, but not to the melancholic extent it was when all the pines closed in on it, and the Hardy-reader's first sight of it is among the great associative experiences.

The regular emergence of bones and stones from the garden gave Hardy a time pattern which helped to console him for the loss of the Christian calendar, which for him became that latest of things. One of his immediate intentions was to fix a sundial on the Max Gate turret which read 'Quid de Nocte?' ('What of the night?'), a question from Isaiah – but it was never achieved until his second wife, Florence, saw to it after his death. It hangs there still, telling good time. What he called 'the Druid Stone' was dug out of the garden while he was finishing *Tess*. It took seven men with crowbars to heave it out of the earth and erect it opposite to what was to be his last study. It had lain for thousands of years among burnt bones and ashes, and now it faced the sun. 'I want to see the deeper reality underlying the scenic, the expression of what are sometimes called abstract imaginings.' Extensions to the house over the years allowed Hardy to write facing new directions and Emma to find privacy from the sight and sound of his fame. Their final work-rooms, his above the kitchen and hers in the roof, are intensely affecting. She, writing the memoir which would after the long, faltering marriage hurry him back to their courtship and a flood of poems, had even managed to cut herself off from the domestic noises of Max Gate. He, on the other hand, wrote *The Dynasts* and most of his best poetry to the muted accompaniment of the maids' chatter and games of ring-board from below. In this room Hardy found his ultimate greatness. The gardener would glimpse the old man from the corner of his eye, wearing a shawl and staring at the Druid Stone and then towards Rainbarrow.

Emma died in her attic boudoir. Her last act – astounding to him – was to break his heart. Florence introduced a bathroom and her own kind of light. But Max Gate now reflects that of the two tough personalities who created it in their middle age. By keeping it in normal homely use, it says more about the lives of Hardy, Emma and Florence, and more about Tess and those other immortals, than ever it could had there been an attempt at keeping everything as it was and roped off. Max Gate had its drawbacks, but it does seem that during Hardy's lifetime it was the done thing to mock it. After a chilly start he and Emma grew to love it. Neither knew much about comfort but they knew everything about symbols, about spirits and about the way in which what lay outside looked in at the window. Max Gate pays homage to the magic of the imagination, and also to the ennui of married life:

> Within the common lamp-lit room,
> Prison my eyes and thought;

Let dingy details crudely loom,
Mechanic speech be wrought.

It has often been said that Hardy's famous sense of irony and of the macabre would have been exercised had he known that his heart and the rest of him would lie some 135 miles apart. To have known that his red study would be cut out of his house and made what he would have called 'a show' in Dorchester Museum might equally have amused and shocked him. But there it is, his study in a glass case for us to gaze into, rather as into an icon, our eyes boring through the smooth surface of his handsome desk to the wonders he created on it. His pens, each marked 'Tess', 'Casterbridge', etc. and put away, lie in their tray. His fiddles and academic robes are respectfully arranged. The calendar is stopped at 1928. The museum itself, like a tiny Liverpool Street station, all fretted cast-iron and galleries, which holds this heart of Max Gate was built by Crickmay, Hardy's old employer. Nearby on a shelf lie fibulae and shards which Hardy preserved from the mounds of soil which his brother's workmen dug out to lay Max Gate's foundations. That he should be laying his own stratum to the remorseless yet beautiful pressed-down stratifications called history, thrilled him. At first he and Emma had watched gloomily as the Roman bones were tossed to the surface. What an omen. In the spring of 1884 the cleared plot became a sheet of primroses and then of 'graegles' – wild hyacinths – and they were cheered.

Holding these two houses in trust, the cottage and the villa, and each of them so much more than this, could have presented untold difficulties had it not been realized that Hardy's 'own people', as it were, should be left to care for them. Bockhampton is a lesson in the understanding of the fragile elements which make up a sturdy Dorset homestead. Max Gate continues its original role of prim bourgeois residence, and wholly fails to conceal the fact that it is still one of the world's most potent literary shrines. Writers' houses sometimes have little to do with the books written in them, but these buildings were in Hardy's blood and so in his work. His sister Kate bought Max Gate for £2,250 when Florence died in 1937 and left it to 'the Nation' in 1940.

It was just a century after Thomas's birth. She also endowed a scholarship of £3,000 so that a Dorchester grammar school boy could go to Oxford. In his eighties Hardy was still being driven over to Bockhampton, once to look at 'fencing, trees, etc. with a view to tidying and secluding the Hardy house'.

Farming

COBBETT'S ENGLAND

(Review of *William Cobbett: The Poor Man's Friend* by George Spater, C.U.P., *New York Review of Books*, 20th May, 1982)

William Cobbett was born the son of a farm labourer in 1763 and became England's greatest radical journalist before he died in 1835. George Spater writes of his genius for exposition, and it is more truth than compliment to add that Spater's own gift for setting out in clear prose the political and social events of a complex era makes his book a key one for any full understanding of Cobbett and his times. Spater had an added advantage in being able to view his subject through American eyes, for Cobbett, who is popularly considered as English as roast beef, was subtly influenced by the years he spent in America during the 1780s and 1790s, and later in the 1810s, and has needed a good American biographer. It is also fortunate that Spater is free of the complexes about class that would tend to tangle a British account of Cobbett.

Not the least memorable thing about this solid (but never dull) life of a very solid man is Spater's own assessment of Cobbett's celebrated or notorious contemporaries. Virtually everybody from the politicians to the royal family gets a reinterpretation that reduces them from outsize characters or outsize statues to flesh and blood, and this without satire. It is because Spater has the measure of men like George Canning, or the ill-fated prime minister Spencer Perceval, or Pitt, that Cobbett himself emerges the correct shape and size. What a figure he was and what nerve he had!

A large part of Cobbett's achievement and character derived from what can only be called a natural emancipation from the traditional handicaps of the 'poor start.' They called it rising from obscurity in Cobbett's day and it was a shaky thing to do. You had to watch your step and justify your temerity. This does not seem to have occurred to Cobbett. Without 'family', as it was termed, he took his place with ease and authority in every level of society; without education, he wrote excellent text-books which were used in schools all over Britain, America, and Europe, spoke easy French, instructed lawyers, edited great newspapers, and perfected a prose style that made the copious advice he gave on every subject, from governing the world to running a kitchen, powerful reading for anybody who could read. His authority was unmistakable, his energies prodigious, even his egotism tolerable.

Physically he was all that agrarian man should be, six feet tall, blond, pink-skinned, majestic (though with small eyes), very upright, strong, and very fresh and clean. In an age in which revolution and reaction created two heady gales of opposing rhetoric, he spoke and wrote a handsome, plain English which had a way of reducing most of the grand arguments of his day to what was either simple common sense or an equally simple idiocy. His passion was for the field workers who during his childhood were the most numerous of the toilers actually producing the nation's wealth. Somehow he either never noticed or could not bear to accept the fact that, from 1820 onward, the factories were swallowing them up in their many thousands, and that the glowing, happy mid-eighteenth-century rural Surrey he remembered had had its day. His dream was not to level hierarchical English society but to force it to create economic and cultural conditions that would make farms the happiest places in which men and women could spend their lives. Instead, he watched while agriculture tumbled into ruins.

Until the present biography of this unique Anglo-American figure, Cobbett studies have been dominated by G.D.H. Cole, whose *Life* was published as long ago as 1924. Not only is Cole's work extended with this new book, but it is extended in a very necessary way. The early United States made its mark on the young Cobbett and it is fitting that what is likely to be the Cobbett biography for the next generation or two should be written by an

American scholar based in Britain. The radical note in Spater's approach particularly is so unlike that of the Fabian Cole and his successors as to alert the ear to previously muffled notes from Cobbett.

William was the third of four sons born in successive years to the Cobbetts, and in common with most village boys until the Second World War he began working when still a child. He never resented this, but gloried in it. The first two fingers of his right hand remained permanently bent because of vast amounts of digging and hoeing before he was fifteen. At home his father's talk was all of the American War of Independence. While working as a garden boy (aged eleven) for the Bishop of Winchester, he heard of Kew Gardens, the sound of which so entranced him that he set off there and then to discover it, on the way spending his last pence on Swift's *Tale of a Tub*. The ploughboy and garden lover settled down in a haystack to read his book, which, as he wrote in his *Weekly Political Register*, 'produced what I have always considered a sort of birth of intellect.' One is reminded of Clare in his early teens coming across half a page from Thomson's *The Seasons* and seeing for the first time what poetry was.

Cobbett did not leave home for good until he was twenty, when his departure was as careless as anything in *Tom Jones*. Dressed in his holiday clothes and about to take some girls to the fair, he boarded a stagecoach that drew up when the driver saw him standing by the roadside, mistakenly thinking he was waiting for it. In a few hours he was in London, with his career sprawling ahead of him.

After a brief spell as a clerk, the only time, he wrote, that he was ever miserable, he joined the army and there, in the barracks, he settled down to teach himself good English. A year or two later he was helping to guard the Canadian border. Then clerk to the regiment, a position of notorious power and influence, he was quick to recognize the ignorance, even the near illiteracy, of his officers, and the stupid muddle of the army generally. At this time Cobbett was deeply conservative, opposed to the American revolution and any other sort of radical change; his motive for getting rid of his regiment's corrupt practices sprang more from seeing that the old order ran honestly than that it should be injected with new ideas.

While stationed at St. John he glimpsed a pretty thirteen-year-old scrubbing a tub in a garden at dawn and he said, 'That's the girl for me.' She was an artillery sergeant's daughter, and before she sailed back to England with her father's regiment Cobbett gave her all his savings – 150 guineas. When he married her five years later she had not spent a penny of it but had kept herself by working as a servant. Although she never learned to read and write, Nancy Reid seems to have made Cobbett an admirable wife for many years until, hardly surprisingly, the marriage caved in under the stresses he later imposed upon it. It was one thing to be the wife of an exciting and ever commanding man, and quite another to be dragged along in the wake of a peripatetic national institution.

Spater is at his best when describing Cobbett's restlessness and heroic schemings, his compulsions and experiments, all of which frequently plunged his bright children and their unlettered mother into chaos. The family side of Cobbett does more to explain the somewhat overpowering element in his nature, and its mixture of altruism and egotism, than a more direct attempt to unravel his psychology could have done. Cobbett himself hid nothing; indeed it was his openness during a particularly evasive time that society found so devastating. His life being such an open book, it was extremely difficult for the swarming government spies of the period to dig up the usual dirt. But this capacity for public candor can be a substitute for personal intimacy, and Spater has been able to reveal this in Cobbett's domestic life.

Like many people who do much for others Cobbett mismanaged his own affairs abominably, and eventually had debts of £28,000. an immense sum at that time. And this was not through idealistic naiveté, such as might be expected of a reformer; but because his farms at Botley and Kensington were run on generous lines just at the moment when British agriculture had fallen into one of its slumps. Although he was arrested for debt and endured every kind of financial difficulty, Cobbett seems to have been more inconvenienced than wounded by these experiences.

Spater shows how, although a small fortune ran through his fingers, and although he had to use conventional business methods as both the leading newspaperman of his day and as a farmer, Cobbett was never really interested in money – 'Nothing so false as figures,' he used to say. He paid his numerous labourers, over a hundred at one time working on his market garden alone, higher wages than anybody else, and was always more patrician than peasant in his somewhat grand attitude toward what things cost, and what he must have, and what he intended to do. This too made him formidable – the absence of apology and caution in him.

Cobbett's literary career began in America, when he joined in the uproar that followed the signing of the Jay treaty in 1794. Two years earlier he had indeed published a seditious pamphlet in London, called *The Soldier's Friend*, an exposé of how it was the practice in the British army for officers to mulct private soldiers of part of their pitiful pay – just an aspect, he charged, of Establishment practices generally, with the rich and powerful maintaining a deliberate policy of subsistence wages, and no more, to the people. (He wrote this after he had initiated and then fled from a court-martial that brought charges of fraud against four officers in his late regiment; he did not dare to make such claims until he was safely discharged.)

Another early work concerned nothing less than the postwar attitudes of Britain, France, and the United States, and was entitled *A Bone to Gnaw, for the Democrats*. This work reveals Cobbett's easy, highly intelligent way with global politics as clearly as *The Soldier's Friend* does his championship of the ordinary man. The two pamphlets can be seen as the beginning of the double-stranded obsession that was to preoccupy him to the end of his life. His aims were rational government and a system that produced a society in which the average person could live happily.

It was in the United States that Cobbett began his work as newspaper owner and journalist. Widely known by the mid-1790s, loathed by the Democrats, he wrote a delightful piece of autobiography in order to refute the wild stories being spread about his life, using the taunting pseudonym 'Peter Porcupine.' Still in his early thirties, in touch with Washington and Talleyrand, he then launched *Porcupine's Gazette*, a daily which almost immediately achieved the largest circulation in America. The tone of the paper was rabidly anti-French and sublimely pro-British, and it was full of invective and abuse. Since many of its leading articles were reprinted in London, a platform awaited him there when he returned, aged thirty-seven, in 1800.

There was unease when he turned down the offer of proprietorship of the government newspaper *True Briton* and set out instead to publish what he had written during his fifeteen years in the United States. To many it seemed that Britain was about to follow the French into revolution, and Tory and Whig politicians alike were desperately seeking a voice persuasive enough to stem the rioting and convince the nation that General Bonaparte, with his 275,00-strong 'Army of England' was about to invade it. Cobbett's answer to all this confusion and despair, hysterical 'war whoop,' as Coleridge called it, and class hatred, was to start his *Weekly Political Register*. It ran from 1802 to 1835 and few other journals have ever possessed such influence and power.

It was also in 1802 that, as Spater writes, Cobbett 'turned his principal attention from the dangers of libertarian doctrine imported from France, to the purely domestic brand of problems relating to the governance of Britain, problems to which he devoted the rest of his life.' He became the people's Cobbett of legend, the devastating critic of institutions and privileges, the spokesman for the villagers, the reformer, particularly of parliament, the scourge of the fixers, the deflater of the 'brilliant speaker.'

Cobbett's ability to speak as he wrote, and to write as he spoke, unnerved his many enemies and transformed him into an oracle where his followers were concerned. The truth was that he dictated much of what he printed. Equally confusing in an age whose sermons and speeches were subjected to rhetoric and mannerism, his unaffected voice, along with a physical presence that exuded wholesomeness, had a plain, direct eloquence which was irresistible. Not the least curious aspect of Cobbett was that in many ways he seemed to epitomize to the British of all classes, from monarch to worker, what they still see as 'good taste' and 'correct style.' He arraigned the 'collective,' as he mockingly called the government, at a time when critics and journalists were being thrown into prison for speaking the truth; he 'assumed the patronage of the poor,' as John Mill put it, at a time when many of their age-old rights were being torn from them.

Spater sees Cobbett's approach as similar to that of Tom Paine, with this basic difference: he was concerned with altering constitutions, not demolishing them. Not that this lawfulness saved him from official wrath, spite and vengence. In 1810 he was thrown into Newgate prison after speaking out against the flogging of young soldiers at Ely. When the Act of Habeas Corpus was suspended in 1817 he fled for a while back to the US. But for the most part he could not be intimidated; he defended the common interest with courage and wisdom. And he did so when his world was in intellectual, military, and social turmoil.

Spater doesn't suggest that Cobbett mastered the cant and confusion of the times like a good, sane giant. He shows that his character and genius as a preacher were formed by one hard decision after another, whether in America or England. He gives a clear account of virtually everything and everybody that concerned Cobbett, whether the rulers of Europe or his New York neighbours, the important writers of the day or the emerging power of the press – which owed more to his integrity than, even now, most of us like to admit. Cobbett's old age and deterioration too are described with an extraordinary understanding of how even the finest of men topple toward the end. Estranged from family and friends, he died nearly alone.

The lasting fascination of Cobbett is that from start to finish his life succeeded in being as much a part of the streets as of the fields, of the halls where rules and money are made as of gardens and wild acres. He continues to interest and inspire us, being both *rus* and *urb* in the fullest sense. Reading Spater's book, you feel that if only a dozen men of his type would emerge every generation, and in every land, we might be saved.

THE MORASS: RIDER HAGGARD

(Introduction to *The Farmer's Year*, Cresset Library, 1987)

'Nowadays the novel is almost everything. If a matter is to be read of, it must be spiced and tricked out with romance. But, rightly or wrongly, I imagine that the generations to come will study our facts rather than our fiction.' So declared Henry Rider Haggard at the close of the nineteenth century as he exchanged the hat of a best-selling novelist for that of a worried Norfolk farmer. The prognostication would not prove accurate where he was concerned, *King Solomon's Mines, She* and a number of his tales bear both reading and examination to this day. Their narrative strength and brilliant imaginative atmosphere, like those of Stevenson and Ballantyne, have kept Haggard's fictions from being carried away on the usual tides. His Africa and his East Anglia were equally potent forces in his literary development, though in severely divided interests. Africa made him an Empire romance-writer of the first water in ordinary popular terms, but two small farms on the Suffolk-Norfolk border made him an agricultural historian not unworthy a place near Arthur Young, William Cobbett and Lord Ernle. Was Haggard himself divided, a part colonialist, part squire? An administrator of the Cape and a J.P. and churchwarden of his English village, a family man and a wanderer, a progressive abroad and a Tory at home, a man of action in Pretoria and a dreamer in West Bradenham – was his a double life? Curiously not. His personality combining an earthy level-headedness with that uniquely Victorian adventurousness and fantasy was all of a confident piece. Which is why his two 'state of the land' books, *A Farmer's Year* and *Rural England* are now recognized as key reading for anyone who wants to know how and why the countryside we see today has emerged. Perhaps more novelists should be set to producing reports on social change.

Haggard took as a blueprint for *A Farmer's Year* Thomas Tusser's *Hundredth Good Pointes of Husbandrie,* a practical guide to farming written by a professional musician in the year in which Elizabeth 1 came to the throne. Tusser wrote his famous advice at Cattawade, Suffolk, where he was sowing and ploughing fields very close to those which would be worked by John Constable's family in the eighteenth century. It is the source of a great number of the rural proverbs, saws and platitudes which are still in use today. Tusser later farmed at West Dereham, Norfolk, which is why he attracted Haggard. Here was a kind of artist whose duty, like his own, it was to understand and explain man's primal toil, the growing and harvesting of crops, and the herding of animals. Except that, unlike Tusser's agricultural scene, Haggard's was one of stagnation, collapse and abandonment. The tragedy was what the politicians and newspapers of his time were calling 'the flight from the land'. When he wrote *Rural England* he placed a text from the Book of Judges on the title-page – 'The highways were unoccupied ... the inhabitants of the village ceased.'

The quote on the title-page of *A Farmer's Year*, the bitter-sweet journal of what was happenning on his own farms as the great agricultural depression descended upon them 'during the last year but one of an eventful and wondrous century' comes from Tom Tusser, the musician-farmer struggling along in the 1550s by the River Stour:

Who minds to quote
Upon this note
May easily find enough:
What change and pain,
To little gain
Doth follow toiling plough.

Haggard called *A Farmer's Year* 'His commonplace book for 1898' and illustrated it with maps, statistical tables and melancholy sepia pictures. A master of 'atmosphere', that here is no less powerful in its way than that which surrounds Ayesha and Umslopogaas. He was in his early forties when he wrote it and was taking stock of his future after having unsuccessfully contested the local parliamentary seat. His career so far had been extraordinary – thrilling even combining as it did the Victorian virtues of action and the ability to describe it. At nineteen he sailed to South Africa to be secretary to the Governor of Natal, Sir Henry Bulwer. Two years later he was on the staff of Sir Theophilus Shepstone and had himself raised the Union flag in Pretoria's main square. Revered by the Africans, detested by the Boers, Shepstone had annexed the Transvaal for Britain almost single-handed – and without consulting the government. The resulting turmoil ended an extraordinary career. Shepstone's psychological approach to black Africa and his great adventures – he had himself crowned Cetewayo King of Zululand – entranced the young Haggard and fed his imagination. Although he was still only twenty-four when he returned to England for good, Africa and daring radicals like Shepstone continued to influence his vision and made him a very unusual member of Norfolk's farming and sporting gentry. Most curious of all was his ability not to allow his reputation as a popular romancer in any way compromise that which he was soon to gain as the tough and realistic recorder of Britain's worst agricultural slump. This his *Farmer's Year*, a format frequently used by poets, diarists and country-calendarists, is a village book with a difference.

Haggard began farming in 1889, a time when many of those who could were getting out of the industry, and especially the farm-labourers. Throughout East Anglia 'Our American relations were bringing villages to poverty by swamping the markets' i.e. newly-invented iron grainships, the oil tankers of their day, were flooding Europe with cheap corn from the prairies of the United States and Canada. And if this wasn't bad enough, a run of wet summers which culminated in 'the fearful year of 1879' washed out what was left of harvests and hope. For Haggard, not long married and also by now fast becoming one of England's most popular writers of adventure fiction, it was not just a question of truthfully documenting the collapse of farming, but a sincere need to reawaken in country people their belief in nature, in the patterns of field-work and of craftsmanship, and most of all a belief in the superiority of village existence to that of the city. 'What kind of places are these cities to live in, for the poor?' What kind of places in the late nineteenth century were Bedingham and Ditchingham for thirteen shillings a week farm labourers and near bankrupt farmers? one might retort.

A Farmer's Year provides answers that are both earthily practical and filled with Haggard's deep love for the land. A few months before he wrote it he had visited Egypt and had seen the paintings and reliefs on the royal tombs at Sakkara, and had thought how very like he was to 'the gentlemen-farmers of the Fifth and Sixth Dynasties who, whilst yet alive, caused their future sepulchres to be adorned with representations of such scenes of daily life and husbandry as to them were most pleasant and familiar.' Egypt had had plagues, but they passed and the joy of the cornfields remained. So he makes his plea to the English countryman to stand firm, 'although how the crisis will end it is not possible for the wisest among us to guess today.' We now know that this crisis ended in the 1940s, when the nation's food requirements inaugurated the second agricultural revolution - and, subsequently, today's embarrassing food mountains.

In all Haggard farmed 365 acres, some two thirds of which were near his house at Ditchingham, a big village of 1100 inhabitants, and a third in Bedingham, a village five miles distant. Some of the Ditchingham land was rented. These farms are immensely ancient and are mostly on 'loving' or heavy land which clings to boots and wheels. When such farms go down it can take years to drain and weed them and bring them back to good working order, and he records his struggles with the dereliction at Bedingham. Ditchingham, where the young Haggards lived in the Lodge, was a very different matter for the situation was one of the most beautiful in Norfolk, where the Bath Hills and the Waveney Valley spread towards Bungay and the grounds of the Lodge were bordered by the river. Close to the village were the extensive woodlands owned by Lord de Saumarez, but whose shooting rights belonged to Haggard. The scene here is that of the successful Empire-builder come home to rest on his laurels – except that it happens to be a scene whose underlying difficulties are preoccupying a landowner-novelist whose idealism and expert grasp of agricultural economy were tearing him apart, emotionally speaking. In time he would produce the kind of report which makes governments act, although those of his own day scarcely raised a finger to help the farmer and his men. But now, as the scale of what was happening became clear, Haggard decided that a personal farming diary in the classic form, a book which everybody connected with the land would be warmed and inspired by, was essential.

A Farmer's Year holds nothing back. The profit and loss of Ditchingham and Bedingham are given to the last halfpenny. So in another sense are those of Haggard's personality as he swings over from being a typical conservative to a highly candid radical. Much of what he longed to happen has happened, a great deal of what he was sensibly proposing nearly a century ago still hasn't been done. The one thing in particular which the modern reader must be struck by is the gulf which stretches between a gentleman-farmer and his labourers. As magistrate, employer, churchwarden and workhouse guardian, Haggard is in total control of them and not at that date less possessive of them than were those Nile farmers of their slaves, whose seasonal tasks he saw carved around the doors of Sakkara. He admires their skills and strength, their stoicism and their character, but with all his imagination he cannot get into their situation, and his book is the better, if the more bitter, for his never attempting to do so. Suitably in the December chapter he describes a visit to Heckingham Workhouse and it sums up his absolute honesty:

What do these old fellows think about, I wonder, as they hobble to and fro round those measureless precincts of bald brick? The sweet-eyed children they begot and bred up fifty years ago, perhaps, whose pet names they still remember, dead or lost to them for the most part; or the bright waving cornfields whence they scared birds when they were lads from whom death and trouble were yet a long way off. I dare say, too, that deeper problems worry them at times in some dim half-apprehended fashion; at least I thought so when the other day I sat behind two of them in church near the workhouse. They could not read, and I doubt if they understood much of what was passing, but I observed consideration in their eyes. Of what? Of the terror and the marvel of existence, perhaps, and of that good God whereof the person is talking in those long unmeaning words. God! They know more of the devil and all his works; ill-paid labour, poverty, pain, and the infinite unrecorded tragedies of humble lives. God? They have never found Him. He must live beyond the workhouse wall – out there in the graveyard – in the waterlogged holes which very shortly ...

In all Haggard employs fifteen men on his farms and gives meticulous descriptions of their many skills. Their dogged strength astounds him. In January he watches two of them bush-draining a huge expanse of clay land. It takes ten weeks and at the end 'such toilers betray not the least delight at the termination of their long labour'. Similarly with dyke-drawing, the toughest of all the winter jobs. This is a book which reminds one that, the ploughing apart, much of Britain's landscape was fashioned by men with spades. Haggard's men work a twelve-hour day in summer and every daylight hour in winter, and without holidays. Minimal though their education is, it 'teaches them that there are places in the world besides their own Little Pedlington' and makes them aspiring and restless. More and more of them disappear, making for the army, the colonies, the Lowestoft fishing smacks, anywhere preferable to a Norfolk farm. It grieves him. *A Farmer's Year* is his apology for agriculture as man's natural activity, the noblest of tasks, and he cites its improved conditions. Now and then, as in Africa, he joins in the labour, although this he finds separates him further from the workers than if he merely sat on his horse and made notes. Whatever he sees or feels or does is written down with total candour, and his journal is at once an important and authoritative compendium of farming practice, private confessional, a history of turn-of-the-century Norfolk and, in its way, an entertainment. The scene he paints is darker than he wants it to be and, for something which sets out as an autobiographical rural calendar about the state of the land at a given date, balance sheets and all, there are highly emotional and intellectual tensions of an unexpected kind.

Sir Henry Rider Haggard's then radical exposure of agrarian decline in this and other books disturbed the profoundly conservative rural society to which he belonged, and, getting on for a hundred years later, it is still capable of upsetting us. But capable of delighting us too, for this is a rich picture of the old landscape and the 'old' people as they were before modern farming and other developments transformed both. It is unlikely to make anyone nostalgic but it will, like a tale by Thomas Hardy, remind us of the tensions, and of the idyll, which not so very long ago were interlocked in the field.

A Farmer's Year first appeared as a serial before it was published in book form in 1899. Its purpose was to hearten the yeomen of England during a time of utter hopelessness and to check the abandonment of the villages by their employees. Haggard pours into the narrative everything which would fascinate the farmer and his men: legends, local history, flowers, sport, the church, games, gossip, weather, prices, customs, country pleasures, hard-nosed profits and losses. Nothing is left out. He said that 'it mirrors faithfully the decrepit and even dangerous state of farming and attendant industries in eastern England during the great agricultural crisis of the last decade of the nineteenth century', and it does.

THE FIELDS OF DULDITCH

(Introduction to *The Fields of Dulditch*, Mary Mann, Boydell Press, 1978)

These bitter and remarkable stories about half-starved East Anglian villagers at the turn of the century were published in 1902, the same year in which the Norfolk novelist Sir Henry Rider Haggard had paused in his creation of exotic tales to issue a devastating indictment of the nation's virtual abandonment of its agricultural industry. Called *Rural England*, Rider Haggard's inventory of the state of the countryside a third of the way through the great farming depression which was to last, except for the First World War years, until the 1940s, gives the economic facts of this disaster. In Suffolk and Norfolk this period was sometimes called 'the coming down time' as many old farming families and rural craftsmen lost their footing and were ruined. The field-workers suffered most of all. During the eighteen-eighties, Joseph Arch, champion hedge-cutter and union organiser, had made Norfolk a hearteningly successful centre for policies which promised to lift farm-labourers out of their serfdom but now, twenty years later, bad harvests, wage cuts and mass emigrations from the land to the towns, the railways, the colonies or the army, had demoralised many of those who remained at home.

Rider Haggard, in *Rural England*, describes village after village with forsaken cottages; Mary Mann reveals the interiors of those that are still inhabited. Although an exciting fantasist where his fiction was concerned, Rider Haggard is down to earth about British agriculture in decline, supporting the 'back to the land' call of the time whilst insisting that farmworkers should have decent prospects to return to. Mary Mann, on the contrary, allows her characters no prospects at all. To do so would be to undermine the tragic situation of what she calls their 'condition'. The almighty, in the role of the great 'Disposer' – the pitiless deity and the general fatalism alike suggest that the author knows her Hardy – has placed these wretched people in Dulditch and they have to accept their place. That, to Mary Mann, is the pathos of their lives.

She was a prolific popular novelist who published numerous country stories, most of them with Norfolk settings. Born Mary Rackham, the daughter of a Norwich businessman, Simon Rackham, she died at Sheringham in 1929. *The Fields of Dulditch* came towards the middle of an output which included such titles as *The Parish of Hilby*, *A Lost Estate*, *Susannah*, *The Parish Nurse*, *Astray in Arcady*, *Rose at Honeypot*, etc. It deserves re-issue because it contains brilliant eye-witness accounts of the intimate life of labouring families at a time when such poverty was not only normal, but was seemingly incurable. Mary Mann's compassion stems from seeing men and women as immutably planted in a location as a tree or a swede. As creatures thus imprisoned, her heart goes out to them. Although she reproduces the picturesque speech patterns of this lowly, grimly-rooted and – for her – blighted society with sufficient colour to entertain the reader, her central purpose is not to show rustic charm but rural plight. Howsomedever (as one of these late nineteenth century labourers would have said), she offers no solution other than the exhortations to endure which provided one of the high-minded supports to the status quo of the time. By enduring the misfortune of their birth, their ignorance, their incessant toil and their malnutrition, her characters receive their own special nobility, and it is this which ultimately concerns her. She describes first the barren soil of a particular life and then the little miracle of its flowering. Her understanding is greatest when it comes to the kind of nervelessness, apathy and inertia which results not so much from being stuck in a rut as from being helplessly tethered to a stunted growth. Although she occasionally comes dangerously near to sentimentalising these field-workers and their families, and sometimes patronises them in the conventional 'lady' manner, all in all she succeeds in being an uncomfortably truthful witness of their difficult existence and her sharp profile of what it was really like to be an ordinary villager eighty years ago challenges any nostalgic vision we may still hold of those days.

Of course, the chief interest to ourselves in such a book as this is not literary in the usual sense – although the actual writing is often very accomplished and vivid – but in its reportage of what were then the humdrum affairs of the farming world but which now can only be pieced together by the social historian. Its stories read less like plotted, imaginatively-shaped fictions of the traditional type than like brief biographies. They are sketched against 'an insignificant landscape, bleak fen-land, gorse-choked heath, familiar ponds and pits and puddles, rank turnip-fields, flat distances...' For Mary Mann, those who work this landscape are destined to find that 'the Book of Life is practically closed'. Yet, in spite of this, it is a far from negative conclusion that she ultimately draws. Her own veracity uncovers the solid worth of others and the reader is not left with a feeling that the Dulditchians are damned. The exposure of their actual lives, however, does contrast unmercifully, for example, with the kind of gentle village fiction known as the 'kailyard school', so popular at this time, in which cottagers displayed rustic adventures in prettily philosophical terms. A Mary Mann tale about what was happening in the average double-dweller in circa 1900 Norfolk bears no comparison at all with such bromides. What occurs in her writing is that, after setting off at a deceptively polite pace into the calm realm of the dialect story, the narrative suddenly ignites into something of more burning importance.

Against the stark facts of their education, religion, diet, illness, marriages, toil and death she constructs the individual shapes of her 'poor units of the brutish, measureless human undergrowth'. Even while allowing for the suppressed horror with which the better-off regarded the fate of the workaday poor and her almost total disregard of what is now called 'job satisfaction' – she dwells on the inscrutable deity 'which toss'd thee down into the field' but says little or nothing about the wonderful ploughing and harvesting that went on in them even at the miserable wage of eleven shillings a week – the cumulative effect of this book is both intriguing and moving. Intriguing because it has all the verisimilitude of an old photograph turned into language;

moving because what happened then can he seen to affect so much that happens now.

Dulditch (situated somewhere between Watton and Norwich?) has an impoverished bachelor squire, Sir Thomas, and a kindly but withdrawn Rector. The squire forgoes his annual holiday so that he can use the money to patch-up his cottages. The Rector is no saint to his maid, who prefers the hideously illustrated bible for which she has exchanged her life-savings to his services. " 'I don't want him a-setting up ter tache me; efso be as ivver I want ter pray, I take it I kin pray without such as him.' She can't read her bible but she adores its 'gays' – its coloured pictures. In the 1860s Edward FitzGerald, the poet, asked a friend to find him a colourfully-plumed cockerel for his hens, stipulating 'only so as he be "gay" according to old Suffolk speech'. The Rector's maid epitomises the wilful East Anglian spirit which stubbornly ignores the rules. The ancient widower, Angel, who unsuccessfully courts her, on the contrary, knows his place. He goes to church in order to 'set under a gentleman' because 'him as prache at chapel bain't no better nor me...'Tis for th' quality to ha' th' haughtiness, and for we to ha' th' manners'. The quality, in the shape of the author, find it witty to call an epileptic Fitz-Brown. The farmyard poultry are ritually stoned – 'everybody stoned them. To 'hull a ston' and lame th' old gander', or to break the wing 'o' th' old yiller hin', being considered ordinary sport. Big families sleep half a dozen to a room, their bed-clothes old coats. For the most part they eat 'light' dumplings consisting of flour, water and baking powder, potatoes, skim milk, peppered and salted bread soaked in hot water, cheese and various fruit and vegetable mashes.

Women, by working all hours, can earn up to six shillings a week stone-picking or singling-out. Men are frequently beer-drunkards. The old live in terror of the 'order for the house' – the workhouse. The sick have the club doctor and all manner of unofficial cures, from comfrey to touching a sore place with a dead hand. Elijah (a woman) has 'a sore', or cancer. The rheumatic are rubbed with horse-oils. There is the pauper lunatic asylum and there is suicide. To the inhabitants of Dulditch and to Mary Mann all this and more, the squalor of the houses and the brutality, is as to be expected as sun in summer. Her lovers and stalwarts, her brave and cunning girls and handsome 'first-team men like Robbud, her cards like Jarge, her intrepids like the gal La'rences, her tragedies like Wolf-Charlie and Ben Pitcher's Elly, and her entire population of the village contend with these tough odds and sometimes overcome them. Like Biller and Becker, 'the unlovely, the loutish, the ungracious, and uncouth, whose births were shameful' as well as the beautiful and intelligent, they are all fixed in these penurious acres and 'are in their own obscure way holding their own there...' It required a special kind of honesty to counter-balance so many black facts with equally relevant actualities such as love, humour and the ability by some to stay undefeated.

A word must be said about Mary Mann's treatment of the old words. She heard them much as they would have sounded centuries before her own day and still untouched by modern influences. As old Angel says, 'These hare be th' wuds' and Mary Mann records them as easily as one for whom they are a second language is able. They tell of some of the side effects of a great industrial calamity when farming failed and an average village went broke.

Dialect and domestic detail aside, what are the issues which motivated these realistic stories and which make them so exceptional for their time? They are the issues which reduced the population of their author's village, Shropham, by nearly a third in her lifetime and left many of its cottages deserted. As wife of Shropham's principal farmer and living at the manor, Mary Mann knew all there was to know about the predicament of the labouring class. In her earlier novels she had kept it in some kind of middle-class check, although dealing with it compassionately, but in the 'Dulditch' tales, begun during the 1890s, she drops the role of the charming recorder of countryside romance and becomes, as a critic of another of her books wrote, 'unsparingly truthful'. Apart from a noticeably crusading attitude towards the evils of drink, she is strikingly non-Victorian about the facts of life in the average rural hovel, seeing in them the seeds of spiritual as well as physical death. She points at the vulnerability of Dulditch to disaster, and reveals its individual root causes in pain, ignorance, endless toil and simply by the fact that there was a group of human beings in her world with the dice loaded against their fulfilment and happiness. Dulditch exercises her radicalism. She sees both the admirable and the feckless brought down by circumstances that are entirely out of their control. She also observes the evil, commonplace by-products of an inbred and isolated community. She writes about fortitude, eccentricity, illegitimacy, animal-like or saintly extremes of conduct, class, alcoholism and, most movingly, about the fate of children. Building-up an inter-related series of village anecdotes in a light, practised but not very distinguished style, she soon becomes fascinating as, unlike the majority of people dealing with the lives of the poor at that date, she balances their entertaining quaintness of custom and talk with accounts of their terrors and triumphs which are disturbingly real. There are many things here which must have shocked the readers of Mary Mann's day – and which provide a valuable record for our own.

It must be added that Fairman Mann, the author's farmer husband whom she married when she was twenty-three, worked hard for the welfare of his parish, particularly where its education was concerned. Living at Shropham Manor and farming some 800 acres around the village, he assumed the responsibilities of a caring squire. Much of what he witnessed among his employees, on the Board of Guardians, as a churchwarden and school governor, etc., must have provided material for his wife's socially accurate reportage. The Dulditch stories stem from the closest involvement with the triumphs and difficulties they describe.

ADRIAN BELL and *SILVER LEY*

(Introduction to *Silver Ley*, O.U.P., 1983)

Silver Ley is the middle volume of a celebrated trilogy of gently novelized memoirs set in the West Suffolk countryside of the inter-war years. Along with its companions, *Corduroy* and *The Cherry Tree*, it throws a revelatory light on the English agricultural scene at a moment when, after the brief subsidized prosperity brought about by food shortages during the crisis, the whole industry sank back into the depression which had afflicted it since the 1870s. The lasting fascination of all three books lies in the contrast between the natural hopefulness of their youthful author and the economic hopelessness of the scene to which he has committed his life. *Silver Ley* describes the conjunction of the idealistic writer's 'new morning' with the old-style farming's good-night. What has taken place in the East Anglian fields for centuries is coming to a muddy halt. Another war will bring the first fruits of an unprecedented recovery and wealth, but neither Adrian Bell nor the farming old-timers with whom he had thrown in his lot would in their wildest dreams have imagined this in the early Thirties, when these books appeared. Interestingly, they were not regarded then as chronicles of the great rural depression but as good green shoots in an area which was producing all manner of strange growth. Bell is the least sensational, the least dramatic of the best twentieth-century country writers, also the least probing, but he is among the most truthful. Everything in *Silver Ley* is in exact focus for his individual eye. He doesn't generalize, doesn't attempt to take in the broad economic and social picture, but by remaining perfectly parochial he manages to capture a memorable view of an entire world in transition.

The landscape of *Silver Ley* is that bulge of the Suffolk border contained by the rivers Stour and Kennett, a still fairly remote district. Stradishall, the 'Benfield St. George' of the story, is a village set in the very centre of a beautiful corn-growing area whose periphery is made up of Essex and Cambridgeshire, and a half circle of market towns, Sudbury, Clare, Bury St. Edmunds, Haverhill and Newmarket. The book's names echo those on the map. There is a Bradfield St. George, a Weston Colville for the 'Mr. Colville' of Farley Hall and a hamlet called Silverstreet for, perhaps, the title itself. Admirers of Adrian Bell are still able to tour the Stour and Waveney valleys respectively, for his latter years were spent in and around Beccles, and discover how well he integrated in his work everything from the atmosphere of a particular region to the character of its inhabitants. *Silver Ley* is especially successful in its creation of West Suffolk at an historic milestone, when there was no way of returning to the tried old ways, and no convincing pointer to the prosperity to come. It is the kind of story which both the historian and those absorbed in human nature stare into, surprised to discover so much. How can such a modest, if stylishly written, account of a middle-class young man's attempt to work a little farm be anything more than yet another competent country-book? A great many were being written when Bell wrote his, so why the lasting quality?

Part of the answer is that the urge which brought Bell from Chelsea to Suffolk in 1920 had nothing to do with the customary going off to write in a cottage but, far more extraordinary, to do with becoming a traditional small farmer: not even an enlightened back-to-the-land emigrant but simply someone who wanted to live as the ordinary practical farmer lived. Just too young for the trenches, ex-Uppingham School and from a literary London home, Bell's motive for abandoning the city for the village could have been the common one of the period – a quest for real values – yet there is little in his writings to suggest that he was searching for more than what his farm apprenticeship would bring him. It was the ancient pattern of toil on the land which beguiled him, man's basic occupation.

It is as well to add here that this sowing and reaping existence, and everything and everybody involved with it, was also beguiling quite a few other pens in East Anglia during these years. Adrian Bell's unique talent is only now beginning to emerge from a whole school of post-World War I writing about East Anglia as something distinctive and rare – the authentic voice of its era. Not a native voice but, because it belonged to someone who by accepting Suffolk as he did was accepted by it, a voice which is singularly honest and percipient. Bell doesn't even attempt to go much beyond the responses of his class, and in his dealings with the fieldworkers and their families it is kindliness, rather than any deep understanding of them as individuals, which makes the connection. But that there is a genuine connection there can be no doubt. The 1920s and 1930s witnessed a great crop of country-books about every corner of these islands, and the Eastern counties' contribution was impressive. Adrian Bell wrote in good company, so to speak. Yet he wrote very much alone, better than the good rural belle letrists, and quite away from the conventions of the good rural novel. When in the late 1950s he wrote his autobiography proper, *My Own Master*, and took a description of himself from the first chapter of *Silver Ley* – 'I was now alone and my own master, and nothing would be done on this holding until I left my bed and did it' – he could as well have been summing up his standing as a regional writer as a man who had 'made it', albeit in the most modest way, on the land. During the decades which saw (for Norfolk) R. H. Mottram, Michael Home, Lilias Rider Haggard and Henry Williamson; (for Suffolk) the excellent and neglected W. H. Freeman; and (for Essex) the brilliant A. E. Coppard, S. L. Bensusan, James Wentworth Day and C. Henry Warren, among many others, Adrian Bell, by means of an accurate vision and subtle simplicity of literary style, was able to write of this much written about province freshly and originally. There was no one quite like him at the time and there have been none at all like him since.

Silver Ley is a very happy book, its happiness that of youth in progress, not of youth remembered. Life sprawls uncertainly ahead, but the war is over and the author-hero, ageing from twenty-one to twenty-eight as the tale progresses, finding his farming feet and working all hours, is buoyant. Sidling through the narrative, barely mentioned, we see the emergence of Bell the writer as well as of Bell the young ploughman, village school manager and taker-on generally of the roles which would then come the way of such as he. By the customary notion of the behaviour of foreigners, his is conventional and he is immediately accepted by his adopted community. He fits, and were he a lesser writer than he is it could have been a disaster. Instead, the acceptance allows him to work from the inside as he quite unpretentiously shares the indigenous outlook. He feels it a privilege to be able to do this, and that it is up to him to see things straight. But there is never any deadening orthodoxy and it is the absence of this, in what to all intents and purposes often appears to be an orthodox situation, which lends the writing its edge. Bell, the newcomer to them, stands witness to the virtues of the yeomanry just when its ancient horse-powered (in the majestic four-footed Suffolk Punch sense) economy is about to vanish. Unlike the majority of artists and writers who have opted for country life, his is a love affair with the land, not the landscape. What we get in *Silver Ley*, and in all his books, is a working farmer's view of Suffolk transmitted via a fine, even elegant, literary intelligence.

'As I ploughed I thought', he says in Chapter I,

> When I rested the horses at the headlands I looked about me. I heard the clock in the village below strike one, but I knew that those who put their hand to the plough did not leave off till two-thirty. And, seeing that to-day I was a ploughman, I continued. But I realised that my present work was more of a gesture than a real attack on the autumn cultivation before me. It was a mere obedience of the first rule of arable farming: that horses must not stand still. At two-thirty I surveyed my work. So narrow compared to the rest of the field looked the strip of dark earth I had been all this while making even so wide. There was much else to be done, and that quickly; harrowing, trimming the grass from the sides of the fields, hedges to cut down, manure to cart

'As I ploughed I thought', and its succeeding anxious pile-up of what had to be done, not only today but year after year until one's strength ebbed; what countless young men alone in their first field must have thought thus. While the farming cycle is certainly not that of the treadmill, this initial sound of 'the plough hushing through the earth' and being pulled along the furrow in a kind of stumbling trot for today and for ever has always brought home to farmer and farmworker alike a sense of being caught inescapably in a current of toil. *Silver Ley* opens with a concise and unforgettable description of the writer, aged twenty-one, waking up on an October morning in the huge iron bed he bought for thirteen shillings, and on the thirty-five acre holding which he would then have purchased for a song, to the chastening realization of his being quite alone and that nothing would be done 'until I left my bed and did it'. It is an inspired start for a farming memoir and one whose only equal in East Anglian terms is to be found in Hugh Barrett's *Early to Rise*. Barrett was only sixteen when, in 1932, he was set down in his first field, all ninety-two acres of it, and told to hoe it. It was sugar-beet, the most detested crop,

> . . . and the land was hard; each chop of the hoe jarred the wrists. Mercifully, the field had been drilled the short way, but even so the rows were over four hundred yards long and neither before or since have I met longer ones. They stretched away past breakfast and 'bait' time, ended at dinner time by the wood, started back in the afternoon and finished at five. In the first two days I hoed precisely two rows a day-eight hundred yards-just there and back, and the rest of the field looked bigger each day, extending into an aching and bent-backed future.

In spite of the gruelling future before them, both writers are honest enough to recall an elation. Bell says,

> My work was about me; my fields were as private to me as my own garden. My work was arduous, but my mind was easy. My hours were long, but I was master of them and did not have to live like a city man, tethered to nine-thirty a.m. like a goat to a tree. I had no reproach to fear save the silent one of my neighbour's fields should they make a better showing than mine when the time came.

The inter-war years were ones of a great dread and despising of cities and anyone who could, from those who forsook their streets for the bright properties of the ribbon developers to those seeking the simple life, as they called it, in the villages themselves, made for the countryside. Adrian Bell's work appeared to his contemporaries as the embodiment of the city-escape ideal, and not idyll – a lesson on how it should be done.

Silver Ley would not be the scrupulous confession that it is if it failed to reveal that villagers themselves frequently have reverse longings. Miss Jarvis, a local girl, asks Bell point-blank,

'But why did you come here?'
'Why, of course, to farm.'
'Yes, but I mean why choose to settle right out here? You came to Farley Hall [where he was taught to farm] for your health, I expect.'
'Oh, it is not as bad as all that ...'
'I didn't mean to suggest that you were ill ...'
'I don't look ill, do I?'
'No, not now. I think your year with Mr. Colville has done you a great deal of good. Only now ...'
'Now the natural thing for me to do is to return to town, you mean?'
'Well, you have your life; it's not as though you were middle-aged and retiring.'

It is a sharp little encounter in a farm parlour, and the writer catches his own awkwardness when confronted by someone who is mystified by his decision to leave Chelsea for Benfield St. George. The only reason for doing so would be poor health and the need for fresh air. Throughout the book, Bell allows these 'point-blank' native challenges to himself and his family. For halfway through the story, impressed by what they are hearing of Suffolk, his parents themselves desert London for Benfield, taking a large house and, although he never says as much, ruining the spartan existence of his bachelor farm. They were to remain in Suffolk, on and off until the end of their lives, and older people will remember Mrs. Bell particularly, a still pretty, amusing but rather formidable woman in her sixties, who became a familiar figure in and around Sudbury just before the last war. Also Adrian's father, Robert Bell, a bent, bookish, charming old man. Adrian's novelist's skill is uppermost when it comes to describing their descent on him, with his mother displaying the kind of panache and fortitude which carried the memsahibs and their households across India. Soon, as the educated townee often does, she is reviving many a method and attitude which Benfield itself has thankfully abandoned. Bell treats her with a kind of bemused admiration and affection, not criticism. Having his family with him, and having to live at impressive Groveside and forsake little Silver Ley, effects a total transformation of Benfield's concept of him and yet, when at last they leave him in peace and solitude once more, life at the farm pursues its way with no acknowledgement of the interruption. 'In truth I felt no older than then; that I had been a little over twenty on closing the cottage door, and was a little under thirty on re-opening it, was a fact without inner confirmation, though it stared at me every time I dated a letter.'

But for all that, as the quiet narrative proves, something of a maturing and impressively advancing kind had happened to Bell during this first decade in a chosen territory. By a means which only a reading of his trilogy can explain he had come into his own. *Silver Ley* is about a stranger turning into an insider and not quite knowing how it happened. The country 'wasn't an escape, as I had thought at first; it was a wonderful grappling influence, like love in its depths and darkness. It wasn't delicate; it didn't tremble; it was like a blundering, uncouth mother with lovely children, one of whom by luck might survive.'

Suffolk's actual children mystified him – those of the poverty-stricken labourers, that 'ragged and chubby throng with angel eyes but acquisitive hands that made a procession of Benfield street morning and evening' and who were found in the fields without shoes or stockings on winter days eating mangolds, some of whose fathers were drunks and some of whose homes were condemned as unfit for human habitation, and some who, for all the hardships, shone from some undiscoverable source of good-living. And he was mystified by their mothers too, 'thin and pale, as so many country wives are'. All around him the new cry on the collapsing farms was, 'Buy a tractor and sack some men.' Towards the end of *Silver Ley*, Bell gives a wonderful portrait of these East Anglian field workers, almost the last of the 'old people', as they are now known. They had come to Groveside to ring hand-bells on Boxing Day, 1928:

> The old narrow bricks used to ring with their steel-shod feet, and their voices to vibrate with an unfamiliar depth and huskiness here within walls. Somehow, seen suddenly away from their usual back-ground of acres and sky, the texture of their lives stood out the more. The brows that one never saw save now, when their caps were off, the wiry rebellious hair like patches of standing corn that the wind had swirled awry, their clean rough shirts and collars, blue and red striped, the heavy festooned watch-chain, the thick waistcoat without points, the leather-bound cuff, the rosy cheek, the swart hand – the roughness and cleanness and well-mendedness of their clothes, the colour of them, and the slow stir that even the small movements seemed to make about them. Their cheeks had been painted by the air and light. They were touched always and all days by limitlessness – by great views, winds. And they brought the stare of it in with them, somehow: it was like the light of the snow in the room.

Such descriptions, there are many of them, are not for the fostering of an idyll but for the heightening of the predicament in which agriculture was gradually discovering itself. This gathering rural storm is what lifts *Silver Ley* from the usual run of ably written village annals and gives it its current importance, for in its quiet pages we have one of the finest records of what it was like to live through the second 'coming down time', as it was known in Suffolk, or the horrible re-emergence of a slump which had first begun to ruin the fields in the 1870s. Portents of this calamity begin to be noted early on in the story, although 'at present no one worried seriously'. But already Farley Hall, the best farm in the village, and the one on which Bell had been trained, and which had been trim, weedless, and rich-yielding under Mr. Colville, but which had been sold to a sharp precursor of many of today's farm-industrialists, Mr. James, was in decline. Soon, 'it came upon the whole valley in the end, till even the best farmers had to allow tangled hedges behind which the harvest sheaves could not dry after rain, while the men had to load them wearing gloves on account of the thistles which the farmers had been unable to afford to hoe out.' Bell's use of this gradualism is very skilful. The mainly middle-class community of which he writes, although its plight bears little comparison to that of the labourers and their families, goes about its business and social pleasures, neither heartlessly nor all that fearfully, but very much as people do when some vast altering of the world's circumstances is beyond their being able to do a thing about it. Repellent politics fill the air, even that of remote Suffolk. The young man slogging away on his few acres, assisted now by the not-so-young Simmons, turned off Farley Hall by its new owner, is openly uncontrite about his turning his back on what is happening. 'The post-war world appeared to me ugly and threatening, overpopulated already with high ambitions, and would-be wresters of power.' In 1918 he had listened to the government declaring, 'The agriculture of England must never again be allowed to fall into national neglect', and here it was doing so after five short years before his very eyes. Being so young, Bell is compensated by the incomparable, if rather perverse-sounding delights of hard physical work in sun and wind. Quite rightly, the message of *Silver Ley* is not that of how to run away from life but how to find it.

The familiar minutiae of his situation, parish meetings and committees, trips to market, tennis parties, the fête, the church, the seasonal round, are all faithfully strung along the narrative in the expected order. Most now possess historic interest. But, unlike such observations and episodes in countless village chronicles, Bell's exist to support and explain his reason for witnessing them. It is an unusual stance for a country writer. On the whole, he is reticent on his emotional development; slight encounters with girls, faint pointers to who or what he is via his responses to his being alone in different rooms, for example, as well as in different fields. Now and then, as when the itinerant threshers arrive at Silver Ley, he rises to a descriptive power comparable to that of W. H. Hudson and Richard Jefferies. Although on the whole it is an error to judge Bell according to the standards of these or other rural masters. Those who are most like him are those who are greatly inferior to him, or who simply deal conventionally with what he deals with so inimitably. Having the perspective of fifty years' distance, we can see very clearly that *Silver*

Ley and its two companion volumes occupy a literary farmscape entirely their own, but exactly how to define this honest property in comparison to all the rest it is less easy to perceive. *Silver Ley* doesn't 'wear well' – it doesn't wear at all. Its strength is the strength of Adrian Bell's own youth. It ends classically in the harvest field and in a scene of traditional beauty and meditation. But just before harvest he and thousands of the farmers and farmworkers of East Anglia had packed Parker's Piece in Cambridge in a huge demonstration to draw the government's attention to the catastrophe now sweeping down on them, and it is this, the modest and unflamboyant pulling together of the practical and the dream, which gives *Silver Ley*, and indeed all Bell's work, its excitement and its authority. He didn't need time to prove that there is no one quite like him, but it has.

JULIAN TENNYSON and *SUFFOLK SCENE*

(Introduction to the 1973 edition, EP Publishing)

Many parts of Britain have their 'Suffolk Scene' a literary work which, while laying no claim to be definitive local history or geography, intuitively lays open the very heart of a particular landscape and its people. Julian Tennyson's book was immediately recognized as a rarity, a genuine and unaffected love story between a young man and a place in which he discovered his real self. All the rest of *Suffolk Scene*, which he called 'a book of Description and Adventure', is incidental to this central revelation. It was written in 1938, the year of Munich. Tennyson was twenty-three and was experiencing, as well as the political confusions of that seedy decade, all the customary upsets involved in becoming a writer. He was as much involved with certainties about himself as with certainties about Suffolk when he set out to search the county by foot and bicycle that year. The result of this double investigation was published in June 1939 and was at once seen to be as something which went far beyond what was expected of an ordinary county guide. The freshness of approach even to such celebrated Suffolk attractions as the Wool Churches, Gainsborough and Constable made readers look at them with a new appreciation, whilst the actual feeling of the county, subtle and notoriously elusive, was captured as it rarely has been before or since. Desmond MacCarthy, enthusiastically reviewing *Suffolk Scene*, correctly predicted that it would be one of those books which would be so constantly praised in talk that for many years to come people would be hunting everywhere for a copy.

This has certainly been the case in East Anglia itself. I remember the excitement with which I read this beautiful personal Suffolk book – the first full essay on the region to make an impression on me – when I was a boy. How it endorsed and ratified so many of the things I saw and heard, all of the utmost importance yet which so often had been distorted or ignored by other local writers. This, of course, explained the war-time fame of the book – six editions by 1944 – and during all the many years in which it has been out of print allowed it to gather its special authority. It put Suffolk history and Suffolk ways into an accurate nutshell but, more than this, it extended its spell far beyond Suffolk's borders by its open-hearted account of its author's classic conversion to the spiritual forces of the English countryside. *Suffolk Scene* is about run-down Thirties' farms, little-visited churches, quiet market towns, boisterous fairs, the old language still undiluted by contacts with the media and the new residents, isolation and nature. It is also about a young man glimpsing his particular earthly paradise before a piece of shell 'about the size of a little-finger nail' killed him in Burma.

Julian Tennyson was born in 1915, one of the three gifted sons of Sir Charles Tennyson, grandson and biographer of the poet. Julian was fifteen when the family first started visiting East Anglia to an extent which began to suggest that the place had a special meaning for him. There had been previous Suffolk holidays and also early indications of his fondness for natural history, but it was at Aldeburgh in 1939 that he began to show signs of having found a countryside which contained everything he needed. When he was stationed in India he was urged by his brother Hallam to try and drop his English attitudes and 'to read Kalidasa, to study the Vedanta, and to do anything that might help him to understand the soul of the country he was in', but, says Hallam, 'He replied very briefly...saying that he was fully taken up with thinking and reading about the things he loved at home, that he had no interest whatever in the East and did not want to go any further East than East Anglia in the future'. What then struck Hallam as typical English indifference to 'abroad' he afterwards came to respect as a memorable example of his brother's character and honesty. 'He would not come to terms with his age and spread himself in our thin, attenuated fashion over the whole world. Rather he went inside himself found the truth there and stuck to it with magnificent obstinacy. His passion for it was unadulterated with modern reasoning, but welled up from the depths as mysterious and free as the joy of the birds and flowers and countryside that he loved so much'.

The books which Julian Tennyson took to war were by George Borrow, Richard Jefferies, De Quincey and Robert Nichols, while in his pocket until the day of his death he carried a manuscript copy of the first part of *In Memoriam*. Between leaving Cambridge in 1933 and joining up in 1939, he had begun that haphazard process known as attempting a literary career. Even without the success of *Suffolk Scene*, there were plenty of indications to prove that there was a future for him as a writer. He had worked for Martin Secker the publisher and on the *Evening Standard*, he had contributed to *The Cornhill*, *The Field* and *The Times Literary Supplement* and had written a cheerful book called *Rough Shooting*. And, ironically for such a stay-at-home, it had been suggested that he might like to edit *The Geographical Magazine* as soon as the war was over.

To speculate on what any writer destroyed by war might have become is not only futile but a form of ingratitude. Particularly if their poems and books have remained living things. *Suffolk Scene* is wonderfully alive. It is Julian Tennyson at twenty-three enthusiastically setting out day after day to inform himself about a land which he has adopted, or which has adopted him – he is never quite sure which – and doing his utmost to put the reader in the picture. He writes of scores of things which have been written about in scores of local books but he does so with such a spontaneity and an eagerness to have one share his youthful vision that his whole account of Suffolk turns into a new tale. He is at his best when describing the small rivers with their vast marshes. These chapters are pure autobiography and offer a link between the Suffolk coast of the Thirties and the desolate 'sandlings' described by Edward FitzGerald in his letters over half a century before. Tennyson was seeing the marshes at the end of their real solitude before the modern repair of their complicated network of ancient dykes and sea-walls, the establishment of bird sanctuaries, and when they were still inhabited by figures similar to those who loom out of the mist in the novels of Dickens. In mentioning the Suffolk people encountered by Tennyson, some of whom became his greatest friends, one must add that his use of dialect stories in *Suffolk Scene* is altogether exceptional. Only somebody very close to the area could have caught its voice so authentically.

But perhaps the most intriguing thing about this highly personal encounter with a place where 'the villages...are remote settlements in a remote land, with no prettiness about them, but a solid, unconventional beauty, an inward warmth distilled by the years and cloaked with an outward austerity' is that, although little more than thirty years old, it is already a period piece. The views so percipiently described are those of the final stages of the agricultural depression. Tennyson was not to witness the economic revival begun during the war and, continuing with a variety of changes, have affected Suffolk's life and landscape ever since. At the same time. he knows that the Suffolk he has fallen for and which he has spent so much of his short life exploring is in the grip of a malaise. 'In 1920 a farm in the next village to mine sold for £2500; in 1927 it sold for £1500; in 1934 it sold again for £750; and last year (1937) it fetched precisely £400. As to the farms and their buildings, most of them have hardly been touched since the day they were finished. It is nothing uncommon to find a barn with the thatch stoved in...a really well-kept building is a surprising sight in Suffolk...It is poor in purse, but in spirit it is strong, solid and persevering...It is supremely and unassailably isolated'.

This book is the account of an endeavour by a young writer to interpret both the strength and the isolation of a county which understood him.

A VISIT TO THE FOUNDER

(*The Listener*)

On a spring-like day in November 1959 John Cripps drove me from Burford to Idbury Manor to have lunch with J. W. Robertson Scott. I was fairly young, he was very old. 'I am ninety-four in the spring, born of Scots parents in a little Cumberland agricultural town, affectionately called by its inhabitants 'the throstle's nest'. He was slight and upright. The house was tall and bookish, that is both filled to the attics with volumes and also the kind of house which gets into novels. It smelled of waxed wood, apple-log smoke and bindings. Hyacinths bloomed in fat pots and a proper housekeeper appeared to lay the table. I think that I had only been to the Cotswolds once before and I remember finding a coolness which was quite unlike that of Suffolk. 'How will you get back to Burford?' I thought that John Cripps would fetch me but feeling that this might sound a rather luxurious answer to the austerities of Idbury Manor, I said I would walk.

'Good. I have always walked. I walked all over Japan when I was not much more than a boy. I was there for six years, avoiding cities, always exploring its rural districts. I edited a monthly called *New East* (Shin Toyo). It was half in English and half in Japanese and was published in Tokyo. And then I wrote a book called *The Foundations of Japan*. He said it was like walking in the Middle Ages. With my head full of ferocious Shinto rites and film-makers' bandits, I said how brave he was. I saw this young Scot from Cumberland in terrible danger as he strode through this pre-Lieutenant Pinkerton landscape. But no. Everywhere he met with exquisite hospitality although hardly anyone in the villages had seen a European before. Should we have a walk now? Oh, yes, oh, certainly. The housekeeper fetched his coat.

'Lunch in an hour – no more!' she warned us, presumably knowing what his walks were. Out into the November sunshine. We took the lane which led from the Manor into Gloucestershire. It ran narrowly through bare fields. Robertson Scott stirred it up, made it lively, spoke to a roadman, showed me the Tree of Heaven which he had planted, and paused at a patch of burnt bank over which was scattered the calcined shells of many snails. 'Fire – a terrible death for a snail'. When we reached a much patched-up barn wall, he leaned against its warmth and we discussed the benefits of co-education. Thin old men turn into pencil drawings, their lines so fine, their skins so papery. Such white, shining hair. On the way back I noticed a swimming pool. He had enjoyed something I had written in *The Countryman* but could not recall what it was.

After lunch he showed me the room in which he had conceived *The Countryman* and, with his wife Elspet, edited it for many years. Again there was this predominance of wood. Although in the Cotswolds the house had been built by a Scottish refugee who had fled his land after the Gowrie conspiracy. It did not seem a house for a man in hiding being so conspicuously airy and open. Not a cosy house but one to be fit and busy in, and beautifully spotless. The bank told him that he was mad to launch a magazine but the manager sent a cheque for £100 with a note which said, 'If you are set on ruining yourself at least take a holiday with your wife first'. Sir Stafford Cripps and a Cotswold neighbour gave £100 a piece, a lot of money, as they say, then. Apart from this practical encouragement the rest of the cost was his own. Journalist colleagues from his days at the *Pall Mall Gazette* and the *News Chronicle* feared for his financial safety and actually came to Idbury to urge him not to go into publishing on his own. It was the 1920s, with farming in the doldrums and mass unemployment. But also, which his friends appear not to have observed, a kind of happiness-seeking flight into the countryside by any one with a good pair of boots or a bike. Though full of rural poverty and hardship, the villages and country towns also contained what was to be the last of a culture which had existed for centuries. There was in fact, when in April 1927, the first number of *The Countryman* appeared, a strong but ambivalent interest in rural Britain which was part love and part loathing, much of it born of the trenches.

This non-party, unsentimental, faintly Quakerish quarterly was, according to Robertson Scott's advisors, the wrong price, the wrong shape and came from very much the wrong address. Its peculiar green cover was made of something called 'Job Air Dried Cartridge', a paper invented for packing cartridges. By taking each fresh issue round London four times a year, the editor managed to pack it with advertising. This is a treasure-house for rural historians, from the Soil Association to Rising Damp, from Ladders for All Needs to Treneague camomile. I used to know the formidable old lady who advertised the latter. She lived in a ravine near Wadebridge, in a little white cottage with a Cornish slate floor, and with faggots blazing in a whitewashed fireplace, and she lived – on camomile. When, at twenty-five, the doctor told her that she would soon die, she got on the Cornish Riviera train, bought the cottage for £50 and grew a plant which became a legend. A poet friend and I would climb down to her deep paradise to have tea with her and the sparks would fly out at us and we would brush them from our clothes, and from her indifferent cat as we ate buttered toast. It was this year, 1959, that John Cripps had suggested a picture-cover for the magazine instead of a list of contents, and I had said that I would ask John Nash for some black and white 'seasons'. John Nash used to visit the Cotswolds as a child when his father, a lawyer, was on 'church business'. He and his brother Paul would draw and paint in the Gloucestershire meadows. John became great friends with the plant collector Clarence Elliott who created the now legendary Six Hills Nursery at Stevenage, and Robertson Scott persuaded them – he was a genius persuader – to collaborate on some memorable *Countryman* features.

Tea followed lunch in the failing November light. I told Robertson Scott that I was writing short stories and he told me that he had interviewed – H.M. Stanley. And that he had dined with a man who had dined with Coleridge, making me do arithmetic in my head, not from disbelief but as though to underline such a confession. I was beginning to wonder how I would get back to Burford, then to Oxford and then to Suffolk, although such a journey appeared petty compared with walking across Japan. Should I telephone John Cripps? Who would dare to ask? All around us were the framed oriental paintings of Robertson Scott's sister-in-law Elizabeth Keith, glinting in the shadows. There was a photograph of Bernard Shaw. Robertson Scott said that he and his contemporaries, W. T. Stead, Alfred Spender and H. W. Massingham had been trained in a tough journalists' world but he hoped that the result justified the effort. He was proud of *The Countryman*. It was a creation like none other on the bookstall he thought. He was, he said, a man in love with language. He had written me a letter on 'how to deal with an elderly gentleman' and I should have made more notes, except that the ambience or atmosphere, or whatever one likes to call it, of the book-laden Manor caused a drift.

The talk turned to Little Easton in Essex where I sometimes stayed with Canon Barnett the far-from Socialist rector who once, when I had returned from a walk to the village asked, 'What is it like down there?' 'What is Little Easton like these days?' asked Robertson Scott, who had lived there when Lady Warwick had gathered all the like-minds she could find to be her tenants, H. G. Wells, Gustav Holst, S. L. Bensusan, A. E. Coppard, Solomon the pianist and Conrad Noel and many others. He listened to the sad tale. The Lodge was no more. Its coroneted gates were doubly locked with rust and spear-grass, the park where Mr Britling saw the Great War through was littered with the remains of a P.O.W. camp.

'But what a tremendous thing to have done, to have found the Gowrie conspirator's house and then found a famous magazine!'

'I get tired,' he said.

The tiredness of old age is unlike all other tiredness. To be ninety-four next April makes one sleepy. John Cripps drives up and tells me, 'Plenty of time, plenty of time!' Whilst he is having tea I return to the shelves on which there is a complete run of *The Countryman*, really to see again some of the early photographs of which I am so fond, and here is a picture of 'Clarence Elliott at Home in the Cotswolds' squatting by a raised bed. Like Robertson Scott he had turned 'his baby' – Six Hills Nursery – over to a successor having arrived at what he describes as 'the rest of the road'. In the spring 1948 *Countryman* he writes, 'Plants and travel have kept me busy and poor enough to be uncommonly happy ... I have now found what I wanted in the Cotswolds.' This distant day hurried back to me as we left the Cheltenham Literature Festival last autumn via a series of by-roads in order to make the most of a rare journey to Gloucestershire. To substantiate its haziness I discovered a letter from Robertson Scott which said, 'First money earned in journalism, 4s. 9d. from C. P. Scott (no relation).' Below it he has scribbled some praise from *The Times*. 'Without *The Countryman* there is a narrowing of knowledge, interest and power'. And this must be true. The photography in the early numbers is a revelation, some of it the kind of thing which now one only sees in a Fay Godwin exhibition, and the articles, although non-campaigning, lack complaisancy. Robertson Scott was a late Victorian and, looking back, I can see that something of the rigorousness of those early days was seeded into his 1927 venture. How pleased he would be to know that it remains a lively one in 2002.

AKENFIELD RECOLLECTED

(Preface to the 1999 Penguin edition)

This book was written in 1966-7 and first published in May 1969. I was then living at Debach, a tiny parish of some eighty souls which adjoined the larger village of Charsfield. I remember walking the ancient boundaries of flat-land Debach and hollow-land Charsfield on a grey winter's day and thinking of the ritual toil which had engaged them, and thousands of villages like them, since those who settled them made the first field. All around were similar settlements with 'field' names, so I called my book *Akenfield* after the oaks which stood in the field opposite my old house. 'Acen' = Old English for 'oak'. Also because I was born in the Suffolk village Acton. 'Actun' = 'the homestead by the oaks'. *Akenfield* is chiefly based on Charsfield, but with the surrounding countryside and myself drawn into it. My excuse for the former extension is that, like man, no village is an island, entire of itself, but has always relied on the blacksmith, wheelwright, schools, transport, butcher, and now priest of the area. The book is more the work of a poet than a trained oral historian, a profession I had never heard of when I wrote it. My only real credentials for having written it was that I was native to its situation in nearly every way and had only to listen to hear my own world talking. Thus a thread of autobiography runs strongly through it. Having been born between the wars during the last years of the great agricultural depression, I was in a kind of natural conversation with all three generations who spoke to me in the mid-sixties, and I was able to structure their talk over farming, education, welfare, class, religion and indeed life and death in terms such as I myself was experiencing these things, although now with a writer's vision of them. I saw the two World Wars as extraordinary intrusions, walling-off two successive generations from each other, and giving each of them a distinctive voice. And I was delighted as always with those who bent the rules, dodged the system and who managed to be 'different' within the rigidities which rural communities like to impose. There is no place like the countryside for the most imaginative – and blatant – non-conformity.

The most unlooked-for change of fortune during the rural sixties would have been that for agriculture thirty years on. Then it was grow all the grain you can, never mind what eccentrics calling themselves 'ecologists' said. An often brutal and ignorant rationalization of the old field system which so upset John Clare when his village was enclosed was government-inspired and paid for. One Suffolk village, Tannington, was in the van of such change, with scarcely a tree or hedge to its name. Although cornfields had to expand to take combine harvesters, it was shocking to see centuries' old hedgerows bulldozed, the pouring on to the land of chemicals about which the average farmer understood very little, and stubble-burning as an economy. Now there is official and social condemnation of such practices, and because of the eventual withdrawal of subsidies, plus European laws, there is a feeling of insecurity among today's farmers such as most of them have only read about and would never have imagined could return. The labour force was small enough then but is now minute. A couple of men on eight hundred acres. The 'old people', that is, those who truly belong to a village, are the least surprised. Ups and downs are in their blood, and although vague about agronomics they don't expect anything to last. But some farmers today are nerve-racked and fearful. Gone is that first fine careless confidence when the grain grew as it never had grown before. Thus a recovered respect for nature, often brought about, I sometimes think, by their children, who have been thrillingly 'ecologized' at school and university, not to mention by television. One of my hardest tasks in the nineties has been to make the villagers *look* at their fields, not drive through them as though nothing existed between their houses and the supermarket. An almost total lack of contact with its growing acres by the majority of people now living in the countryside has, more than anything else, brought about its increasing urbanization. The old work ground is seen only when it becomes a playground. But the locals as well as the visitors are walking more, which is something they would have found difficult to do during the sixties when the ancient village paths petered out in seas of grain.

My father had fought at Gallipoli in the Suffolk Regiment and it was while listening to Len Thompson about what to me, as a boy, was a half-glamorous, half-terrible experience, that I recognized the 'iceberg' quality in those I thought I knew pretty well. Only the tip of them showed, all the rest ran deep. A similar revelation occurred when I listened to our retired district nurse. She was the secretary of the P.C.C. and I was a churchwarden, and we had every reason to believe that there was not much we could tell each other which was not already known. Many years after *Akenfield* I sat by her death-bed and watched the old 'authority' come and go in her dark eyes.

The earlier poet of this region was Edward FitzGerald who lies buried under rose-trees seeded from those which grow round Omar's tomb at Naishapur in Boulge churchyard, just a mile or two from my house. How often he would have seen it, and how often I sat in what was once his lodge-cottage distributing our Flower Show prizes – mainly to two grimly competitive farm-workers who yearly cleared the board. Tramping and cycling about, I frequently found myself haunted by FitzGerald. Many of his lanes had been obliterated by the American bomber base across which the Welsh rector and myself would take our blowy walks. The poet in *Akenfield* is James Turner, my first writer friend, who lived three miles away, and with whom over many years I explored Suffolk – a vivid, sometimes testy man whose wife moved him on and on until he reached Cornwall.

There was the question of dialect. 'Suffolk' being my first language, so to speak. I did not find it wholly impossible to write even if it is thought to be notoriously hard to get right. I sat with the wheelwright's nephew as we asked each other the meaning of words in Forby's *The Vocabulary of East Anglia*, 1830, and found that we were rarely stumped. Eventually I decided to keep to what was being said, and to a certain personal rhythm in each speaker, using a story, 'Tom-tit-Tot', from the Suffolk Folklore Society's collection to give a wonderfully accurate example of our dialext. It has always intrigued East Anglians how their speech gradually broadens out between the Stour and the Wash. This is one thing which hasn't altered much since the sixties. In fact, certain 'country' groups may be re-establishing the local speech of their grand-parents.

One can compare the economics of then and now but it would need an expert to explain the real difference. The Rural Dean's annual stipend in 1969 was £1,175; in 1998 it is £15,000. The farm-worker's weekly wage then was £11.11; now it is £200 with overtime. But the long struggle against the poverty wages and grim conditions of the inter-war years continues to lie like a barely credible memory at the heart of today's prosperity and leisure. The middle-aged, let alone the aged, have to shake themselves to admit that things were so. There are various ways to describe a time, a place, a condition. One can come to them from outside and say what one saw. Or one can emerge from within a community, as so many rural writers do, and be at a particular moment its indigenous voice.

Pictures

FIRST STEPS: THOMAS GAINSBOROUGH

(*New York Times*, July 17th, 1988)

If John Constable's is the most familiar of all British artists' home territories, Thomas Gainsborough's is among the least. The comparison would not have been such a pointed one had not these territories joined or, they sharing the same river, overlapped. The two great painters were born some twenty miles and fifty years apart in the Stour Valley but due to Constable's naturalistic (he called it 'scientific') treatment of its gentle scenery he had siezed it all, popularly speaking. The Constable Country is now as much a must on the tourist itinerary as Bath and Stratford-on-Avon. Whilst the Gainsborough Country can never be so easily accessible, it is there and not to be missed. The young John Constable, who was twelve when Gainsborough died, walked every inch of it and revered it. And, as it is not entirely extravagant to ask, 'would there have been a John Constable, landscapist, had there not been a god called Gainsborough only a walking distance upstream?' one might say that the Stour Valley's enormous role in the development of English painting can only be understood if one starts at Sudbury.

This is where Gainsborough was born in 1727 and where he dominated my childhood in somewhat the same way as he dominated Constable's. The artist's forcefulness and inescapability had much to do with the excellent statue erected to him just before the First World War, a life-size bronze, palette and brush in hand and his gaze on his birthplace. As a boy, this monument seemed to draw up all the little town's little preoccupations and put them through a process of transfiguration. I had nearly forgotten the power which Gainsborough's statue had over me until, only the other day, I read a biography of Helen Waddell and learned that a huge carved Buddha in the street of the Chinese town where her father worked as a Presbyterian missionary, filled her as a small girl with a strength and radiance which remained with her most of her life. William Golding, brought up under the spire of Salisbury Cathedral, was permanently influenced by this soaring symbol. Similarly, Thomas Gainsborough, rearing above the market-stalls and backed by the tall wool church which itself was the last word in local grandeur to my child's eyes, his plinth with its swag of violins and flutes lit at dusk by the naptha lamps of the banana-sellers, lifted me out of a market-town's humdrum into the magical realm of art.

But the key to why so many people came to see the Constable Country and scarcely any to see the Gainsborough Country, a still virtually unexplored land, did not arrive until a member of the catchment board asked me to help him organise a little book he had written about the River Stour. I was about to become a writer and he was a descendant of the Cavalier poet Edmund Waller, thus intriguing me. Colonel Waller's *The Suffolk Stour* revealed what John Constable was really painting in his superb 'six footers', as he called them, which was the river which ran through his family's farm and which drove its mills and was an industrialised waterway. His many pictures of the Valley were intended to be of an immediately recognisable and desirable place for human existence – albeit that during the time that they were being painted the starving agricultural workers were rioting. Constable wasn't being hypocritical, he was providing powerful and beautiful statements of what we now call man's place in the ecology. Everything in these native scenes, from the work to the plants and the weather is spiritually true and scientifically accurate. The countless visitors who come to East Bergholt every year are shocked to see so exactly what Constable saw, and to breathe his air.

What would these same sightseers find if they drove, preferably via the river-hugging lanes, upstream to the Gainsborough Country? In terms of art-related topography, little which could be discovered without the aid of books, which would have made Gainsborough, who hated reading, laugh. Yet it was rural Suffolk, even during the half of his life spent out of it, which inspired his ravishing landscapes, so beloved in their day – which poor Constable's never were when they first appeared – and which seem to be purposely designed for us not to enter or walk in. Except for a few magnificent instances such as *Cornard Wood* or the surroundings of Mr and Mrs Robert Andrews, or a few views along the River Orwell near Ipswich, Gainsborough Country cannot be pin-pointed on the ordinance survey. Its geography was shaped on a table-top from bits of cork, broccoli, twigs and looking-glass, and then subjected to a transfiguration. The rustic scene which so repeatedly emerges contains so many similar elements that we can only conclude that it represented a human condition which was of private significance to the artist. It is of a secluded peasant world where life is rough and ragged, yet mysteriously blissful. There are the usual village tasks, yet an indifference to them seems to prevail. Is it the classic idyl? No – there is never a Virgillian quote in sight. The actual farming is terribly muddly and a far cry from that on Robert Andrews's estate. These landscapes are Gainsborough's escape from where portraiture had taken him, Georgian society. Some were called his 'fancy' pictures and they fill a section of that frustrating atlas which contains the geography of *Le Grand Meaulnes*.

But, having got to Sudbury, and before setting foot in his birthplace, drive through the town and up Ballingdon Hill to a house called Auberies. It has stone cats on the gateposts which we, as children, were told changed posts at midnight, although we were never allowed to stay up and watch it happen. This was the home of Robert and Frances Andrews who were married in All Saints' Church below in 1748 when he was 22 and she 16. Their portrait painted by Robert's schoolfriend Tom Gainsborough during the harvest was most likely a wedding-present. The couple look across the Stour Valley on a panorama of fields, woods, medieval towers, water-meadows and river twists which, after two and a half centuries, has changed hardly at all. All that this view includes, and it stretches bluely to the Cornards, is the Gainsborough Country. Further reaches of it are in and about Ipswich, a county town crammed with associative surprises from Chaucer to George Orwell.

And so from the setting of what many believed to be the finest English domestic portrait to Gainsborough's House in Gainsborough Street, Sudbury, curiously, considering the nation's many literary shrines, the only artist's birthplace open to the public. Like countless houses in ancient town centres, it is a timber and plaster building made elegant in the 18th century by the addition of a brick facade. Gainsborough's father built this improvement in 1723 and there could hardly have been designed a more perfect backdrop, as it were, for such a son. Not that its history is of the purely residential – far from it. Gainsborough père ran his various trades from it, most interestingly his shroud-weaving business. In a forlorn hope to revive the once prosperous wool trade a Charles II law required everybody to be buried in a woollen shroud. This law did little for the industry or for Gainsborough's father, who went bankrupt. I have found myself less thoughtful about this than of that lad sketching below the room where those lengths of warm cloth for the Sudbury's corpses were run off the looms.

The Gainsboroughs were an extraordinary lot, father an Independent, mother an Anglican, two sons inventors and the whole atmosphere of the home a strong mixture of entrepreneurial effort and the wildly impractical, genius and the kind of eccentricity which the English admire. John Gainsborough – 'Scheming Jack' – the artist's brother, invented a cuckoo which sang all the year round, a cradle which was self-rocking, a waterwheel which turned in still water and wings which failed to let him fly when he took off from the roof of the summerhouse. Their mother painted flowers, their uncle – her brother – the local curate and schoolmaster, the Reverend Humphrey Burroughs, was the member of the family to whom posterity is most in debt, for it was chiefly due to this percipient man that Tom, aged thirteen, was sent off to London to learn to be an artist. The robustness of the house during the Gainsborough's occupancy had utterly vanished by the time of my first awareness of it as a boy. For it had become, after much else, a refined small hotel whose bedrooms had the titles of Gainsborough's paintings instead of numbers. Guests were told that 'we have put you in Mrs Siddons' or 'in the Blue Boy'.

The fortunes of this old house were dramatically and courageously changed in 1958 when a handful of local people managed to buy it and, by degrees, turn it into one of the nation's most evocative and fascinating art centres. Until these roomfuls of his drawings and paintings appeared in their midst, Sudburians paid their homage to something and somebody they knew almost nothing about by having a Gainsborough cinema, street, road, and various commercial enterprises, although even now the sense of association, of being in immortalised scenes, remain thin when compared with Cezanne's mountain, Monet's garden – or Constable's mill. Gainsborough has been, in popular terms, an artist in abeyance. No one would have thought that by creating an art centre in his birthplace that he would have been drawn so far forward so quickly and made so much more recognisable. But this is what has happened. There will never be any general admittance to his landscapes, for these are very private views. But the range of the Georgian faces is a very different matter. An entire society, squires, bankers, royalty, beggars, priests, actors, children, the aged, aristocrats, farmers, musicians, the clever, the beautiful and the wild, surged through his painting-rooms at Sudbury, Ipswich, Bath and London, and were given all the glitter and profundity which life demands. It is only just that the first portrait he painted, a small boy in his finery, should now hang where he grew up.

Having allowed Robert and Frances Andrews's grand view of Sudbury and its hills to give them a broad Gainsborough Country perspective, and having felt as much as seen the house, the pilgrim should walk down the street to the river. On the left, up School Lane, is the school which stands on the site of that in which the artist was taught by his Uncle Humphrey. Opposite, on the right, the road leads to St Gregory's Church, where his grandparents are buried. Straight ahead lies the Stour and its common-lands, the swimming, games-playing, idling, courting meadows for Sudbury's youth for many centuries, and maybe the initial path to Gainsborough's personal countryside. The disused track of the Cambridge train runs across it like a barricade. Distantly to the north is the tower of Borley Church below whose altar lies Humphrey Burroughs. This descent past the houses of the rich medieval wool merchants to the Stour, the tow-path to the Croft, the lanes to the Market Hill and confident Tom high above it, has been my Gainsborough Country since I was not much bigger than whoever he is in the pretty waistcoat in the picture. This walk and another on the high ground at Little Cornard, an adventurous spot in my boyhood, full of pits and gulls where the teenage Gainsborough painted his first landscape in which, through the oaks, distantly, points the spire of the church in which his parents were married. It is strange to think that had he widened his view to the left it would have included Constable's grandfather's farm. Not quite so odd, perhaps, that this early landscape, *Cornard Wood*, now in the National Gallery, used to belong to Constable's Uncle David. Or that Gainsborough's brother and Constable's father attended river navigation meetings together, seeing that their vision was shaped by a single stream.

A PERFECT INTERPRETER: JOHN CONSTABLE

(*Horizon*, Spring, 1975)

Great artists are often seen as people who have been forced to struggle against enormous disadvantages in early life. John Constable is one artist who had no such struggle.

He was born at East Bergholt, Suffolk, in June of 1776, the second son of Golding and Ann Constable. The Constable family had farmed in the Stour Valley for generations and had gradually acquired more property down-stream until, at the time of John's birth, they owned a prosperous string of mills and were among the leading agricultural merchants in the river trade. The business was so successful by the 1770's that Golding Constable was able to give up living in the hollow at Flatford Mill and build a 'mansion house' in the village. The Stour villages – East Bergholt, Dedham, Stratford. Stoke, Nayland, and Bures – are fine villages full of magnificent architecture from the days of the medieval wool merchants, and during John Constable's boyhood they were being expanded by the Georgian gentry. These crucial years of the eighteenth century, which the artist could barely recall but which moulded the character of nearly all the people he knew, have been described by agricultural historians as the golden years of English farming. For John Constable, the essence of this glorious scene had been set down in paint by Thomas Gainsborough.

There was, to Constable, something overwhelming in the fact that Gainsborough had once walked the lanes that he now strolled in his slow, deliberate, country fashion. He saw Gainsborough 'in every hedge and hollow tree,' and soon, scarcely daring to think about the consequences, he too was making up his mind to become an artist. 'For long I foundered in the path and tottered on the threshold,' he wrote, 'and there never was any young man nearer being lost than myself.' This was certainly a boyish self-dramatization, for when we see what actually happened to John Constable (once he had convinced his practical East Anglian parents that neither the church nor the flourishing family business was for him), we will find that he was shown 'the path' by some of the most helpful guides anyone could wish for. What was even more extraordinary, these people were living, as it were, on his very doorstep.

Although his advantages were remarkable, John Constable, a man whose favourite word was 'placid,' had been born into a world of violence and change. The American, French, and Industrial revolutions all occurred during his lifetime. And he himself, while seeking to prove the spiritual harmony of the natural universe, would be too revolutionary a painter to be understood.

But it was only where his painting was concerned that Constable was a revolutionary. In nearly every other way he was a conventional Tory gentleman who believed that the land is the source of all the best things in life, a God-given commodity that the landowners had to revere. The farmers worked for the land-owners and the villagers worked for the farmers. It was all part of a divine pattern. His long and bitter struggle to be accepted as an artist by everyone, from the inhabitants of Suffolk to the members of the Royal Academy, was a wish to be an accepted part of the civilized world he so strongly believed in. His difficulties – and ultimate triumph –stemmed from his refusal to give the public what it wanted as the price for easy entry into that world.

'Painting,' he said, 'is a science, and should be pursued as an enquiry into the laws of nature.' But the public did not want painting to be a science; they wanted painting to be a kind of magic. They did not want straightforward descriptions of the countryside they knew so well: they wanted stories and mystery in paint. They wanted to look into a picture as they could look into Virgil or into one of their favourite poems, *The Seasons*, and see an idealized existence. Constable bewildered – and annoyed – them by leaving out these literary and emotional references and painting instead the natural realities of a certain place at a certain moment. This now seems a reasonable thing to do, but when Constable, at the very beginning of his career, confessed to his friend John Dunthorne that he intended to be a 'natural painter,' one of those rare peaks of total originality in art came into view.

Dunthorne was six years older than Constable and lived nearby in East Bergholt. He was one of those 'odd men out' that so many villages produce, a plumber-glazier who was also an artist and a freethinker. Constable was still a boy when Dunthorne taught him to grind colours and encouraged him to sketch. The association between the miller's rather dandified son and the 'atheist,' as Dunthorne was called, was disapproved of in some quarters, though Golding Constable seems to have found it amusing. To him they were 'Don Quixote and his Man Friday.' 'I shall endeavour to get a pure and unaffected manner of representing the scenes,' his son confided to Dunthorne. 'Nature is the fountain's head.' And, every evening after work at the mill office, he carried sketchbook or easel into the fields and painted until the light failed.

In 1796, when he was twenty, Constable met J. T. Smith, an antiquary who encouraged him to make drawings of old cottages in the Stour villages. These beautiful little pencil sketches were made in a book small enough to be held in the palm of the hand, and Constable acquired a habit that he would have for the rest of his life. William Blake was amazed by the perfection of these sketchbooks. 'Why, this is not drawing, but *inspiration*,' he told Constable. '1 meant it for drawing,' replied Constable in the sharp way that was to unnerve so many of his fellow artists.

How far this good-looking, steely, and, at the same time, deeply spiritual youth had to go in order to persuade his parents to let him study painting is not known. But in 1799 he left Suffolk with an annual allowance of one hundred pounds from his father and a student's pass for the school set up by the Royal Academy. Three years later, in 1802, Constable returned to Suffolk, trained and expecting to earn a living. His first step was to buy a cottage-studio away from his parents' house; his second, to find some sort of answer to the barrage of criticism that now began to pursue him. Inevitably, the trouble had started in his own family; with typical Suffolk common sense, they thought that he should provide the neighborhood with what it required – namely, portraits. Constable was willing to do them, but his rough, impressionistic brushwork was an immediate cause for complaint. His rich uncle, David Watts, summed up the general feeling when he advised Constable to 'Paint a little starling on your easel with the words, "Finish! Finish!"'

One neighbour, a Mr. Reade, did commission a painting of his house, and *Old Hall* was the first of what Constable called his 'house portraits,' the most superb of which is *Malvern Hall*, painted in 1810. Constable asked ten guineas for *Old Hall*; with *Malvern Hall* he would ask the world to see a new vision of art.

But in 1802 it was still Thomas Gainsborough and the old vision that enthralled him, and his great problem was reconciling the traditional landscape, which in many ways he admired and respected, with the 'natural' truths he saw whenever he glanced out the window at Flatford Mill or looked across the water meadows to Dedham. One thing he never worried about was finding a subject. His home valley, a six-mile stretch of East Anglian river scenery with church towers, huge trees, industrial buildings, and brilliant light, was an incomparable challenge. Later he would say he never wanted to paint any scene where he was not a 'welcome guest.' And, when the time came for him to show people what kind of artist he intended to be, he would choose the valley he knew so well as the subject for his first big picture.

In *Dedham Vale* (1802), Constable looks through Gainsborough to the old seventeenth-century masters of landscape. The painting is also evidence that Constable had formed an influential new friendship, for its composition is remarkably like that of an exquisite seventeenth-century work by Claude Lorraine entitled *Hagar and the Angel*.

Sir George Beaumont owned this painting and was so fond of it that he had it hung in his carriage when he travelled. His mother lived in Dedham, and it was inevitable that the man who was about to be the greatest patron of the Romantic movement and the man who was to be its leading painter should meet. It was an important friendship, for Sir

George – whose collection would be the nucleus of the National Gallery he helped found – introduced Constable to the Rubens landscape called *Chateau de Steen*, to the paintings of other Flemish masters, and to the work of such 'modern' artists as Thomas Girtin. When Sir George asked one day whose style he would choose for his own, Girtin's or the old masters', Constable replied that it would be neither. His, he said, would be 'God Almighty's style.'

Dr. Johnson once said, 'We all know what light is, but it is not easy to tell what it is.' Dissatisfied with that kind of vagueness about something so vital to humanity, Constable set out to paint light. He saw that when the light changed, a place changed. It was his earliest and most important discovery. 'The world is wide,' he said, 'no two days are alike, not even two hours, neither were there ever two leaves of a tree alike since the creation of the world, and the genuine productions of art, like those of nature, are all distinct from each other.'

He worked hard now, both to discover himself and to establish himself. He sent pictures to the Royal Academy, he copied family portraits for aristocrats, he even travelled about England to paint, as landscape artists were expected to do. In the Lake District Constable met William Wordsworth and, although they were never to become friends, he found in Wordsworth's poetry a perfect statement of the 'natural' values he sought for his own art. His search would, of course, be successful. As one modern critic has said, 'Few painters had Constable's power to bring the infinite facts of nature into one single idea, and, with almost unconscious naturalness, to translate them into a poetic image.' Wordsworth and Constable, though they had little to do with each other, were the channels through which the English Romantic movement was to express itself in its most profound terms.

But it was a lonely course Constable had set for himself. 'I see him silhouetted,' wrote Charles Leslie, his friend and first biographer, 'coming from nowhere, going nowhere, but producing work of wonderful quality within lines sharply distinct from the ambiance of history.' There have been artists and writers who have prided themselves on being 'distinct from the ambiance of history,' but Constable was not one of them. From the very beginning he worked to be understood and accepted.

In 1810 Constable came of age as a revolutionary artist. He had been struggling since about 1806 to free himself from the rules governing traditional landscape painting. Fortunately for art, Constable's new 'realism' was brilliantly suffused by his romantic imagination, and his work, with its broad sweeps of colour and movement, reveals a man who saw poetry lying at the root of the everyday things of life. He had emerged, too, as an artist who had a keen double vision for what was happening around him. One part of him saw what most people saw when they set off to labour in the fields or factories along the River Stour; the other part of him invested these humble sights with a profound spiritual significance. It was a way of looking at life that Wordsworth described as 'far more deeply informed.' Constable himself was fond of quoting a couplet by the Suffolk poet George Crabbe:

> It is the soul that sees: the outward eyes
> Present the subject, but the mind descries.

Constable's 'outward eyes' were those of a gentleman farmer, a corn merchant, and, since the sea was so near, a sailor. They were also the eyes of a naturalist and meteorologist. He was a dreamer who constantly demanded hard facts. He crowded his sketchbooks with the facts – carts, ploughs, sailing tackle, notes about the weather – and then, in his paintings, made them all subservient to 'nature,' the wonderful and mysterious force that controlled everything.

He was fascinated by time. When work on a picture continued long past the hour or day to which it belonged, he would go to great trouble to get every detail correct. *The Cornfield* (1826) is a view of the Stour Valley on a hot July day, but it was later in the year when Constable began to work on the foreground. We find him consulting one Mr. Phillips, a botantist, and receiving this advice:

> At this season all the tall grasses are in flower, bogrush, bullrush, teasel. The white bindweed now hangs its flowers over the branches of the hedge; the wild

carrot and hemlock flowers in banks of hedges, cow parsley, water plantain, etc.; the heath hills are purple at this season; the rose-coloured persicaria in wet ditches is now very pretty; the catchfly graces the hedgerow, as also the ragged robin; bramble is now in flower, poppy, mallow, thistle, nop, etc.

Constable's religious attitude toward landscape, his 'inner eye,' was obvious even as his career began. Sometimes it overwhelmed him and made him doubt everything he was trying to do: 'Nothing can exceed the beauty of the country,' he wrote, '– it makes pictures seem sad trumpery, even those that possess most of nature.' Sometimes it humbled him: 'Remember the great were not made for me, nor I for the great. ... My limited and abstract art is to be found under every hedge, and in every lane.' When he saw the kind of landscape that was popular at the Royal Academy, he saw blasphemy: 'Good God! – what a sad thing it is that this lovely art is so wrested to its own destruction – only used to blind our eyes and senses from seeing the sun shine, the fields bloom, the trees blossom, and to hear the foliage rustle – the old black, rubbed-out, dirty bits of canvas to take the place of God's own works.'

The art world Constable set out to enter – rather than conquer – was dominated by members of the Royal Academy, most of them portrait painters and what were called 'history' painters. The acknowledged leader of the portrait painters was Sir Thomas Lawrence, who captured the elegance of Regency England and gave his sitters the heroic attitudes that the long years of war against Napoleon had made popular. History painters turned out stories, morals, and ancedotes. Battles, national events, idealized cottage scenes, episodes from the Bible, Shakespeare, or the classical poets – these were the subjects people liked to have hanging on their walls.

The Royal Academy, which had been in existence for nearly forty years, set the standards for what was acceptable as art, serving a clientele drawn mainly from the middle class. Constable and the Academy – and its customers – were at odds from the very start. He flatly refused to be what he called 'a ladies' and gentlemen's painter,' and Academy clients objected to what they called his 'low' art. His brushwork offended them, and they could not understand why anyone would want pictures of ordinary barns, mills, and labourers. They wanted theatrical pictures like *Belshazzar's Feast* by John Martin, which resembled a glittering scene from one of Handel's operas. *The Blind Fiddler*, by David Wilkie, allowed them to indulge their Christian compassion for the poor, and they enjoyed huge, action-filled canvases like Benjamin West's *Battle of La Hague*. The public's eagerness for glossy miracles of technique and pictorial novelty shocked Constable. 'In an age such as this' he declared, 'painting should be *understood*, not looked on with blind wonder, not considered only a poetic aspiration, but as a pursuit, *legitimate, scientific* and *mechanical*.'

Fortunately for Constable, this period saw the foundation of another long-lasting friendship. Friendships with John Dunthorne and Sir George Beaumont had each led to remarkable extensions of his art, and now, a chance meeting with Dr. Fisher, the rector of Langham, led to the friendship that was to sustain him in the long days of rejection ahead.

The parish of Langham lay to the south of Dedham Vale, and it was on a hill not far from Langham church that Constable sat to draw his favorite view of the river scenery below. Dr. Fisher liked to make watercolour sketches of the same lovely farmland. After he became bishop of Salisbury, Fisher invited Constable to visit him there. Constable was to find a scene he would make almost as famous as Flatford Mill—the tall, pale, dizzily spired cathedral rising out of the water meadows and the sluggish river, the kind of river he liked, winding over Salisbury Plain. And there, too, in 1811, he was to meet the wisest, most understanding person in his life – John Fisher, the bishop's nephew and a newly ordained minister as well.

Constable spent these formative years not only in discovering 'his path'; he was also busy doing all the things other young artists of the time did. He showed paintings of the fashionable Lake District at the Royal Academy, and he entered into the spirit of the Napoleonic Wars by going to Chatham and painting *H.M.S. Victory*, May, 1803.

At Chatham I hired a boat to see the men of war, which are there in great numbers. I sketched the *Victory* in three views. She was the flower of the flock, a three decker of (some say) 112guns. She looked very beautiful, fresh out of dock and newly painted. When I saw her they were bending the sails.

Superb sea painter that Constable was, with an expert knowledge of shipping, he found the sea itself formless and horrifying. He never sought it out. His magnificent sea pictures were nearly all painted when chance circumstances brought him within sight of the ocean.

Although Constable was at the height of his power between the years 1810 and 1818, particularly with his *Boat-building near Flatford Mill* painted entirely in the open air during the summer of 1815, it was not until the end of that decade that he set out to force the public to accept him as an important landscape artist. His aim was to produce for the Academy a number of very large pictures of Flatford Mill and Dedham Vale that would incorporate both his scientific view of nature and a remarkable new painting technique. The canvas size was deliberate, calculated to impress the Academy and test himself: 'A large canvas will show you what you cannot do, a small one will only show you what you can do.' And so we find him cheerfully writing to John Fisher, 'l do not consider myself at work [unless] l am before a six-foot canvas.' He called this venture his 'canal' pictures, and the series was undertaken during what were probably the happiest years of his life.

The basis of this happiness was his marriage to Maria Bicknell. She was the granddaughter of Dr. Rhudde, rector of East Bergholt. a fierce, rich, authoritarian old man who seems to have distrusted Constable long before the artist met Maria. The dislike was so obvious that when the two fell in love they lived in dread of the rector's finding out about their relationship and disinheriting Maria. The lovers were forced into a miserable and frustrating secrecy that Constable found particularly distressing. He was thirty-three when this secret courtship began and thirty-nine when the wise John Fisher persuaded the unhappy couple to stop worrying about Dr. Rhudde's money and get married. He performed the ceremony at Saint Martin-in-the-Fields on October 2, 1816. John Fisher himself had been married a few months earlier, to

Wordsworth's niece, and now the four of them left London by coach for a honeymoon in Dorset – bringing Constable to one of his chance meetings with the sea, and to the subject of his most profound sea painting, *Weymouth Bay*.

On their return from the honeymoon, the Constables set up housekeeping in London, first in Bloomsbury, then at 35 Charlotte Street in Soho, and Constable began travelling to Suffolk to make oil sketches for pictures he later painted in his studio in town. It is these oil sketches that contain the essence of his genius. In them we see art entering a new dimension. Executed entirely for his own instruction and joy, they are masterpieces that fuse the elements of the natural scene – light, earth, and water. Other painters had sketched their first ideas in oils rather than pencil or chalk, but none like Constable. Something unique and amazing happened here. A moment of time in the open air was transposed to canvas, or to the specially prepared sheets of paper he often used. Constable once said, 'If I were bound with chains I should break them, and with a single hair round me I should feel uncomfortable.' In these tremendously immediate paintings, each a complete statement in itself, he found the total artistic freedom he needed.

In the six 'canal' pictures of 1819 to 1825, which grew out of these sketches, Constable combined his inspired vision of landscape with, he hoped, sufficient traditional feeling to make the canvases acceptable to the public, and particularly to the artists at the Royal Academy. But his colours hadn't been blended properly, people said, and the white flecks of paint he used as highlights were dismissed as 'Constable's snow.'

The Hay Wain, completed in 1821, was the third canvas in the series to fail to find a buyer at the Royal Academy. It was hanging in a gallery called the British Institute when two young leaders of the French Romantic movement, Tbeodore Gericault and Charles Nodier, saw it and were overwhelmed.

French painting was dominated then by a facile style known as classicism, a mixture of militarism and 'Grecian' sensuousness that reached its peak in the work of David (which Constable thought derived 'from the brothel'). It was in 1824, when the war between official art and Romantic art filled the Salon with controversy, that a dealer named John Arrowsmith, learning of Constable from Nodier, brought *The Hay Wain* to Paris.

Constable had been reluctant to sell, although, as he said, 'I need the money dreadfully.' As a conservative English patriot who had lived through twenty years of war with France, he could think of the French only as enemies. He also held the Englishman's traditional view of Paris: 'Think of the lovely valleys amid the peaceful farm houses of Suffolk forming a scene of exhibition to amuse the gay and frivolous Parisians!'

Amusement was hardly what *The Hay Wain* provided in Paris. Constable didn't read French, but his wife translated the news for him. He could hardly believe it. 'My landscapes have made an epoch there,' he wrote. 'They wonder where the *brightness* comes from.' The commissions rolled in, and the critics raved; two pictures, *The Hay Wain* and *A View on the Stour*, were placed on special exhibit at the Louvre, and Charles X awarded him the Salon's Gold Medal. Constable was overcome. 'What a feather!' he exclaimed. It was the first official acknowledgment of his genius.

No one knows why Constable quarreled with Arrowsmith, but suddenly, just when it seemed that he might become a leader of European art, he flatly refused to let 'the French man' have any more pictures. Certainly Constable disliked having to work on a commissioned basis. Commissions were 'jobs' and having to do a job irritated him. Arrowsmith seems to have been neither very generous nor very tactful, and one day, with the short temper for which he was famous, Constable sent him packing.

The break with France came at an unfortunate time. A few months later Constable finished the sixth and last painting in the 'canal' series: *The Leaping Horse* is his most dramatic canvas and a superb culmination to the group of paintings with which he made his bid for fame. Yet, 'no one picture ever departed from my easel with more anxiety on my part,' Constable declared, and his premonitions were correct: the Academy was outraged and the painting was not sold.

Nor was *The Leaping Horse* shown in Paris. Nevertheless, twenty of

Constable's canvases had gone to France and there they forged a link in the chain that would result in an altogether new concept of art. Delacroix changed his palette because of them; a group of landscape painters working in the Forest of Fontainebleau was influenced by those brilliant East Anglian views, and the generation that followed the Barbizon School, as it was called, would make wonderful use of Constable's discoveries. Would the Impressionist movement have been hurried forward had Millet, Corot, and Delacroix seen *The Leaping Horse* or Constable's oil sketches? The 'ifs' surrounding Constable's moment of glory in Paris have intrigued art historians ever since.

Constable was never again to know fame in his lifetime. As though even this brief success had to be tempered with disappointment, the first serious signs of Mrs. Constable's tuberculosis emerged in 1824. They went to Brighton for her health, and while she rested he painted sea pictures, including *Brighton Beach, with Colliers* and *The Marine Parade and Chain Pier, Brighton*. Indeed, it was here that he heard of the sensation his work had created in Paris.

His wife's illness, his increasingly large family (they were to have seven children by 1828), his problematic position with the Royal Academy – all contributed to a new seriousness in Constable. He worried about money. The collapse of agriculture after the Napoleonic Wars was ruining the prosperity of his beloved Stour Valley, and it was a great shock to Constable, faithful believer in the old social order, to hear that the starving villagers of East Bergholt were rioting. The financial situation was sometimes so bad that the mill, a source of income for Constable, failed to make a profit.

Now and then there were hints of fame. Constable described one of them in a letter to a friend:

> In the coach yesterday coming from Suffolk. were two gentlemen and myself, all strangers to each other. In passing through the valley about Dedham, one of them remarked to me, on my saying that it was beautiful, 'Yes. sir, this is Constable's country!'

Most important, there were the pleasures of nature: 'The trees and the clouds seem to ask me to try and do something like them, and that's no small return for a life of labour.' Words like 'light,' 'dews,' 'breezes,' 'blooms,' and 'freshness' run through his letters and lectures, making us feel the very air of George IV's England. Everything connected with the weather fascinated Constable. 'As I rode home a complete arch of rainbow came down to my very feet: I saw my dog running through it.'

As a miller's son, Constable was proud of having a miller's weather eye, but it was not until the publication in 1820 of a book entitled *The Climate of London* that Constable – and indeed, all the writers and painters of the Romantic movement – discovered what might be called the meteorological facts of life. Luke Howard, the author and the first modern weatherman, classified clouds into categories – cirrus, cumulus, and so forth – and gave a scientific basis to the atmospheric changes that painters had used for mood or simply as decoration. While Shelley was writing 'The Cloud' and Goethe was writing to Luke Howard himself, praising him for discovering in meteorology 'a symbol of the universal law,' Constable was out 'skying,' recording the sky in all its moods. He worked fast, sketching on sheets of oiled paper in the lid of his paintbox, and in 1822 alone he executed more than fifty brilliant little pictures. 'It will be difficult,' he said, 'to name a class of landscape in which the sky is not the keynote, the standard of scale, and the chief organ of sentiment.... The sky is the source of light in nature, and governs everything.'

Having freed himself of the literary feelings that surrounded conventional landscape painting, Constable now realized that an artist did not constantly need to seek fresh scenes: the mood, form, and tones of a single landscape were in a state of everlasting change and permutation because of the effect of light. Howard's book helped him to explain things for which there had previously been no correct language, and now he was able to say in one of his lectures that landscape painting 'is scientific as well as poetic; ... imagination alone never did, and never can, produce works that are to stand by a comparison with realities.'

Constable's sky sketches were made in Hampstead. In 1820, when he first went to live there, it was a large, comfortable village, only a shilling coach-ride from London. The Heath, with its ponds and gravel works, was still very wild. 'Our little drawing-room commands a view unequalled in Europe,' he wrote to John Fisher. His favourite sketching and painting spot was near Branch Hill pond. Foggy, noisy London lay below. It was while watching the effect of the clouds from these heights that Constable formed the corollary to his ideas about light: 'I live by shadows,' he said. 'To me shadows are realities.'

Like the Stour Valley and Salisbury Plain, Hampstead Heath was to become an important personal landscape for Constable. But when his beloved wife, Maria, died in November, 1828, he chose none of these for his astonishing memorial to her.

Many years earlier, during his frustrated courtship, Constable had discovered an ancient tower overlooking the Thames estuary at Hadleigh. He had told Maria about it in a letter: 'At Hadleigh there is a ruin of a castle which from its situation is a really fine place.' He had never revisited the spot but now, his wife dead, he remembered it and how it had seemed to represent the futility of human endeavour. The majestic sketch that he made for the picture of this castle, which he entitled *The Nore*, is overwhelming in its grief. One critic has said that nothing equals its sense of desolation except Van Gogh's last paintings of empty fields. Although more than a century was to pass before the importance of the finished work was understood, the luminous *Hadleigh Castle* of 1829 marks one of those great and rare advances in the history of painting.

Constable was elected a member of the Royal Academy a few months after his wife's death. It was his fourth attempt to join the Academy, and he had been accepted by a margin of a single vote. His great contemporary J. M. W. Turner came around to tell him the good news and was full of congratulations. Sir Thomas Lawrence, president of the Academy, was, however, genuinely surprised. Constable, he commented, 'ought to think himself lucky.' Although Constable had once remarked that 'the Royal Academicians know as much about landscape as they do about the Kingdom of Heaven,' the election meant a great deal to him. A man who honoured institutions, he believed his acceptance by the highest art institute in the land meant people would look at his pictures with new respect. He felt vindicated at last.

Gradually the depression following his wife's death lifted. He travelled to the English places where he felt himself a 'welcome guest' during these last years. 'I must again repeat the necessity of keeping one's mind alive to that external nature with which we are surrounded,' he said. 'We exist but in a Landscape and we are the creatures of a Landscape.' At Coleorton he stayed with his old friend Sir George Beaumont. The Romantic movement was now nearing its end, and Sir George, in a truly romantic gesture, had erected in his garden an ornamental cenotaph to Sir Joshua Reynolds. Constable painted this elaborate garden scene, introducing a stag that seems to link the eighteenth century with the Victorian age, now so near. It is a strange picture, almost academic in its artificial sadness and unusually finished brushwork, as if Constable were making an effort to please a sentimental public.

In 1832 he exhibited his most ambitious attempt at history painting. He had worked on *Waterloo Bridge from Whitehall Stairs* for thirteen years, and the subject – the new bridge over the Thames being opened by the Prince Regent to celebrate the defeat of Napoleon – was a popular one. But the picture was not popular. Constable's wonderful description of light playing on the water and on the crowded banks was, as usual, dismissed as 'spotty.'

In 1835 he sold the last of his great Stour scenes, *The Valley Farm*, for three hundred pounds. He spent most of the money fitting out his son Charles for the sea. In February, 1837, he gave his last lecture at the Royal Academy school at Somerset House, and was cheered by the students. He walked home with a friend who said, 'We parted at the west end of Oxford Street, laughing – I never saw him alive again.' Constable died suddenly at about midnight on March 31, 1837, after a long day working on a picture called *Arundel Mill*. There was a Rubens print near his feet and Cowper's *Letters*, his favourite bedside book, near his hand. He was sixty-one years old. He was buried near the wall in Hampstead churchyard, beneath the clear skies from which he had learned the profound truths that fill his landscapes.

Nearly all his work remained in storage until 1888, when his daughter bequeathed it to the nation. Thereafter, most Englishmen would see John Constable as the perfect interpreter of their countryside; indeed, *The Hay Wain* became, as one modern critic has said, 'part of the landscape of every English mind.'

It is ironic that as total acceptance of Constable's vision of landscape art was beginning, the French impressionists – Cezanne, Monet, Manet – were struggling against the same kind of official hostility that Constable had encountered. But in time, they too would enjoy the public adulation that their English forebear finally earned.

THE ARTIST AND THE FARMYARD

(*Country Life*, 5th January, 1989)

Art – and religion – originated in the fields, and any age other than our own would not have needed reminding of it. So, although it should not be surprising that there exists a vast collection of farming art to select from, nevertheless the exhibition 'This Land is Our Land' at the Mall Galleries, in London, is likely to be a revelation to most people, especially to that huge new population of country-dwellers for whom the symbols and rituals of agriculture mean nothing unless reduced to the entertainment language of the theme park.

The strength of the exhibition is its unselfconscious display of the old realities. It ranges from high art to naive art, from the sublime to a kind of workman-like art for working folk. Here is the everlasting circle, the non-stop seasonal round which for most of the inhabitants of these islands was, until the beginning of the 19th century, part bliss and part treadmill. No wonder artists, writers, scientists, moralists and craftsmen followed its revolution so imaginatively and so hypnotically. For, again until our own day, there was no way of completely avoiding such a powerful slipstream.

Growing food, in the earth and on the hoof, was an activity which carried everybody to harvest and celebration. Cities did not feel themselves exempt. Cattle and poultry filled their streets on market days: London's Cornhill was the capital's barn. There could be no better way of initiating this 'British Food and Farming Year' than bringing us face to face with what was genuine, if often harsh, in rural life. Perhaps unwittingly, we have imported much that is phoney into the countryside these past few decades. This exhibition could prove a powerful antidote.

Agricultural painting was at its zenith in the 18th century. It was then that the experiments and inventions of Jethro Tull, Robert Bakewell, Lord 'Turnip' Townsend and many other modernisers attracted the entire nation to the plough. 'Farmer George' might be a landowner, his tenant – or even the king – but the common interest in agriculture united them, and artists both brilliant and wonderfully awful served all three. In farmhouse and country house, oils of immense pigs and sheep, and horse portraits, hung in gold frames beside the family pictures.

The classically educated managed to live with a double vision of what lay outside. Virgil told them one thing and their common sense another. But when the culture of the educated agriculturalist and the rich, indigenous culture of the village people encountered science, Arcadian views and saws and traditions began their obsolescence. The exhibition follows it step by step: a sad farewell to shepherdesses, a thankful goodbye to profitless practices.

It leads to the present where, in the ever-widening commuting areas, the new villagers know less about what happens on their local farms than they do about the Great Barrier Reef. In a sense, the exhibition is an extravagantly illustrated history lesson which enables us to make sense of our surroundings. Artists, too, suggests the catalogue, might take as realistic a look at farming as did their predecessors. *Discussing the Milk Quota* and *Artificial Insemination Day* are subjects awaiting a debut at the Royal Academy.

Not that the old artists painted everything they saw. William Vaughan reveals this in his essay *Leisure and Toil*, which covers the century 1750 to 1850, and links two 'golden ages' across the post-war miseries of the 1820-40 slump, with its violence and near-starvation. East Anglian labourers were firing ricks when John Constable was at work on the great series of a working landscape with which he hoped to establish his reputation.

Both his and John Fisher's letters are full of agrarian distress but there is no sign of it in those Stour Valley masterpieces which, as one critic has said, are 'the landscape of every English mind'. Nor was this hypocrisy. Constable, who was to see his father's beautiful brick house pulled down because of the Depression, and the ruination of so many of his poor neighbours because of enclosure, was offering a milling-farming scene of hope. Gainsborough's *Mr and Mrs Robert Andrews*, which Sacheverell Sitwell called the greatest English domestic portrait, has similarly been misread by historians.

The catalogue says it represents ownership of farming land in a particularly direct way and that its main point is to emphasise the wealth of their possessions. This is not so. The picture is thought to have been a wedding present from Tom Gainsborough to his old school friend. They were taught by Gainsborough's uncle in the little market town shown below the figures in the picture, which indeed encompasses the whole world of the artist's boyhood. The newly-weds can also see All Saints Church, where they were married, and where Gainsborough's daughter had recently been baptised. The ownership here is of a shared view of home.

Gainsborough's *The Morning Walk* is queried for its absence of agricultural activity but, since it was painted in Pall Mall, and its setting is most likely a London park, this is not surprising. Concepts of the idyll and the actual in rural art and literature are full of pitfalls. For example, our farming forebears and their recorders existed in a religious climate of whose intensity we know next to nothing. Samuel Palmer and William Blake created holy fields and flocks. The catalogue says that the disturbingly erotic figures in Holman Hunt's *The Hireling Shepherd* of 1851 were intended to remind his contemporaries of some religious controversy of the times. In fact, it was intended to remind them of St John 10:12 – and with a shock. One needs to have read *The Books of Kings, Ruth* and *The Psalter*, as well as the history of rural Dorset, in order to understand Thomas Hardy.

Farmers today frequently claim to have made Britain's landscape; in fact, this was achieved only with the help of hired labourers, wives and children. As with so many things, the lot, as they philosophically called it, of the farm worker and his family over the years is hard for us to comprehend. The hard toil, the wages so minute, most of all the lowly status – when it was upon the multiple skills and crafts and energies of such people that the entire national economy depended until the

Industrial Revolution – give us cause for thought.

Yet their history is one of injustice and deprivation. Not only Cobbett but Shelley and Byron rallied to the farmworkers' defence. This exhibition does the labourer proud. We see them scything under misericords, as popular models for mantelpiece ornaments and fairings, busy at Lord Leicester's internationally celebrated sheepshearing ('Holkham Clippings'), crowding market days in the towns and thick on the ground in the stackyard. We are reminded of how numerous they were and how few they are today.

There is an enchanting engraving of a harvest scene at Hackney in 1814 by William Walker. The immemorial task is being done without fuss in a field near the church. White smoke belches from summer chimneys as the evening meal is being cooked. Constable would draw in his father's fields until he saw such smoke and then pack up to go home and eat.

There is too a photograph of the hedgecutter who founded the National Union of Agricultural Workers, Joseph Arch, four times Member for north-west Norfolk. The making and maintaining of Britain's hedges and field walls has gone on since prehistory, together with countless miles of ditch-digging – that beloved patchwork stretching from Wick to Zennor involved incalculable labour. Bulldozers tore parts of it to pieces in hours.

Some of the finest paintings of farm work are by Evelyn Dunbar. Her milking scenes contain the rich, sweet heaviness which filled the dairy and she captures the stillness and roundedness of the beasts and seated women. She is one of the few artists who recognises the isolation of such jobs as picking vegetables or singling-out, with the body unsheltered, straining all day against wind, soaked by rain or scorched by sun.

Perhaps the most sensitive of mid-20th-century agricultural artists was Thomas Hennell (*Country Life*, November 24, 1988) who died during the Second World War and who has been much neglected. He was commissioned to draw Britain's agricultural war effort. An American administrator of Lend-lease told of our drastic measures: 'The several times I flew over Britain, I looked down on a country where almost every acre of land was being used. Forests that had been carefully tended for centuries were being cut down ... golf courses and parts of great estates were being ploughed up and tilled. Marshes were being drained. Family 'victory gardens' had been planted on every vacant piece of land round the cities. Farms large and small were everywhere... the new inexperienced farmhands would plough by day, the old hands after dark ...'

Hennell, S. R. Badmin, whose work is well represented in the exhibition, and many other artists painted and sketched the astonishing rural phenomenon of a Britain increasing its acres under plough from nearly 13 million to almost 20 million, and its food output by 70 per cent, in the space of four years. It was this wartime encroachment by the plough, so necessary then, which contributed to the destruction of the sanctity of certain parts of our ecology and allowed much of the devastation of the 1950s and '60s to proceed without too much conscience. Amends are now being made, but only in the nick of time. Wars have always had a far greater effect on our farming than we realise. Napoleon's wars, the Civil War and pre-eminently and most poignantly, the First World War, all marked our fields.

It is only recently that we have come to admire the scenes which agriculture has created. There were long periods when people turned away from them, as we might turn away from some of the industrial sights of the present. (Queen Victoria is said to have ordered the blinds to be drawn when the Royal train passed through certain towns in the North.) For much of the year farms were rough and ready places, and those that worked them were marked by toil. Better the farms of poetry and the paintings that poetry produced, those of Claude Lorraine above all.

Brian Stewart, in his excellent catalogue piece on livestock portraiture, tells of the gentleman-tourist with his 'Claude glass', a smoked convex mirror which turned any homely English scene reflected in it into a 'Claude'. Mr Stewart writes of the long-held passion for the Picturesque. Sheep might be included in the Picturesque, pretty peasant children, gypsies and contented old folk.

Contentment was the quality most required of the countryside. Yet the pattern which millennia of farmers have left on the map of Britain nowhere shows a socially manageable group of people who simply went the annual round of seedtime and harvest, but a driving and imaginative force, and one which produced not only the nation's food but – since until about 1820 everybody was closely related to the land – most of the nation's great men and women.

So much emphasis has been placed on the role of the plough in the making of the landscape that we tend to forget that large parts of it have been grazed, munched and manured into what we see now. Cattle tracks became lanes, and lanes, main roads. Until the advent of modern fertilisers it was livestock which went the rounds on the farm and increased not only the harvests, but woodlands and pond life.

The exhibition's tribute to the beasts who did so much to make the landscape is chiefly astonishing in its revelation of what our ancestors thought their livestock looked like. It also shows their doting regard for some individual horse, pig, cow or dog which brought them fame. Animal artists were paid so much an hour to paint what appear to us to be thin, ill-proportioned horses or pigs, and bullocks of such obesity that we should relegate the achievement of their production to the category consistent with that which produces huge, inedible vegetables for the village show. But how dear these mountainous sows, sheep and cattle were to their owners. The affection in which they were held is framed with them, and who are we, cholesterol-panicked Man, with our little packet of all-lean meat from the supermarket, to question it?

Feasting the eye on these animal portraits, one might ask, what has the artist of *The Fat Pig of Northleach* to do with George Stubbs or George Moreland? Well, what has Gainsborough's portrait of the squire got to do with some travelling likeness-catcher's daub of his wife? In the country, genius and naivety have always hung side by side, and the exhibition stresses this. Over the centuries the farm has encouraged a delightful crop of bad pictures, and what a treat it is to stare into them and, through their rigid faithfulness to some stackyard or stable, see the land in the making.

Fatstock goes to market and there are prints of Smithfield, drawings of butcher's shops – one complete with a Victorian butcher's wife at the cash desk – and two of Peter Coker's superb 1950s paintings of the way we used to buy meat. The better off one was, the more meat one devoured. For the rural poor, meat was minimal and as so few of them possessed ovens, it would have floated in the stew pot. For generations the men who physically shaped the land with their spades, drained it, piled up the field headlands, mended the roads, kept the water courses flowing, and pollarded the woods, carried with them a 'bait' or 'elevenses' of chunks of fat bacon, onion and bread.

Mr Stewart writes on the artist Bakewell and how he led the advance in accurate pictures of pedigree animals. Before such realists as Bakewell, an ox in a painting would more likely be depicted as a garlanded creature surrounded by nymphs in a glade, than as a good breed standing foursquare in a meadow. There were some million horses working in agriculture by 1900 and their role in fashioning the pattern of the land remains incalculable. They were to be dreadfully culled on the Western Front. A horseman was the prince of farmworkers and he ruled with a mixture of inherited skills and mysticism. The late George Ewart Evans has written the best guide to this complex world.

But what of the landscape when the machines took over? Little changed until the Second World War and after. The first machine was Tull's drill, which allowed plants to be sown in neat, exactly spaced rows. By the early 19th century Ransome's of Ipswich were into a miracle of inventiveness which would fill the fields of Britain with mechanical reapers, binders, threshers, steam ploughs and all the forerunners of the labour-banishing gear which pack farms today. Another Suffolk firm, Garrett's of Leiston, made traction engines, surely the most enchanting of all mechanical farm vehicles?

As they wore out, these pre-1940 machines rusted in derelict corners, play-things for village children, tangled with ropes of convolvulus and spear-grass. Artists like Eric Ravilious and his friend John Nash enjoyed the stillness of a once-busy machine, and old harrows, pumps and engines lie around in their tidy watercolours. Both men looked for the bones of landscape, the austere foundations of the surface. They liked to see them breaking through.

Agriculture in art must include agriculture in literature, where it has always found its fullest creative expression. With religious beliefs filled with pastoral metaphor and imagery, and religious feasts that run parallel with farm work, it is hardly surprising that fields and stock, and the human existence decreed by them, have in particular dominated our poets, from Caedmon to Seamus Heaney and Ted Hughes, with John Clare and Thomas Hardy articulating in the most wonderful way the philosophy of our land and those that formed it. Ted Hughes has written a specially commissioned poem.

The literature on display includes such rarities as a tithe-table, satires, farm plans and maps, petitions, government papers, contributions to an agricultural journal by 'Ralph Robinson' (King George III borrowing the name of his shepherd), advertisements and most of the classic works on practical farming.

The first printed book on the subject was the *Liber Ruralium Comodorum* by Crescentius (1471) and the first on English farming, Sir Anthony Fitzherbert's *Husbandry* (1523). The organisers have raided the library at Rothamsted Experimental Station for most of the treasures displayed: Thomas Tusser's' *Hundreth Good Pointes of Husbandrie* (1557), of course, but also such volumes as Charles Butler's *The Feminine Monarchy or the Historie of Bees* (1623); Walter Blith's *English Improver* (1649); and Maxall's *First Book of Cattel* (1587).

There has never been anything quite like 'This Land is Our Land – aspects of agriculture in art', though goodness knows why, considering the vast quantities of pictures, tools, records, literature and artefacts that lie around in our private houses and public institutions, rather like those old Ransome harrows on the farm wastes.

Anyway, nobody who is part of rural life, or who has recently come to share it, should miss this unusual and telling exhibition, beautifully mounted by Demelza Spargo, who also edited the catalogue. The latter alone is worth a visit to London.

P. H. EMERSON AND THE COASTAL LENS

(*Times Literary Supplement*)

The name P. H. Emerson drifts around in East Anglia's subconsciousness in a still quite powerful way. His masterpieces, 'Gathering Waterlilies', 'Yarmouth from Breydon Water', 'Women Raking', 'Towing the Reed' and especially 'Coming Home from the Marshes' have acquired the icon-like properties of pictures into which a community stares in search of its soul. The late Nancy Newhall, whose major work was this biography of the great and strange nineteenth-century photographer, says Emerson's interpretarion in words and images of what she calls 'the Netherlands of England' is worthy to stand beside Atget's Paris, the geological surveys of the American West and the Farm Security Administration's America in the 1930s.

She sees him as the first true photographer-poet. Arriving as he did on a frenetic photography scene in which so many talents were striving for artistic reputations on a par with those of painters and engravers, it could not have been a better moment for a young man with his cantankerous mixture of patrician aloofness, invective and inner conviction to state his case. He was twenty-seven, a qualified doctor of medicine, a New Englander as well as English (American law allowed him this duality), married, a novelist, tall, fair and stylish. Together with these assets – and that of being the cousin of Ralph Waldo Emerson – he had the good fortune to find in Norfolk and Suffolk, on a first visit, his special territory of the imagination. This was in August 1883 when he first saw Southwold and Great Yarmouth.

It had all begun in Rome, where the Puritan, agnostic and analogist in him were each profoundly shocked by Italian art. With a naturalistic philosophy curiously similar to that expounded by Constable in his lectures, Emerson at once set about finding his own truth-to-nature creative responses, particularly with respect to human beings rooted in a landscape. The year before he found both his people and his place on the East Anglian coast, he had bought his first camera, and it was the revelation he received through its ground glass which gave him what Nancy Newhall calls his answer to Rome, to the unnaturalness of painting and sculpture. This intensification of the view in the lens was to remain for him the camera's ultimate glory, more marvellous than any print. He agreed with his East Anglian 'peasants' when he allowed them to put their heads under his focusing cloth and they caught their breath with delight at a brilliance which they had never before encountered, and said, 'Ah, if we could only get it like that!' Life, they meant.

Emerson had some lessons in photography, not from a photographer but from his old tutor in physics and chemistry at Cambridge. On the whole, though, he served no apprenticeship. He was one of those artists who need only the merest outlines of instruction. Julia Margaret Cameron, of course, was another. Presented by her daughter and son-in-law with a lens and dark box – 'It may amuse you, Mother, to try to photograph' – she turned her coal cellar into a dark-room and a glazed henhouse into her glass-room and began to take pictures. Emerson revered her and his account of her work, included here, is fascinating. Although only half the age she was when she began her work, he was for a while equally obsessed and single-minded. He gave up medicine, brought his family to Southwold, found a local artist and naturalist (T. F. Goodall) to guide him about the region and began work at once on the great series of pictures which were to fill *Life and Landscape on the Norfolk Broads*, *Pictures of Life in Field and Fen*, *Idyls* [sic] *of the Norfolk Broads*, *Pictures of East Anglian Life* and *Wild Life on a Tidal Water*.

These remarkable albums were received with every kind of hostility and criticism, and with some awe. The new photographic establishment, with its proliferating journals and medals and its attempts to place itself as an equal among the traditional arts, saw all that it preached and practised threatened by what Emerson called his Naturalistic Photography. Primarily, what the Photographic Society and its academics objected to in Emerson was his 'differential focusing' as he himself called it. He said:

> The principal object in the picture must be fairly sharp, *just as sharp as the eye sees it and no sharper*, but everything else, and all other planes of the picture must be subdued ... lightly out of focus, not to the extent of producing *destruction of structure, or fuzziness*, but sufficient to keep them back and in place.

But it is in another statement that Emerson sums up the genius of these enthralling work-portraits of men and women labouring in and around the Broads a hundred years ago:

> Nothing in nature has a hard outline, but everything is seen against something else, often so subtly that you cannot tell where one ends and the other begins. In this mingled decision and indecision lies all the charm and mystery of nature.

Nancy Newhall backs her long, detailed and utterly absorbing portrait of the conflictingly high-handed and humble Emerson with a witty account of the late nineteenth-century photographic world. She concentrates on such figures as O. G. Rejlander, Alfred Stieglitz and, most of all, on the uncrowned king of English pictorial photography, Emerson's *bête noir* Henry Peach Robinson, whose 'Autumn' she says, was the most be-medalled photograph in the world. Robinson had begun as a painter. Turning to the camera and adapting the techniques of genre-painting to it, he became enormously successful. 'Any dodge, trick and conjuration of any kind is open to the photographer's use ... It is his imperative duty to avoid the mean, the bare, the ugly, and to aim to elevate his subject, to avoid awkward forms and. to correct the unpicturesque', he advised. Paraphrased and streamlined, says Nancy Newhall, Robinson's ideas and devices are overwhelmingly still with us.

The wealthy Emerson christened Pedro Enrique on his father's Cuban sugar estate, was as far from this skilfully manipulated and profitable photographic scene as anyone could be. But he was a man with a message who had a taste for dissent and even for a quarrel. He attacked the Robinson school and it reviled him. In the long course of this row, splendidly documented here, all the confused business about art-and-photography comes to the surface. Although he stirred it up and kept it on the boil for nearly twenty years, Emerson was never deeply upset by the battle. It allowed him to exercise a far from offensive high-and-mightiness and it drew him close to the subject of his controversial vision, the half-marine, half-agricultural society and its watery acres.

Having no other criterion by which to judge such a triumph, those who admired his work talked of artists such as Courbet and Millet. The East Anglian press was in no doubt about what he was getting at and its columns were filled with Tory rage by his exposure – in captions and essays, as well as photographs – of the miserable conditions in which the poor lived. Emerson, unlike the genre-photographers who combed the alleys and seafronts for beautiful or striking faces, published his studies of a coastal people in order that they 'would help in the understanding of this peculiar region and add to the outcry against abuses'. He set down the local dialect and made himself familiar with all the local crafts and customs. And as a doctor he was expert in gauging standards of health and welfare in the district. His albums, though among the finest aesthetic achievements of the camera, are also early sociological documents. In Nancy Newhall's words, they were to make him 'a prophet crying in a strange, dry, mechanised and mercantile wilderness'.

In 1891 he gave it all up. In a letter sent to every photographic magazine he said that the medium must rank the lowest of all arts ...In short, I throw my lot in with those who say that photography is a very limited art. I regret deeply that I have come to this conclusion'. There was no overwhelming private grief in this repudiation. Emerson had tired of hobbies. tired of houses and places, tired even, it seems, of what he so uniquely was, an artist of the ground glass. He lived on until 1936, still taking some pictures. But the high period of his achievement was to be the 1880s. The second half of this lovely book consists of a great sheaf of pictures from then, the now familiar bulks and features of his 'peasants', all taken on a grey day 'when possible'; the wherries 'which Old Crome painted in some of his pictures', and the toil, and cold. The beauty and strength of it all too, such as would have naturally existed in such labour and in such a countryside.

REMEMBERING PAUL AND JOHN NASH

(Lecture to the Cheltenham Literary Festival, Autumn, 1989)

This recollection is primarily about my long friendship with John Nash and his wife Christine, both of them among the most influential people in my life. I never met Paul Nash and his wife Bunty, but, over the years, heard much about them.

I first met John Nash in 1951. He was collecting paintings from Essex and Suffolk country houses for a Festival of Britain exhibition at Colchester. His assistant was Maureen Hull, a friend of mine, and she introduced me to him. Maureen's father was the distinguished archaeologist Mark Hull, who was curator of the Colchester Castle Museum. She herself was very pretty and John Nash, who liked pretty girls, liked her. I recall how easy and casual the lending of masterpieces was in those days. John and Maureen would go into some mansion and ask, 'Have you got any good paintings we can borrow for our exhibition?' And the owner would say, 'Yes, here is a Gainsborough, or a Romney'. And they would be loaded on a van and hung up in Colchester Town Hall for month or so.

I had met John's wife Christine some time before this and we had become friends. She used to lunch with Esmé Pissarro in a little cellar-like cafe in Colchester where lunch cost 1s.-6d., and which we all thought very sophisticated. Esmé was the daughter-in-law of Lucien Pissarro. She was tall and beautiful – and poor. Or at least careful, searching her handbag for the 1s.-6d., which amused us, as we knew that she and her husband Tommy owned lots of Pissarros, Camille's and Lucien's. Or so it was said. Christine Nash was tall and plain, but with a voice which fascinated us, very beautiful. She too was careful with money, sharing Esmé's austere tradition. One often hears of the dreariness of the fifties, but they were never dreary to me. Although none of us possessed money in today's sense, and our houses were somewhat elementary by today's standards, we ourselves – a small group of painters, writers and gardeners living on the Suffolk-Essex borders – felt rather stylish and privileged. I found it all very exciting and not once did it occur to me that life was grey or limited. Very much the reverse. I half thought of myself as an incipient artist, although all the artists recognised me as an incipient writer.

I was born and brought up by the River Stour, that thirty or so miles of countryside immortalised by Gainsborough and Constable. Later on I became friends of Constable's descendants. The landscape was so dominated by these two great artists that Walter Sickert used to warn painters off it, calling it a sucked orange. All the same, although there was never a local 'school', as at St Ives, many artists were living in the area when I was a boy and, as I grew up, I also grew into their orbit, as it were. They all lived very simply in old cottages and farmhouses, and they all knew each other. The largest group was at Great Bardfleld. It included Edward Bawden, John Aldridge and Michael Ayrton. John Nash always referred to them as 'the Bardfield boys'.

The Nashes themselves belonged to Buckinghamshire, where the family had been farmers, lawyers and clergymen for generations. Both John and Paul – and their sister Barbara – were born in Kensington. They returned to Iver Heath, then at the turn of the century still a remote village, when they were very young. The Chilterns' ecology and the Thames Valley were to provide John and Paul with their early symbols, notably the tumuli known as Wittenham Clumps, which were to haunt Paul all his life. John was educated at Wellington and Paul at St Paul's, and both brothers were equally miserable at school. They talk much about child abuse these days, but could there have been much worse experience than that met with at the average Edwardian public school? John showed signs of his future genius by winning the Botany Prize at Wellington but was relieved when his father allowed him to withdraw from the school and train to be a journalist on the local paper. Also, there were emotional and financial difficulties at home, due to Mrs Nash's mental illness. Nursing homes sapped the family income. Mr Nash became the Recorder of Abingdon and, after the death of his wife, married again. But before all this, talking to John, or rather listening to him, I always sensed a kind of darkness in his childhood. Even when he was old, I realised that part of Christine's role in their marriage was to drive the shadows away.

As a youth, Paul became friends with the north country poet Gordon Bottomley and, as an artist, became influenced by the Pre-Raphaelites and by the 'open road' philosophy of writers such as George Borrow. He studied painting and drawing at a school in Bolt Court, and later at the Slade. It was while at the Slade he met the artist who was to change his brother John's life. This young artist was Claughton Pellew. I have always found the seemingly casual coincidences of life – that running round the corner and running into somebody who, in retrospect, is seen to have changed everything – enthralling. All that happened here was that Paul and Claughton were going on a walking tour in Norfolk, when Paul suddenly found that he couldn't make it and said, 'Go with John instead'. John set off with Claughton, a trainee journalist (and already learning shorthand) and returned an artist. But what about the training for this career? Paul's advice was daring. Having seen that the orthodoxy of the art schools would almost certainly have crushed his brother's exciting freshness and naivety, he said, 'Don't go. Teach yourself to draw and paint.' Their father, now with two sons, set out on what was to him the most precarious of all careers, cleared a space on the dining-room table and told John, 'You had better do it here'. John was to paint his watercolours, and to draw and engrave, on a *kitchen* table all his life. Older friends now and then taught him certain basic skills. Harold Gilman, who would die in the terrible flu epidemic of 1919, showed him how to use oils, and that near-forgotten master etcher, Francis Unwin, showed him how to cut and print wood-blocks.

Paul and John's first show was a sensation and a sell-out. John told me that they were walking down Pelham Street, Kensington, when they saw a lampshade shop run by two young men. There were spacious walls. They went and asked if they could hang their pictures on them. John made a poster and, amazingly to them, Sir William Rothenstein found his way to this two-brothers show and made it famous overnight. I remember Sir Charles Tennyson showing me a John Nash given to him as a wedding present which had been bought at the exhibition. Paul was at this time, John told me, a dandy. And Barbara, their sister, told me in old age how Paul's extravagance over money – clothes, wine, etc. – caused much anxiety at home. But never 'Jacko', as she called John, who remained utterly indifferent to personal display.

When the War came, Paul joined the Artists' Rifles and eventually was commissioned as an official war artist. John couldn't get into uniform at first because of his health, so he went to work in the White City, making tents. My mother, as it happened, was also making tents there, before she became a VAD. John said that the White City was a dreadfully rough place. Eventually, by 1916, he was fighting in the trenches. He was a sergeant and newly engaged to a Slade girl named Christine Kuhlenthal. He never expected to survive. It was the Somme. After two years of the worst battles, Paul and Eddie Marsh managed to extricate him, and in the spring of 1918 he returned home to join his brother as an official war artist. Their task was to paint the war for thirty shillings a day, which was riches. They worked side by side in a seed shed in Chalfont St Peter. There they created the great pictures, 'We are Making a New World' (Paul) and 'Over the Top' (John). They must be honourable, Paul said, and paint the war pictures until six, then they could be free to paint their own work. John painted his 'The Cornfield' under these conditions. He painted it, he told me, to celebrate his coming out of the trenches alive. It is a glowing Buckinghamshire harvest field in the late daylight. Eddie Marsh bought and left it to his friend Ivor Novello on the condition that he would leave it to the Tate Gallery, where it now is. Before he began work on the Western Front pictures, the War Office asked John if he would like to return to Flanders to refresh his memory! He said that all he needed was some corrugated iron, barbed wire and duck-boards, etc. so that he didn't make errors regarding such official supplies. A lorry-load of these were sent to the seed shed by the government. John would regale me with these grim facts with a certain pawky amusement. He and Paul both married during the War, Paul to

Margaret Odey, the daughter of an Anglican priest. Known as Bunty, she was partly Arab and wholly formidable, a suffragette and a keen advocate of women's rights. Also very attractive, she and Paul were married in St Martin-in-the-Fields and, as a friend and helper of 'fallen' women, the church was filled with some very strange ladies. Or so said their friend Lance Sieveking. John married Christine Kuhlenthal, who was half German and half Scottish. She had been introduced to him at the Slade by their mutual friend Dora Carrington. Christine had shared a flat with Carrington just before the war. John, like so many boys, was a little in love with Carrington, who wrote him marvellous letters full of witty drawings. 'Did you ever sleep with her?' I once asked. 'My dear fellow! What a question! The nearest I ever got to her was when we shared a mackintosh apron on the top deck of a London bus. It was the thing to take a girl upstairs on a bus so that one's knees could joggle against hers under the apron. Very exciting.'

Shortly after finishing the war paintings, Paul became unwell. The aftermath of the war had caused all sorts of strange illnesses. Paul was also asthmatic. He and Bunty went to live at Dymchurch, and for the next few years he drew and painted the vast sea-wall. Also Romney Marsh. I was there recently to walk both the wall and the Marsh, and to think of Paul. The wall had been added to since Roman times, and the Marsh itself retained its loneliness and solitudes. There was a sense of melancholy, and also a sense of exhaustion because of so much concrete. Paul's wall drawings and paintings are absorbed by the geometry of water and concrete. Later on they moved down the road to Rye, then the centre of E. F. Benson's comic novels and full of the originals of his characters. Here Henry James had written his last novels and Radclyffe Hall her scandalous *Well of Loneliness*.

From then on they moved as people who are never very well tend to move in what is underlyingly a search for health. John and Christine Nash were all against moving – although they shifted about, one way or another, more than they liked to think. When I first became a writer and began a modestly drifting progress from Skye to various addresses in Suffolk, they shook their heads. Surely I wasn't going to be a mover? How could I ever write if I never *settled*? And I was aligned with Paul and Bunty, and other drifters. Many years later I had to edit and introduce Tolstoy's *The Death of Ivan Ilyitch*, that amazing novel about the inescapability of death, and learnt how Tolstoy himself had once believed that he could find new health by simply finding a new address. But Paul, of course, was pursuing landscape and its symbols in his – not all that many moves.

During the 1920s he read an old book which was to provide the philosophy and imagery he craved. It was Sir Thomas Browne's *Urn Burial* and *The Garden of Cyrus*. This book offered him a whole new world of freedom and concepts. He sent a copy to John – I still have it, the Macmillan edition of 1929, inscribed, 'John with love from Paul' – insistent that he read it. It had been first published in 1658. Some thirty years earlier the excavation of a Roman cemetery at Walsingham had drawn from Sir Thomas Browne, a Norwich doctor, his exquisite prose-poem *Urn Burial*. For Paul, haunted by death, and with his asthma getting worse, it offered a comforting – and grand – language. In 1930, whilst on a visit to Matisse in France, a French doctor had persuaded him to accept his condition and from then on he began to look, not so much for cures, as for some progression from deathliness. You see in his paintings of this period objects being released, as it were, from the earth's thrall. Sir Thomas Browne, like so many seventeenth-century writers, was intrigued by such 'heliotropian' or sun-turning objects as bloodstones, sun-dials and sunflowers. He also discovered that much of nature was 'quincuncial' or five-sided: seeds, petals, fruit, etc. Nets were quincuncial, so were honeycombs, so were some of the classic divisions of armies, so were atoms. I then realised that one of John's favourite roses was called the Five Brothers. Paul, having discovered this extraordinary geometry, began to use it in such works as his 'The Soul Entering the Mansions of the Dead'.

In 1930, too, Bunty gave Paul a Kodak camera. It was one of those weighty but neat folding cameras which could be carried in the pocket. He at once became a keen and good photographer – John never advanced beyond snaps with a Box Brownie – and altogether Paul was to take over a thousand pictures. The most influential of these were of

Avebury in Wiltshire and some fallen trees in a Gloucestershire field. The latter provided the inspiration for his 'Monster Field' paintings, and the former for his surrealistic 'Megaliths'.

By this time the brothers had discovered their own distinctive territory. They remained loving but apart. During much of the 1920s John was teaching at the Ruskin School in Oxford, and living, first at Whiteleaf and then at Meadle, Buckinghamshire. Both brothers had become first-rank wood-engravers and were illustrating books. Each, in fact, was in the van of the great book-illustration movement of the inter-war years, along with Claire Leighton, Blair Hughes-Stanton, Eric Gill and David Jones. John's friend and neighbour in Whiteleaf was Francis Unwin, among the finest of all the etchers of that period. When Francis died from tuberculosis in 1925 he left John his sturdy Talbot car – the car in which, ten years later, John and Christine's small son would be killed. It was Christine who told me of this disaster; John never mentioned it until after her death in 1976. This little boy, William, had slipped from the hard leather seat as the door flung open, and had hit his head on a rain grid in the gutter. He had been their only child after a number of miscarriages, and his loss was the greatest tragedy of their lives. Neither Paul nor their sister Barbara had children, and all their branch of the family vanished in just a few years, but leaving behind art and gardens.

The first thing I learned when I met John Nash was that if you wanted to be an artist, you painted, and if you wanted to be an author, you wrote. It wasn't so much the work ethic as the actual doing what you were supposed to do. The notion that one had to have certain conditions to write or paint, or be a musician, was to both him and Christine absurd. Of course, one might not be able to do it – that thing which one was put into the world to do – but that was another story. A sad one. To not do it when one could do it was to be a bore. Much was expected of their friends, their 'dear ones', and yet nothing was demanded of them.

Christine and Bunty Nash, sisters-in-law, never got on. They were often caustic about each other, and told tales about each other in a very candid fashion. 'Now, now', John would say. So far as I could tell, it was the old story of loving our families whilst not actually liking them. The unhappiness and the falsity comes when you believe you have to like as well as love where a family is concerned. I never heard John in any way decry his brother or subscribe to the popular view that he had been wounded by Paul's fame. He outlived Paul by thirty years and I think that all the post-Second World War work distanced John sufficiently from the period when as, the Nash brothers, their careers (where the critics were concerned) ran in a kind of parallel, not to say race, with Paul always winning. John's admiration for his brother showed clearly when BBC2 made a programme about him. He and Christine watched with horror an actor being Paul and saying words from his book *Outline*. They saw the necessary juxtaposition of his pictures, and inserted photographs of themselves, and held their heads in their hands at the travesty which had been made of Paul's life. In vain did I attempt to explain the documentary process. I had made a film – directed by John Read for BBC2 – about John in 1968 and, mercifully, it had been received with delight. But then it had no actors, only John Nash enjoying himself in his truthful way.

Among John's and my own closest friends were Sir Cedric Morris and Arthur Lett-Haines. They lived about ten miles away at Hadleigh in a Gallicised Suffolk farmhouse, around which Cedric had made his famous garden. Cedric and Lett had opened their East Anglian School of Painting and Drawing at Dedham during the late thirties, after some sensational years in Paris. They taught in the old French 'atelier' manner, their students picking up their craft by attending the studio of the master. The poet James Turner first took me to Benton End, with its great iris garden, its charming if slightly threatening owners, its garlicky meals and riotous talk, and its students ranging from teenagers to octogenarians. It was the first time I had eaten off a single wooden plate which had to be scrubbed up with a bit of bread for the next course. One of Cedric and Lett's early pupils had been the eighteen-year-old Lucian Freud, who had accidentally burnt the school, then at Dedham, to cinders. John Nash said that when Sir Alfred Munnings heard that it was in flames, he drove by, like Mr Toad, shouting, 'Down with modern art!' My visits to Cedric with John Nash were entirely confined to gardening. After Dedham, and shortly after the last war, Cedric and Lett moved to Benton End, much at the same time when John Nash was settling in at Wormingford. Thus Cedric's garden and John's garden were being created at the same moment. His iris-breeding apart, Cedric filled his garden with exotics which he collected whilst painting abroad during the winter. Some of these exotics found their way into John Nash's garden, but chiefly his was a wonderfully expanded version of the Victorian cottage garden. None of Cedric's irises, for instance, was allowed in it. Cedric didn't mind. He would walk round John's garden mumbling, 'Not a boring thing!' Which was high praise. When John and I went to Cedric's garden, I could only trail behind these learned creatures. Their botany and their horticulture were quite beyond me. But I did begin to understand what the reality of flowers meant to them as artists. Both of them painted flowers all the time, Cedric with a Fauvist dash and vividness, John with a kind of poetry mixed up with botanical accuracy.

During the 1920s, when Paul was discovering himself via the magical prose and the metaphysics of Sir Thomas Browne, John was finding his path as an artist via gardens and farms, woodland and ponds. It was at this time that John became friends with Clarence Elliott, whose Six Hills Nursery at Stevenage, and whose gardening essays in the press, were rapidly making him one of the most influential horticulturalists of the period. Until he met Clarence, John used to go to the Physic Garden in Oxford for 'models' to paint. Now he began to grow his own plants. He remembered when he was a boy at Iver how two old sisters lived nearby in a garden which was utterly unlike his father's garden. His father's garden was simply a space – with a few herbacious things round the edge – to play croquet in. The old ladies' garden, on the other hand, was a rich muddle of lovely, precious specimens tucked into plots, each one some treasure, and understood. When John eventually made his garden of gardens, at Bottengoms in the Stour Valley, the old house in which I now live, he never called himself a gardener, but an 'artist-plantsman'.

I remember when he was teaching botanical illustration at the Flatford Mill Field Studies Centre how he would carefully select the models for the day before driving up the rough track. How they rode rather precariously in jam-jars and potted-meat jars. These would be their thrones when the students drew them. At the end of the day they would be awarded to the best artist in the class. He spoke against the roar of John Constable's millrace, his voice gentle and courteous in an old-fashioned sense, but faintly sardonic as well. John was a much loved teacher at the Ruskin School, the Royal College and at Flatford. Paul, I have heard, could be forbidding, even cold, as a teacher. One of John's noticeable traits was his essential lack of interest in the work of other artists, living or dead. It wasn't pride or hubris. Watching him not looking at pictures when I accompanied him to various shows, I began to realise that, without believing it to be superior, he was somehow trapped or locked in his own vision. He would say, jocularly, and even once to Henry Moore, an old friend, that he had been getting down 'to some art-work'. He once told me that if he could have his time over again he would be a musician first (he was a good self-taught pianist), a gardener second and an artist last. But this, I think, was just a kind of banter regarding himself. It was always obvious to me that when he was working, either on some bank or in his gloomy studio, that he had entered a world where none of us could follow, and that he knew it.

Christine alone understood this fully. She had actually given up her art so that there would be no other 'art-work' going on in his presence, and which had to be acknowledged. When she and Carrington were at the Slade in 1913 it was accepted that she would one day be a very good painter indeed. After her death in 1976 I looked again at two large oils of hers which had languished, face to face, in John's studio for half a century. One was of a picnic by the Rhine in 1913, with a self-portrait, the other, a nativity in a Buckinghamshire barn. Each is a captivating work containing Tonks's emphasis on good drawing and Christine's true promise. Carrington found it quite unbelievable that Christine should give up her own painting when she married John Nash in the spring of 1918, and wrote her imploring letters. But she never did paint again. Instead, she created the somewhat strict environment required for his life and art. She did this unslavishly and with a certain wit. It was impossible to say with any certainty that she had in any way 'lost out'. Her enchanting Rhine girlhood painting, with the lilies and Liberty blouses, the cropped heads and her mythic 'moon-apple tree', and which half suggests an illustration to a story by Kathleen Mansfield, tells me more about her every time I look at it. Which is every day. When I first met her she was immersed in amateur theatricals in the village hall, along with Guy Hickson, 'Miss Marple's' brother, who lived just up the lane. Both she and John liked fancy-dress, and I was often decked out in Tudor or Georgian clothes for some party or other. And I still possess the costume which Paul Nash wore at the Colchester Pageant in I91I.

Although Paul died just when John and Christine were taking up residence at Bottengoms, and just when I myself was beginning to become part of the life there, he too remained present. Not in any ghostly or even sentimetal way, but in the natural way he dogged the talk. And also because he had been a brilliant writer and, now that many of his papers and books were in John's possession, I often found myself reading him in order to get to know him – and to understand John better. Here is part of a letter from Paul to his wife Bunty from the Western Front:

And here in the back garden of the trenches it is amazingly beautiful. The mud is dried to a pinky colour, and upon the parapet and through the sandbags even the grass pushes up and waves in the breeze, while clots of bright dandelions, clover, thistles and twenty other plants flourish luxuriantly, brilliant growths of bright green against the pink earth. Nearly all the better trees have come out and the birds sing all day in spite of shells and shrapnel. I have made three more drawings of these wonderful ruined forms which excite me so much here ... I feel very happy these days, in fact I believe I am happier in the trenches than anywhere out here. It sounds absurd, but life has a greater meaning here and a new zest and beauty, and is more poignant. I never feel dull or careless, and I am always alive to the significance of nature ... I think that this has been the most significant week of my life ... I have seen things that would last me my life as food for paintings and drawings. Oh, these wonderful trenches at night, at dawn, at sundown, ... As night falls the monstrous land takes on a strange aspect. ... As the dark gathers the horizon brightens and vanishes as the Verey lights rise and fall, shedding their weird greenish glare over the land, and in acute contrast to their lazy flight, breaks out the agitated knocking of the machine-guns as they sweep the parapets....

Later he would write:

Sunset and sunrise here are blasphemous, they are mockeries to man ... the guns plunge into the grave which is the land, one huge grave, and cast upon it the poor dead. It is unspeakable, Godless, hopeless. I am no longer an artist, interested and curious. I am a messenger who will bring back word from the men who are fighting for those who want the war to go on for ever. Feeble, inarticulate, will be my message, but it will have a bitter truth and may it burn their lousy souls.

This shows real literary power. As does the following:

As we were about to enter the village there was a cemetery on the left side perched up on the higher ground. ... It was a wonderful sight, little wooden shrines over each grave filled inside with some sort of wire wreaths and small flowering trees, a little bower pale green in colour, and always there was floating a little cherub doll upon a thread. Wind and weather had washed the white shrines to a moist delicate grey – had faded the flowers to a mysterious pale blue. The wind passing through the place set the cherubs flying gently over the wire trees and flowers, set the foliage whispering and the little doors that had sprung open, creaking. Never have I seen such curious beauty connected with graves and burials. The uncompromising slabs, a brown-coloured marble, rise before my mind, monstrous piles, a hopelessly grey black granite with chiselled words in gold of some vapid hymns, the circular glass cases with white wax flowers, the poisoned-berry yews, all conveying the idea of death for death's sake. I turned from this to the windy churchyard of waving trees and shrubs and little tinkling shrines ...

During the late thirties Paul attempted, not so much to write his autobiography proper, as to set down his beliefs. His book *Outline*, which he never finished, is one of the most successful attempts by a twentieth-century artist to put his creed into words. John Nash never attempted this, but he could write about botany in a way which was self-revelatory. And both he and his wife read a great deal. As they grew old and their sight failed, I used to read novels to them after dinner. Favourites were *Miss Mole* by E. H. Young, the *Eustace and Hilda* stories by L. P. Hartley, Jane Austen, and *The Spoils of Poynton* by Henry James. They also loved whodunits, and I was much praised if I found some detective-story writer new to them. I read John's final weeks away, with Jane Austen, parts of whose novels he knew by heart. He was shrunken and full of arthritis, but angry about dying and about it being all over. Christine had died in her typical no-fuss way, simply vanishing at eighty-two. John went clingingly. He'd totter round the paths saying, 'The garden's going, and I'm going!' He was at first simply put out by Christine's sudden departure, saying, 'What does she mean – going off like that!' They had been married for nearly sixty years. Cedric Morris brought a great bough of cotoneaster berries to her funeral which John brought back to the house and put in water. He said, 'Everything shouldn't die'. I buried their ashes in Wormingford churchyard, walking with a spade from the shed and digging them in among the Constables – John's uncles, aunts and cousins, who all lived in the village and whose mill ground the Bottengoms corn. John Nash had painted his last picture, a watercolour of Skye, a few months earlier.

It is a rewarding yet at the same time unnerving experience to have oneself recognised in some potential way by an established artist or writer. John and Christine Nash set me to work. They were exacting, disciplined. My most influential friend when I met them was the poet and novelist James Turner. They rapidly expanded my local circle so that it soon included Benjamin Britten, Imogen Holst, John O'Connor, Mary Potter and many other people. I wrote a book about the Aldeburgh Festival for Ben, and numerous catalogues, etc. for the artists, whilst at the same time writing my own stories. Looking back, it seemed a miraculous time. The general rule was one of extreme simplicity, both in lifestyle and in the way one worked. We lived in and out of each other's houses. I lived with almost no money – or so it now appears.

Figures from the past, such as Paul Nash, although unknown to me, entered my normal every-day existence because those who had been close to them continued to talk about them. I was surrounded by Paul's pictures, his binoculars, lots of his letters and books, and even by some of the furniture which appears in his drawings. Barbara Nash, the sister, also made an unconscious linkage. She and I spent her last Christmas together when all the others were dead, putting up holly from the garden, cooking a duck. She and her friend Enid had been classic maiden ladies of the inter-war years, running a nursery in the Chilterns, and running their house austerely, if not actually stingily. She was pleasantly grumpy and I loved her and was at ease with her. She could be very sharp when discussing Paul and melting when she talked of 'Jacko'. The long friendship of nearly forty years has brought my world into theirs, and theirs into mine.

Outposts

SLIP-SLIDING AWAY

(*The Independent Magazine*, 4th December, 1993)

It has taken the North Sea a thousand years to gnaw away more than two miles of Britain's eastern coastline. So one might have thought that the inhabitants of these uncertain acres would have learned that edges crumble, that tides sweep in, and would have preferred to step back a bit, rather than fight an ocean. Who ever defeated a sea? Well, the Dutch, replies East Anglia, which has a long and admiring record of Low Countries' ways. As masters of sea walls, drains and sluices, it was the Dutch who showed flat, eastern England what could be done, although, long before these lessons, there is much written and watery evidence to prove that holding the sea back was the preoccupation of generations of those who lived in these parts.

So when the Ministry of Agriculture, Fisheries and Food last year published its *National Strategy for Flood and Coastal Defence*, with the revolutionary suggestion of a 'managed retreat' from the flood (a policy welcomed by the National Rivers Authority, whose head of flood defence, Christopher Birks, remarked, 'It is right to give back land to the sea; we nicked it in the first place'), it could not have come as more of a shock to the determined East Anglian seaside than if it had been put out of bounds.

The Government initiative was poignantly timed. Forty years ago, 307 people were drowned and 180,000 acres of property were submerged in Britain's worst natural disaster of modern times, when, on the last day of January 1953, the Great Tide swept in. A near-victim of the deluge in Essex muttered to his rescuers, 'To lie in sleep and awake to drown.' Similar flooding is bound to occur again, if not with similar death rates – for who can contemplate, with the eastern seaboard at a tilt and sea levels rising due to global warming, the constructing of adequate defences stretching from the Thames to the Humber?

Now the Government's advisers are telling the North Sea, 'Come in if you must'. Which means saying to such remnants of the ancient prosperity as tiny Covehithe, in Suffolk, 'You may stay undrowned until 2030, or for ever, but that will be up to the sea.' For farmers, landowners and every other kind of native, such an invitation is as outrageous as it is craven.

Just as some national calamities become history's afterthoughts (the Great Tide, the flu plague of 1919), so all that remains of a once-flourishing community can tell the whole story of what happens when men are in the way of the water's path, be it in Suffolk or Bangladesh. Seen as surrender, it is to East Anglians quite shameful that yet one more of their habitations should be devoured by the sea. When Wilkie Collins arrived in Aldeburgh in 1862, he began his novel *No Name* with what he believed must be obvious to everybody – 'The most striking spectacle by the Shores of Suffolk, is the extra-ordinary defencelessness of the land against the encroachments of the sea', never realising, being a stranger, that the last thing that would strike an East Anglian was his helplessness when it came to a deluge.

Covehithe has been gradually dwindling through means other than just the sea. A victim of trade and water, it represents the fate of so many villages and boroughs which once prospered all down the great arc of the East Anglian shore. Yards full of small ships for short journeys, hythes busy with exports, vast churches humming with prayer and pride, some of them – such as St Andrew's, Covehithe – the most brilliant gull-cages ever made. Those who built it could never have imagined that their descendants in the 17th century would be so broke that they would have to seek permission to wreck the church and sell the stone. Twenty years later, a similar self-ruination occurred a few miles south at Walberswick. The poverty, the cold, the watery miseries, the isolation and desolation of this coast, until in recent times it became 'the sea-side', can hardly be described.

One of the curiously depressing aspects of East Anglian coastal erosion is its sordid treatment of plants. Hanks of grass or wheat lie around like heads from the guillotine. Blackthorn and blackberry bushes tangle in ruin with their roots exposed and, although they were next-the-sea, with evidence of little moisture. The locals always go to look at the latest cliff-fall, boys standing not at all gingerly on the fresh edge; and, should a house have 'gone', everybody wondering, as always, why there is so little which can be retrieved. It is as though desiccation calls to desiccation with the split, parched quality of each tumble to the beach.

Whilst one can meditate on the majesty of the Atlantic overcoming Cornish granite, the manner in which, every now and then, a few tons of East Anglia slip away leaves one with little more than a sense of temporary bewilderment at the havoc, rather than awe at the forces of nature. There is no imperious motion, just slither and crump, dribble and aridity. Should anything like a building or an old road or track be involved, the sight is less archaeologically interesting than just plain miserable.

Land-wreckage, like sea-wreckage, drifts, and scraps of one parish sometimes make their way to the next, or become caught in the 'maramels', which is what Lowestoftians used to call their marram-grass dunes. Broken concrete in a cliff-fall presents the most hideous picture of human futility, but broken brick walls are another matter. The sea likes a nice hand-made brick to suck and makes a good job of smoothing it away.

Where erosion is constant, new surfaces are not given a chance to clothe themselves decently in vegetation; so piles of sandy earth, with the promise of plenty more to come, disfigure the coastline. Erosion looks what it is, a mess which can never be entirely cleaned up.

Here and there, one sees items to provoke thought. Often it is a scattering of graveyard bones, or Second World War litter, of which there is still an enormous amount, as it was thought that Hitler would invade Britain in 1940 from these easy beaches, or Western Front-like trench soil, which helps to suggest the shelled landscape of the modern battlefield. And then there are the whole and perfect scenes of sea and land through which the cliff erosion runs like a scar. These offer plenty of balance to what would otherwise be a hopeless perspective.

In the famous light which illumines these spectacles, one could say that coastal erosion is no more than a nibble – not more than a mile or two in a millennium. It has its good points, too. It turns cliffs into beaches. It lets the ocean have a dip in the marshes. Has our mistake been to live too much on top of the coast, so that we are bound to tremble when the ground gives way? If so, it is because all along the coast paths, from north Norfolk to the Stour estuary, there is still so much to remind us of this shoreline's once-solid worth.

Most noticeably, there is the grand parade of all-purpose medieval churches with their high towers and enormous naves, in which boats might be sold and theatre staged, buildings through which the Reformation flowed on its way to Cambridge. One could start with St Margaret's, Cley (pronounced Cly but meaning clay). Here is stone and glass-encased air, with windows set in pairs to divide the full force of the east wind, just as groynes and breakwaters cut through the strength of the sea.

Below is the River Glaven and the marshes which are a part of Norfolk's unrivalled kingdom of birds. Silt fills the harbour where the wool-ships loaded, but a flinty prosperity persists, and, although those who retire here could get blown away, they are unlikely to share the fate of the coast south of Cromer. Here, after many years, two villages, Overstrand and Sidestrand, famous before the First World War as Poppyland, suffered massive cliff falls. In the 1880s, the theatre critic Clement Scott ('Ibsen's *Ghosts* is a loathsome sore unbandaged') captured all the popular fantasy surrounding drowned churchyards, or, in this case, a soon-to-be-drowned churchyard, in a poem called *The Garden of Sleep* ('In my garden of sleep, where red poppies are spread/wait for the living, along with the dead./For a tower in ruins stands guard o'er the deep./At whose feet are green graves of dear women asleep').

The conquest of church towers by the sea was to local people something extraordinarily poignant. It was quite a different feeling to that experienced when mud-filled harbours and poverty forced the dismantling and neglect of some of the finest of these relics of a golden age of trade. The parishioners of Sidestrand had taken the main body of their old church down, stone by stone, and re-erected it far back from the dangerous edge, where it still stands. But they left the tower – and the dead.

Submerged Dunwich remains, as it has done for centuries, the capital of erosion. The sea began to gulp it down in 1286, when it was at its most splendid, and went on devouring it until the tower of the last of its 18 churches toppled in 1919. A Roman Dunwich probably floated away before this. The Dunwich which remains is little more than a sandy ledge for contemplating what was and what is. Longshoremen cast their lines towards streets and squares. Somewhere, fathoms deep under the far horizon, is the spot where St Felix walked ashore with the Gospel for Suffolk. Somewhere beneath that wall of water lies a see, a parliamentary division, a city. Girton, Henry James, Britten, FitzGerald have stood by the Franciscan gate and allowed their fancy free rein. But for the coast-dwellers of East Anglia, Dunwich possesses something akin to the Aborigine's song-line. Romantic marine archaeologists descend to it in utter blackness to feel for its treasures on the sea-bed. This dark veil is caused by suspended sand and earth particles. A few years ago, it was briefly drawn aside and divers saw St Peter's church, lost during the 17th century. But traditional finds at Dunwich are amber among the pebbles, flowers descended from monastery gardens, and the ability to hear bells ringing beneath the waves.

Local records, such as those belonging to the commissioners of sewers, reveal a whole industry dedicated to keeping the sea off the land. There were juries for viewing sea-banks, levels-men, wall-men, marsh-men, men for 'bottom-fying' and general labour, pumping-plant-men, sea-breach commissioners, ditching gangs, sluice-cutters and every imaginable toiler and specialist for blocking what they described as 'the inroads of the sea'. Each river had its own government and the ocean itself its alert tide-watchers. The bones which plunged from their graves to the beach were re-buried, some of them over and over again. Now they are left for the sea to have them.

Meanwhile, the Countryside Commission (East Anglians can hear their wicked old sea laughing) believes that the Government's policy of 'managed retreat' would enhance Areas of Outstanding Natural Beauty, and that to check erosion by constructing sea walls would not only bring much ugliness into this beauty but also stop fallen soil from renewing the beaches, and would bring floods and crumbling to other parts. All the same, the proposed budget for sea and river-wall defences for the coming decade is £370 million.

One idea is to build more off-shore concrete reefs, such as those proposed to break the seas between Happisburgh and Winterton. Piles of pine logs from the gloomy forests nearby have proved effective in preventing the banks of the Orwell estuary from slipping away. Looking around, one can appreciate all over again the predicament of one's first sandcastle and why, in spite of everything, the very next day one built it again. Putting money and sweat to one side, there is something compulsively satisfying in holding back the sea – if only for a lifetime, if only for a yard or two.

IN ROMNEY MARSH

(*The Sunday Times*, 23rd May, 1990)

The Romney Marsh and the East Anglian Fens have long been my special Low Countries, though rarely visited. The lower the earth, the more towering the skies. The Romney Marsh in late spring is at its level best, a land lacking its own horizons, for what terminates the view has to be what rises above these watery flats, the cliffs and escarpments of the old Kentish shore, now miles from the sea, or the English Channel itself, tall and metallic in the distance, as if waiting to fall on these thousands of pastures which have been claimed from it over the centuries. They feed solitude as well as sheep and the Marsh, I was glad to sense, was steeped in its ancient quiet.

The whole area from Hythe to Rye, and reaching back to Appledore, is actually made up of two huge marshes, Romney and Walland, and little Denge Marsh, practically surrounded by stony beaches, and the old marshmen would have insisted upon the distinction. They would never have forgotten on which side of the Rhee Wall they had been born. Like the Fenmen, their best music was made by sluices and drains. Wandering above the dykes, I heard little of this after such a summer-like winter, only skylarks and the hornet-like buzz of the microlite plane going nowhere particularly in the languid afternoon. Many of the ditches flowed under a coverlet of crowfoot and other flowers, as in Millais's *Ophelia*, reminding me that he had painted his *Blind Girl* above Winchelsea. The most prevalent sound throughout the Marsh was that of its celebrated sheep, flocks of which grazed in every other meadow. From Abraham to Cobbett they would have spoken prosperity to the traveller. I tried not to let them speak sentimentally to me, but it is hard with sheep.

Beatrix Potter, a good shepherdess in Cumbria, once remarked, 'Every lamb that is born is born to have its throat cut', though not in her children's books.

The Marsh, some 50,000 acres of it, is contained between this part of Kent's old and new coastlines. The new coastline makes a wide V from Hythe to Rye Bay and the old one contains two of England's most earnest attempts to prevent invasion from the Continent, the Saxon Shore Way and the Royal Military Canal. Here and there they run side by side, and with their romantic history and leafy shades, not to mention their challenging distances for the walker, for the whole length of the Saxon Shore Way from Gravesend to Rye is no less than 40 miles and that of the Canal over 20 miles. They are a reminder that from the Romans to the Battle of Britain the Marshes have watched for, or watched the enemy. It was William Pitt, talked into it by an army officer and the Duke of York, who sanctioned the digging of the Military Canal in 1806 to stop the French army. It was to be 70 feet across and 9 feet deep. Contemporary critics were hilarious. That an army which had swept across all the great rivers of Europe should be halted by Pitt's ditch! Whatever else it failed to be, the Royal Military Canal, especially where the Count of the Saxon Shore's 'Way' happened to coincide with its banks, must be the most charming of all our military follies. Moreover, it taught the marshmen a lot about drainage. Tramping along beside it, noting its Georgian bridges and locks, admiring the handsome stands of angelica and the lush grass, I thought, 'Good old Pitt!' – thought too about the Channel Tunnel being scraped out further along the Kent coast and of what our ancestors would have said. The Royal Military Canal creates a somewhat urbane approach to the workaday marsh, like a feature from a country-house park which offers one a prospect of a broad reality which has had to be fought for all the way.

The opposite limits of the Marsh are coastal, the sea itself, the East and West Roads curving around the desolate projection of Dungeness, and at Dymchurch staved off by one of the most massive sea walls in Britain. Paul Nash had left his native Chilterns to live by it in 1921, where for the next four years its geometric concrete would dominate his imagination. He was close to me because of my half a lifetime's friendship with his family but, dying in 1946, I had just missed him. He was ill at Dymchurch, unspecifically upset, a delayed nervous reaction, maybe, to what he had witnessed in Flanders. In his numerous and compulsive pictures of the wall, its severe length is bent like a concrete crossbow aimed at the Marsh. Concrete was elegant and optimistic in 1921. Now and then he allows wraith-like figures to parade Dymchurch wall. But the echelon shape repeats that of the board-walks which made it possible to cross the morass of the battlefields in his lithographs of the western front. The seawall at Dymchurch is the ultimate Marsh wall. Charles Rennie's early sea defences are encased in it. With its groins and steps and miles of protection, it holds on to a kind of Cubist purity which could not be in greater contrast with what happened to Dymchurch during the 1930s when the architecture of 'the uninhibited seaside' spread, according to one's tolerance, either like a rash or a nice bit of folk art for much of its length. Beyond the little holiday houses, the Romney Marsh, most of it 'inned' long before coast became recreational, lies open but mysterious. It is one of the paradoxes of flat country that it is able to hide itself.

On the Marsh I was briefly reminded of Paul Nash again when I stopped to watch a microlite take off from a still pasture. It had a Dymchurch-wall shaped wing which was more like a sail, and it took off like a bee from a flower, straight up and away with a buzz. The unexpected sudden disappearance of its two passengers from a secret meadow into the blue left a vacuum. Eventually, Paul would paint a war plane crashed in a marsh and, towards the end, sunflowers cart-wheeling back to the sun.

Although there is a fair amount of arable, the Marsh retains all the character of a classic sheep run. When Cobbett rode across it in the summer of 1823 it was grass as far as the eye could see, an emerald table-land glinting at the edges, and pullulating all over with sheep as white 'as a piece of writing-paper'. When I rode over it this total pastoral was broken up by corn, leaving the beautiful white sheep in their scattered squares. My neighbour, a Scottish farmer now in his nineties, remembers the last great days of the 'Kents', as he calls the Romney Marsh breed. How they were cared for either by a shepherd or a 'Looker', a shepherd being an employed man, a Looker being a man on his own. Both spent half their lives like hermits, sitting alone in a tiny brick sheep-house. A few of these remain, plus their last graffiti – 'A. Booth lambed down 276 ewes, 1930', '17 men of the Rye Harbour Lifeboat were drowned Nov. 15th 1928', 'Rained like hell today'.

Did he have Suffolks as well as Romneys? I asked a farmer at Fairfield. 'Just a few'. His lambs, he said, are now a delicacy for the French and cross the Channel in their hundreds. My neighbour said that in his time that ageing Marsh sheep were examined for falling teeth and sold at Ashford market. The buyer walked them to the Thames, ferried them over it, 'finished' them on his Essex farm, after which they were fed to the Lascars who crewed the ships at Tilbury. The Marsh shepherds 'croned' their flocks. To crone was to pick out and reject. An old ewe was the original crone. I described my walks along the trim empty Romney lanes and he remembered them dusty or muddy as the Lookers trundled down them in their carts, with sheep-dogs curving and dancing excitedly a yard or two behind the axle. He remembered the marshland farmers' traditional loneliness, although 'they liked it that way'. Their sheep, too, were strongly territorial and a dried-up ditch would never tempt them to wander off into the pasture of a neighbouring flock. I thought how tragic it was in the full Blakean sense that these guiltless creatures should, in old age, have to walk all the way to Essex and be devoured by Lascars when their universe was a Romney meadow. But at least it was a world which did not call mutton lamb or either 'sheep meat'.

At St Mary-in-the-Marsh – a lovely ragstone Norman tower, Haffenden Farm, a row of council houses – I made my way to E. Nesbit's grave. There she lies, under a nice wooden memorial made by her husband Mr Tucker, a marine engineer. The memorial is in the form of a bedhead and is inscribed 'Resting'. I thought of *The Wouldbegoods*, the *New Treasure Seekers* and *The Railway Children*. The Romney, Hythe and Dymchurch Railway – no connection –

rattled along in the distance. This 'The world's smallest public railway', as it was billed when it was opened in 1927, three years after Edith's death, has remained a delight for the denizens of the uninhibited seaside and the Marsh traveller alike. Its first steam-engine, made by Davey Paxman of Colchester, was suitably named Green Goddess after the 'Twenties'most popular cocktail, maybe. In the St Mary-in-the-Marsh pub I sat with a cat named Snargate, after a nearby village, and recognised the continuum of marshland music which immemorially has robbed Romney of its expected silence, baaing and lark-song. It was in this pub that a fire burned all night during lambing-time, so that the shepherds and Lookers could cosset the weekly new-born creatures by its hearth, and themselves too for that matter. Outside ran the Haffenden Farm flock, white as wool, of course. It was in this hamlet that I recognised how peripheral to the Romney Marsh proper have remained all the holidaying, military and late 20th century development activities of its coast. Although it has its conservation groups, there is no obvious sense of protection; it is as though the Marsh itself forces the pace, which is in some way defeating and unmanageable to those who would like to change it.

In so many ways it is all contradiction. It is austere, for example, as plains tend to be, yet it is luxuriant, though not in the Kentish sense. It draws the imagination up into the high arc of sky which complements low-lying land, and also sucks it down into mire and darkness. As with the Fens and the Essex saltings, one becomes gradually conscious of the watery ground's stripped clean look, of there being little of what is useful still lying around. Tidy marshes inevitably remind me of sensible Dorothy Hartley in her book *Water in England* (how one would like to have a piece of her mind on its privatisation!). She quotes Thomas Tusser who wrote his *Good Husbandry* on a water-logged farm just down-river from my home:

> What ever befall
> Amend the Marsh Wall.

And then goes on to say why there was never the customary

agricultural mess lying around where there was a marsh wall. Broken hurdles, dead trees, tumbled buildings, big stones turned up by the plough, domestic odds and ends, pottery, etc. old gates, horse bones, all were stuffed into it where sea or stream threatened to seep through. She herself had excavated a lump of 14th century chapel. Whatever falls down, mend the wall with it. Romney's early farms and altars, animal skeletons, smashed boats and most of the debris of its inned existence are undoubtedly within its walls. They are a pleasure in themselves, like my East Anglian ditches, creating patterns and abstractions which provide just the right accompaniment to cross-country walking. The variety of marshland walling in Romney must be unique. And again like the ancient ditches of Britain generally, it is easy to leave out the cost of the labour which made them. The sheep are to blame. They spell ease and the folded security of a religious language.

Most visitors enter the Marsh to look at its churches. There are no less than fourteen of them, none alike, and yet all sharing the homogeneous quality which Romney imposes on everything within its limits. They are all Norman and early Mediaeval buildings standing on artificial mounds to escape the floods and damps. New Romney – St Nicholas – is the grandest, Fairfield – St Thomas à Becket – the most remote. How remote and inaccessible Fairfield was is revealed by an old writer: 'the church for the greatest part of the year is to be approached only on a boat, or on a horse, passing with great danger up to the middle girths'. I walked to it over a bone-dry causeway, circumnavigating the lambs in my path, to find a touching amalgam of antiquity and the Edwardian arts and crafts movement. Little red and blue brick walls, an immense roof; box pews, festal white frontal, and a great many unanswerable questions. It was a sunny morning, but what when the tempests swept the Marsh and its waters roared? What when agues and malarias made themselves visible in the congregation, and where did it live, anyway, there scarcely being a house in sight? And where does it rest, there being no graves? 30 people lived in Fairfield in 1801 and 61 in 1931. Sine then they haven't bothered to give this village a separate census.

The last person to have her funeral here, on a June day in 1859, was Kate Tolhurst. I see her resting, usefully, under the causeway. The records harbour some interesting complaints. 'The Chaplain pastured sheep in the churchyard, and allowed a WOMAN to serve at the altar. He agreed not to do this in future, except in Harvest-time.'

St Mary's, East Guldeford has fascinating credentials. All of brick, it was built by Henry VII's Master of the Horse, who had drained part of the Walland Marsh and felt obliged to provide a place of worship for the people who had come to live in it. As with so many of the Marsh churches, it is box-pewed, so that the parson in his pulpit stared down at a human version of the sheep markets in the surrounding towns, his flock penned, family by family, below him, their feet in winter in clean straw. St Nicholas, New Romney, has long been the church of the Cinque Forts administrators. Their 'Jurats' were elected by the stone which still exists in the south aisle. I drift on, as travellers in the Marsh do, from tower to bellcote, recognising an entity rather than a succession of parishes. What these houses of the spirit have in common is a disobeying of that injunction about not building on sand, or in their case, on shrinking peat. But what was the option? Getting out of the Marsh to go to church, or just to get to one's neighbour's church, was often virtually impossible. Hence these fourteen altars spread over a land where folk had to stay put. Canterbury, so near, seems to have had a hand in it. Could the Saxon authorities have seen the Marsh, then more a delta of islands, as a 'desert' for hermits to practise their disciplines in? Architecturally, the foundations are nearly non-existent, and the piling-up of such enormous masses of stone in a bog could come into the divine foolishness of saints. Yet here they stand, All Saints, Burmarsh, just, St Augustine's, Snave, defiantly buttressed, Snargate, with a painted Tudor galleon sailing on its inside north wall, in spite of having to soar over what was once a sea creek with its sluice gate, and which has been ever since deep marsh below the Rhee Wall. Richard Barham, who wrote *The Ingoldsby Legends* used to be the rector of Snargate, a place full of marsh fever then. This reminded me of the health hazards of Cambridge University before Parliament got the Dutch to drain the Fens, the mosquitoes, the 'humours', the endemic sickliness which hung around the beautiful colleges. 'Love and a cough cannot be hid', wrote George Herbert, who was employed to oppose the scheme because they thought it would spoil the Cam. I thought too of our current love for the Wetlands and our petitions to save them. 'Wetlands' – how disagreeable a word this would have been for any age other than our own. But a marsh, curiously enough, used to spell high living and an individualism bordering on lawlessness. So the good life if the damps did not penetrate the flesh. Although the general feeling I got from considering the lives of the old Romney Marsh community was of a quiet robustness and buoyancy. There is an inscription in Snargate church which says, 'J Bourne, (Churchwarden), Warrington Romney plumber, T. Apps carpenter and all his jolly men' mended the roof in 1780.

The locals called the Marsh 'the fifth quarter of the globe' which suggests that they did not think of themselves as being on earth in the normal sense. The people on the innings always knew themselves to be outsiders. Novelists from Dickens, Conrad and Victor Bridges to Graham Swift have been drawn to them. The most popular of the Romany Marsh storytellers was Russell Thorndike, Sybil's brother, who invented Dr Syn, the kind of gentleman who, in Kipling's poem, it was best not to see:

> Five and twenty ponies
> Trotting through the dark –
> Brandy for the Parson
> 'Baccy for the clerk –
> Laces for a lady, letters for a spy
> Watch the wall, my darling,
> While the Gentlemen go by!

Smuggling was more than a Marsh romance; it was big business, as profitable in its proportion to drug smuggling now. Vigilantes known as Riding Officers were often killed during their mainly hopeless efforts to halt the 'runs' and an undercurrent of quite non-fictitious violence pierces the history of most of the villages. Brookland, for instance, where a wall painting shows the ferocious slaughter of Becket by four knights, and where in 1821 the Coast Blockade, the forerunners the modern Coastguard Service, fought a smuggling gang known as 'The Blues' in a bloody battle. It was winter and the heavily uniformed Blockaders slipped and sank in the mire. The smugglers, as always, were guided through the dark Marsh by their 'pilots', men who by day were shepherds and knew every sinking inch of the way.

I thought of this, the most sensational of all the smugglers' fights, with the gallows busy afterwards, as I walked a friend's dogs over Camber Sands, for there is no other comparable corner in Britain where invasions of one kind or another have left so many evidences, oral or otherwise, no place so littered with defensive clutter. The Marsh has such a complete range of military installations that it could be the proto-Imperial War Museum. From the Roman fort of Lemanis hanging like a great molar under Lympne ('Lim') to the War Office's ranges below Lydd, there seems to be something from every period. The Cinque Ports themselves – Rye, one of the extra ones, glittered across the sands like a night painting by Edmund Dulac, – were a cluster of naval bases armed against the French. The Camber friend mentioned the mnemonic without which even a marsh-bred child would have a hard time remembering them:

> Some Danes Have No Homes
> Sandwich-Dover-Hythe-New Romney-Hastings.

Before us, like an enormous sandcastle about to be flattened by the tide, loomed Henry VIII's contribution to the defences of Kent. To the east stretched the darkening shore where they held the first trials of Churchill and Flamethrower tanks, and above this the marvellously strange triangular ledge of loose shingle, over 6,000 acres of small stones perpetually in re-arrangement at their edge, which was Dungeness. But behind us, as much as sixteen feet below the sea in places lay the quiet Marsh levels. The Lords of the Level used to meet at Dymchurch to rule them, now they are administered by the Southern Water Authority. So, whether from the inland escarpment or from the English Channel, one descends to this openly withdrawn country of 'court' farms, broad rhines or ditches, more trees than one expects and pond plants, acutely aware, as in all tended marshes, of flood, shift and impermanence. The joy of the Romney Marsh is that there is so much of it, and that one can tell exactly where one stands when it comes to knowing if one is in or out of it. I realised that its 'pale warmth', as John Piper described it, could become an addiction.

THE LAND OF LOST SHIPS

(*The Independent on Sunday*, 30th January, 1994)

A place that holds us in its spell is often a native place, now and then a personally discovered landscape, or somebody else's special territory which we simply had to annex. I suppose that for me north Cornwall has to belong to the last definition. Thirty years ago two old friends left Suffolk for Trethias, a hamlet near Constantine Bay, where I followed them for a few weeks each winter or spring, to write, to talk, to walk and quite unintentionally to allow that powerful moorland and seaboard secretly to become part of me as it had become part of them.

At first I thought we shared its impact, that it was saying more or less the same thing to each of us. But being so much alone there – they were for short strolls, myself for long hauls over St Breock downs or the coastal paths – I soon knew that where this dramatic scenery was concerned I was not their guest. It had roared and blown and burnt itself into me. Then equally unexpected and surprising, after I had wandered all around this wonderful region, came the invitation from P N Furbank for me to work on the New Wessex edition of the works of Thomas Hardy, 'my' volume being none other than *A Pair of Blue Eyes*, that fictionalised account of his courtship in and around St Juliot, every land and field of which had by this time become as familiar to me as those at home.

This task necessitated thorough travels through the north Cornwall of Hardy's youth and widower-hood, when his attempt to come to terms with a failed marriage resulted in a sequence of love-and-landscape poems which have no parallel in the English language. He called it 'the land beyond the land' and one of 'those sequestered spots outside the Gates of the World'. Emma, his unfortunate, immortalised wife, had said: 'All this should be seen in the winter to be truly appreciated.'

That was when I was always seeing it, although occasionally I was there in May. My friends were 'movers', shifters about in the same few miles, makers and forsakers of gardens, and enthusiasts for a year or two of almost any fresh view. I used to envy them their up-sticks energy and panache, and there was always the thrill each Christmas or Easter of being shown the new house. Praise for it poured from us. They would never leave it, never move again. But they did. I loved them for their fickleness.

Where I was concerned, the chief effect of these moves was to set me down in the next square of the six-inch Ordnance Survey map. I would check on the revised position of Brown Willy from my bedroom window, or hark for a changed note in the sound of the sea. The first explorations from the new base were intensely thrilling; even the glimpse of yet one more wintering holiday bungalow called Tamarisk or Spindrift on the edge of the new village would create runs of speculative thought. There would be my friends' latest church, latest pub. At the early service Suffolk churches strike dry cold, the Cornish dank cold. My friends' Cornish churches often stood among swaying rookeries and huge shrubs which clawed against the windows, their painted roofs were carved from bog oak and the granite preaching-crosses of their founders stood tall among the dead, whose memorials were elegantly engraved slate visiting-cards. Miracles of penmanship carried out with a chisel.

There is nothing like slate for making a good flourish and I never grew tired of searching the hilly Cornish churchyards for these refined letterings of grief. The slate came from Delabole, arguably the biggest man-made hole in Britain. where it has been cut and split for many centuries. The abandoned surface machinery gives no real warning of its immensity. They said that the best slate lay 24 fathoms from the top. Men abseiled on ropes to reach it. This went on headstones. But the main product of this recently vanished industry roofed the Cornish for life.

Beyond St Austell, not far off, rose the milky mountains of the china clay trade, and I remember thinking how amazing it was that two such manufactures, the one so deep and blue-black, the other so high and white, and both so vast, should exist below the moor. Industrial Cornwall – and it includes the fishing and the pittance farming of the recent past, the tin-mining and the quarrying – may be 'another country' to the holidaymaker, but to me it was an integral part of what made this county such an unforgettable experience. I would clamber about in old workings and find my way along the tinners' tracks, all this side of Cornwall captivating me.

But the ultimate influence was the sea itself, the Atlantic brought to a crashing halt by a dizzy granite barrier along whose face screamed wild hosts of sea birds. These tall cliffs offered pleasures that were shot through with fears, terrors even, if one knew only a little of their history. Below them are the lands of lost ships and a turbulence which, like the tides themselves, alternately drags one towards it and drives one back. The towering headlands – Trevose, Pentire, Tintagel – jut from it, and broken-away islands such as Quies and Gulland provide a kind of staying point for the eye in so much movement.

In spite of Cornwall's 'otherness', writers like Sir Thomas Malory in his *Morte d'Arthur* and composers such as Elgar, Bax and Malcolm Arnold were to establish what we now accept as 'Englishness' out of what they imagined here. I vividly recall my first lonely encounter with this coast. It was on Trevose Head on the afternoon of the shortest day. I had walked there from Trethias, which was not far in mileage but at that particular moment as far as one could go from a secure hearth. It was haphazardly light, with spumy mist and yet a clear enough path. A foghorn brayed and farm dogs barked and for a while there was no sound of the ocean. Then, just below, it announced itself, not violently as I had expected but rather like the sound of the sea which we heard in a shell when we were children. Behind me stretched the tees and hummocks of a golf links and a neolithic burial ground. All around me were the coves and bays with their mocking names: Booby's, Stinking Cat's, Mother Ivey's. I looked down from various edges. The air which blew in from the water was mild and phosphorescent. The map in my head was saying this is only the beginning. There is everything to look for from here to Hartland – when it is light.

I went to St Juliot with no feeling of pilgrimage. Although heart-breakingly signposted in Hardy's novel and poems, the village itself and the immortalised Valency Valley leading to it would tell one little if one had not read his work. The wits used to say. 'Thomas Hardy loved women – Yes, *dead* women,' yet he went back to St Juliot to come close again to the vital Emma, not her ghost.

In *A Pair of Blue Eyes* one reads their story between the lines, in the poetry along love lines uneqalled for their openness. They met here on Monday 7 March 1870, both aged 29, she boisterous and close to being an old maid by the standards of the day, he slight and private, an architect's assistant sent from Weymouth to 'restore' the parish church where Emma's brother-in-law was the rector. Four years later, on the strength of *Far from the Madding Crowd*, they were wed, to the inestimable benefit of English literature but apparently doubtful benefit to each other. Yet who can tell? The spots they shared in north Cornwall do not attempt to and stay, in Hardy's words, 'old love's domain'. The stream and its waterfalls, the bluebell banks and the woodland walks of Valency appear quite undisturbed by time since they courted there. I noticed when my friends were with me how conversation had to make way for the silences needed for such a unique journey.

With Emma gone and old age come, Hardy had to acknowledge that St Juliot held the key to his existence. Bits of discarded stone from his restoration still lay in the churchyard, as did Emma's sister. The small fields combed with winter wheat rested safely from the sea. The day after Emma's death Hardy found her description of the place which was to be both providential and fatal:

> Scarcely any author and his wife could have had a much more romantic meeting with its unusual circmstances...with the beautiful sea-coast, and the wild Atlantic rolling in with its magnificent waves and spray, its white gulls and black choughs and grey puffins, its cliffs and rocks and gorgeous sunsettings sparkling redness in a track widening from the horizon to the shore. All this should be seen in the winter to be truly appreciated.

As well as to Valency I would walk along the crest of Beeny Cliff towards Crackington Haven. Beeny was where Hardy set the first cliffhanger, when he makes a young intellectual in *A Pair of Blue Eyes* hang by his fingertips from wet shale above a boiling sea. The Cornish cliffs rise to their nerve-racking zenith at Beeny, which is no place for the vertiginous. A girl (Emma) eventually hauls her unloving 'lover' to safety. It is a great scene.

Boscastle, just under St Juliot, also had its appeal. It had not quite lost its workaday roots when sailing ships would be towed into its swan-necked natural harbour to be loaded with Delabole slate. The gloss of tourism never quite smooths away the industrial grittiness of Cornwall, as harshly toiling a place as one could find anywhere.

One of my friend's moves – he was the poet and novelist James Turner – took him and his wife to their own 'Valency', a secluded farm-house near Wadebridge where unseen brooks could be heard coursing through the trees and there was never a minute during the year when wild flowers were not in bloom. The formidable Miss Seward, who had re-introduced camomile lawns, lived nearby in a low-set cottage whose tiny rooms were filled with birdsong and the sound of rushing water. It was from here that I was to discover north Cornwall's exhilarating wilderness, Bodmin Moor.

The approach to a great moor is one of the excitements of travelling. Mine to Bodmin was via St Breward and Altarnun. Admiration for moorland is a modern notion; traditionally there was never a good word to say for it. Travellers needed to have a hard time, now and then, and crossing Bodmin Moor could be proof of their nerve. They peopled it with horrors and shut their eyes to its loveliness.

The moor's twin peaks are Rough Tor and Brown Willy, and these crests must have been the holy mountains of neolithic Cornishmen, whose huts and hearths and cromlechs are scattered all around them. Wild horses shelter where they must have stood out of the wind. Far off the Atlantic is cameoed in distant bays. Nearby is Cornwall's only inland lake, Dozmary, the tarn from whose depths a hand caught King Arthur's sword, Excalibur.

But my romance was with the early dwellers on this granite platform who were clearly careful to put the boggy downs between themselves and the terrible sea, and who must have been folk of wonderful perspectives and clarity of vision. When I find traces of this old society, I don't so much think of what it fed on as what it sang. Rails for the tinners' trucks remind me of another race of Cornish highlanders and their liberating songs – by the Wesley brothers.

Rough, rude and elevating, Bodmin Moor with its strong scents and racing air has marked me for life. Just mentioning it makes me long to walk there again, and then to the raging January shore, and finally to Treneague to see the mild lanes and the harts-tongue fern curling from the banks. There are special compensations for covering the same ground.

SOMETIMES IN WALES

Never go back, they say, though sometimes one must, in order to convince oneself that one was ever there. It is one of the ironies of travel that certain places which permanently secure themselves in the imagination are the least substantial when it comes to setting down the hard facts of what one actually saw during the brief visit to them.

Yet there they are, the big and lasting names on the crowded map of one's journeys. My brother and I were staying in Shropshire, a county he had taken a fancy to and wanted me to see, when for no reason either of us can now recall, we found ourselves walking up and up the Pony Track from Dolgellau, our old car abandoned by the wayside and our eyes fixed on the astounding scenes ahead.

There lay Cader Idris, the towering walls separating the chieftainships of Gwynedd and Powys, the seat of wisdom and a landscape which shook and nonplussed our East Anglian souls. My brother, having wandered through the Ardennes, could afford to be as much interested as impressed, but, this being my first mountain, I was so overwhelmed that for ages afterwards I could only recall its emotional effect and not its views.

Like W J Turner's *Chimborazo, Cotapaxi*, Cader took me by the hand, and so doing caused me to take leave of my senses. As the ranked peaks broke on me, I wasn't in Wales at all but in another dimension. This proved to be far less satisfying in the long run than it sounds, for as somebody who likes his travel feelings to be supported by plenty of history, geography and botany, not to mention literature and art and the local brand of human behaviour, Cader Idris soon became one of those frustrating journeys which we all make but which have to be repeated in order for us to see where we have been. Some people take a short cut to this kind of verification by taking photographs, but this would never do for me. I have to make the repeat trip, usually on my own, and with all my wits about me.

So, gloriously blinding Cader Idris was filed away for future exploration. I went to Wales many times afterwards and saw many mountains from which it was impossible not to glimpse Cader itself, but this did not count. A time had to come when this first mountain of mine would renew old ties and explain itself, as it were.

It did so via one of those coincidences which – unless one was Thomas Hardy – one would never dare to use in a novel. About three years ago a clergyman friend invited me to stay with him at Arthog, his new parish overlooking the exquisite Mawddach estuary. Across the estuary lay Barmouth, sedate and remote in the evening sunshine, and neither it nor Afon Mawddach giving so much as a hint of their industrial past, but each reflecting the arresting stillness of an Edwardian viewcard.

Behind us and thrusting high above the vicarage garden, causing its orchard and terraces to cling tenaciously to its boulders, was the first of the vast sills of volcanic rock which, only an hour or two's walking and clambering away, climaxed as the summit of Cader Idris. Scattered sheepfarms, indeed, made it a perfectly ordinary fact that my host's ministry extended to stony miles of my delectable mountain. There had been no tradition of clinging safely and sociably at its feet. Ancient homesteads and giddy runs of dry-stone walling ascended its fastnesses and had dragged some kind of living out of its solitudes for centuries, and I was struck, as I had not been on my first visit, by Cader Idris as an inhabited region. The bards thought of Idris as a giant intellect, thus making it possible for the people to dwell in his titanic realm rationally and unthreatened. It takes a visitor some time to appreciate this.

I came to Arthog again this summer, not only to see my friend but to look at Cader with all my tourist might, to settle it in my experience as a favourite bit of geography and not leave it floating about in my sub-conscious. There are many routes to its pinnacles, all of them spectacular and none of them over-difficult. From the south there are paths from Tal-y-Llyn, Dolcae and Abergymlwyn, and one can also climb up by tracks at each end of the main range, the one leading from Cross Foxes and the other from just by Bird Rock. But the quickest way up is by the road from Minffordd, and quite the easiest and most popular is the way my brother and I took along the famous Pony Track from Dolgellau, and by which so many generations of Cader Idris pilgrims have journeyed. There is also the Foxes' Path, which involves a strenuous half-hour climb over broken rocks and the crossing of a spring containing, some say, the coldest water in Wales. And finally there is the incomparably lovely ascent from Arthog itself, with its beginnings in the dense elegance of Victorian country-house gardens, all secret walls, rhododendrons, peacocks and hidden, crashing streams.

The ultimate rewards of Cader Idris are the cone lakes on the summit of Pen-y-Gader, one in its north cwm and the other in the south. The latter, Llyn-y-Cau, is the subject of Richard Wilson's haunting painting in the National Gallery and is among the most extraordinary features of the natural history of Britain. Wilson's interpretation of it is highly personal and strange. Critics wonder why he pastoralised this jagged scene by letting shepherds pipe in the foreground and by painting the lake in such a way that it half suggests the crater of Vesuvius filled with water. As a Montgomeryshire man, though, to whom the darker side of the mountains would have been very real, I sometimes wonder if he had the alternative notion to Cader as the seat of poetry and philosophy in mind when he worked on this celebrated picture. This was that Gwyn an Nadd, the lord of the underworld, lived within the mountain. Gwyn with his pack of hounds, the Cwn Annwn, had to round up the souls of the new dead and shepherd them into its shades.

I have to admit that, although scenery on this heroic scale can make me feel insecure and even fearful, what affects me most of all are the alternating emotions of reckless freedom and exhilaration which it produces. Wind passing over large expanses of corn and grass in Suffolk or becoming half-drugged by staring through tall trees at scraps of intensely blue sky is its East Anglian equivalent.

It means that even as I set out for the heights of Cader Idris I was on a trip which was going to make me see quite a lot further than Worcestershire and Ireland, which is the marvellous view offered from Pen-y-Gader (3,100 feet), its highest peak. For me a mountain walk is a mounting excitement whether I make the final gradients or not, and often the greatest pleasure is in the first hour of setting out, with the long day ahead and knowing that there are hours of nothing to do except walk and look and let the scenery filter its way through me.

Before climbing or walking anywhere, I always think it makes sense to understand something about the people who have lived in the grip of a vast landscape, in Cader's case for some three thousand years. Though way beyond any form of complete domestication or industrialisation, this mountain never seems to be above the inhabitants of Dolgellau, Arthog, Minffordd and all the fascinating settlements which have sprung up by the woods and rivers at its feet, but a part of them. The ease and intimacy derives from the nature of its mountain agriculture, which involved herdsmen and their families in a complex network of lonely journeys between the isolated cottages, and the citizens of Dolgellau itself, until recently the ancient capital of Merioneth and the centre of its wool trade, in a commerce which depended upon the Cader Idris flocks.

Arthog remains for me the gate of knowing to these steep pastures. So out of the vicarage garden, wired high against the sheep, and turn right for a little stroll along the estuary road which is so enchanting in itself as to tempt me to forget mountain-climbing. Incredible to think that just over a hundred years ago this was the wild highway of the sensational Dolgellau Gold Belt, where 24 gold mines were spaced out all along the Mawddach valley from Barmouth to Clogau, attracting miners from Cornwall, Australia and America. A few hundred thousand pounds worth of gold was extracted, including that used for the Prince of Wales's investiture regalia in 1911, and the wedding rings for Queen Mary and the Princess Royal, but it was all over by the First World War and the chief mines at Gwynfnydd and Clogau, where locals and foreigners alike scrambled for a fortune, are silent glades.

The salmon river they briefly polluted runs diamond pure once more beneath miles of conifers.

At Maescwm the Forestry Commission have brought together many of the aquatic plants of the area, along with the abjuration:

> Leave nothing but footprints,
> Take nothing but pictures,
> Kill nothing but time.

Well, let those kill time who like it better dead, as Rose Macaulay said, I was in a decidely time-vitalising state of mind as I walked off the fortune hunter's road and began the long and steady rise. Soon I was high enough to be looking straight down the chimney-pots of the village and down too through a crack in its slates into the forsaken interior of a big chapel, imagining those vanished miners singing of golden cities and gates and corn. It was far above the huge sweep of Cardigan Bay, which now appeared as though it belonged to another sphere altogether.

Mountains are like that. They draw one up into their own element, set their own rules, make their own demands. They look down on the sea. But, 'great things are done when men and mountains meet. This is not done by jostling in the street'. Did Blake actually ever set foot on a mountain? He should have climbed towards Tyran Mawr (Great Towers) via the Arthog waterfalls with his face to Pen-y-Gaden, miraculously only two miles on. Between them runs the old narrow Dolgellau-Towyn road, where the cautious modern traffic is dwarfed into insignificance by their mighty banks.

I climbed Tyran Mawr first because I had been told that its views were considered by some to be better than those from Cader Idris itself. Below was the ancient grass track called the Black Road. Probably Roman in origin, it makes an arc around the west bastion of Cader, winding seven miles down into the Dysynni Valley, a fabulous and unforgettable walk. Below, too, lay the Crogenen Lakes which, like all corrie lakes, look too deep and still for comfort. They are 800 feet up and I, my head resting on the barren brow of Tyran Mawr, am 2,167 feet above the sea which, from up here, flashes blue and illimitable.

One of the lakes has an island with larch trees and the other a white edge which dips and shrieks. Hundreds of gulls are riding its shallows. There is barking and shouting as a shepherd and his dogs bring the flock down and there is so much birdsong that once I began the complicated process of identifying a fraction of it it occurred to me that, what with their sonorous sounding-board like acoustics and this huge mixture of calls, Cader should be deafening. Yet it contained some central silence which held itself aloof from the racket. This was, perhaps, its great mystery, its apartness from all that happened on it, above it and beneath it.

One of those strong winds which have an existence outside the weather forecasts blew up suddenly as I lay there, and soon I was down on the soft turf of the drove road amidst the larks' nests. Mountains don't tolerate one for long.

From Cader Idris itself I saw what looked like the photographic negative of a city taken from the air. It was an acre of burnt gorse. And there to the south was Pumlumon and, to the north, Snowdon.

The Cader Idris passes and tracks are noticeably solitary in comparison with those of Snowdonia. It is an accessible, magical country of luxuriously foliaged lowlands and sharp finials, a walker's dream.

ONCE IN ORKNEY

(*The Sunday Times*, 9th October, 1988)

Why, when one has crossed the world, do certain places comparatively near at hand keep their distance? What is most remote is often not very far. Why, I ask myself, is Sydney so near and Stromness such a long way?

Finding myself at last in that great paved-over Georgian street which is Orkney's second town, and through which, disconcertingly, cars are allowed to pass, their tyres slapping against the granite, I experienced that old 'journeying' feeling. I knew Stromness well because of some books in which it is often called Hamnavoe, its original name, and via which I had made an un-met friend, the poet and novelist George Mackay Brown.

Orkney is fortunate in the strength and variety of its continuities, in its thousand years' run of the best authors, for instance. From the saga-writers (Icelandic actually) to Edwin Muir and Eric Linklater, and via generations of stylish historians, the 70 or so islands which lie scattered in the northern waters beyond the Pentland Firth have received no ordinary documentation. Their ancient sagas seem to have flowed into today's literature without the usual historical break, creating a kind of continuity of soul.

George Mackay Brown and I approached in the suddenly deserted street like characters in an old movie. I expected to see him, but he didn't know about my Orkney journey, although he was less astonished than amused. We stood, not explaining and making plans, in a chasm of fine houses with stepped gables built end-on to the sea to escape the full force of the easterlies, the homes of the men who supplied the Greenland whalers, the Hudson Bay Company's fleet and Captain Cook. Water from the well just up the road would have had to last for months, and would be carried over the Atlantic. The buildings frustrate the full force of the spring wind, as they were intended to do, but where they break into sea-steps and alleys, it knifes through and cuts one's head off.

I am sailing to Hoy and George and I will talk later. But first I walked the length of Stromness again and again, half in Scandinavia and certainly never wholly in Scotland. It clings to a rock called Brinkie's Bray, which is tumultuous with birdsong and the school playground. 'The Tours' – spoken of with the courteous fatalism of Celtic monks expecting raiders – had not begun, but neither had any obvious preparation for the tourists. Orcadians have fine manners and laconic responses.

Hoy, the high island, looms for miles, and is part of the archipelago which encircles Scapa Flow. I reached it on Mr Mowal's *Scapa Ranger*, a bouncy 12-seater crammed with children, ornithologists and sturdy ladies reading *The Orcadian*, my aim being to walk to Rackwick which, I was assured, was one of this earth's most lovely scenes.

We passed under the bow of the sunken block-ship off Graemsay and it was from here that one could see the full significance of Stromness as a provisioning last call for sailing vessels. The pack-horse path to Rackwick did indeed take me to an exceedingly beautiful, but also an abandoned, situation. Those who had farmed and fished there for generations had fled to better livings. Their dry-stone homes yawned emptily in the small gardens, although there were signs of return. The hilly nature of Hoy has restricted the modern farming which has so transformed Orkney generally. No more that old subsistence agriculture which was itself a multitude of green islands struggling to survive in an ocean of moor, harsh and story-filled, but perfect fields from shore to shore. The small scale of the expansion and its openness – no hedges, low boundary walls – creates the feeling of something blessed having taken place. Wheat and barley, pastures with flocks and herds and horses all carefully set out like those painted lead animals in the toy farms we had as children. This new fertility shines against what looks like a background of wild blue and grey heights, but which are a succession of distant islands equally fully farmed. The trim low-lying buildings do their best for a handful of cringing trees and provide a landscape which no Orcadian prior to the last war could have imagined. A distinctive feature is the Nissen hut bar, Orkney's version of turning swords into ploughshares.

Loot and litter from both wars are thick on the ground, poignant, intriguing and now, in some strange way, an Orkney asset in their own right. They reach their crescendo of meaning and utility at Scapa Flow, that huge, sad, enclosed water full of drowned navies. The mess left here must at one time have driven to despair those Orcadians who knew the state of the archipelago before the war-men descended on it, but now it is no longer mess, it is elegy.

Walking for the first time from Kirkwall to Scapa, or driving over that Cubist marvel (or horror) which is the Churchill Barrier, is a very thoughtful business. The latter is a vast tumble of squared concrete which was tipped into the sea between the islands of South Ronaldsay, Burray, Holm, Glims and Mainland after the sinking of the *Royal Oak* in the autumn of 1939. The barriers provide a grandstand view of the cold expanse where one of the factors which caused the first world war, the navy race, ended. The road-stead designated as safe anchorage for the British fleet in 1905 became the graveyard of the Kaiser's fleet in June 1919 when the skeleton crews of 74 ships opened their cocks and scuttled them. A few miles from Stromness is Marwick Head where, on June 5, 1916, *HMS Hampshire* went down with Kitchener and his staff.

Many thousands of British soldiers and sailors, and hundreds of Italian prisoners crowded Orkney during the last war and have left an indelible mark. Nothing written in concrete becomes discreet. But, as everyone must, I did visit the lovely Italian chapel on Lambholm. The inspiration of a prisoner captured in the North Africa campaign, Domenico Chicchetti, it is the apotheosis of the Nissan hut. Nowhere in Britain have the two wars left a more eloquent residue than in Orkney. I was unprepared for its impact.

But so much seemed to hold its power for ever here, as the Ring of Brodgar proved. I had longed to see these celebrated standing stones. They stand in a more intimate relevance to the lives of those who raised them than any other group of monoliths in Europe. For nearby on the shore of the Bay of Skaill is the intact Stone Age village of Skara Brae, 10 houses filled with their original beds, dressers and seats, all linked by covered passages. Wild weather in 1850 washed the sand out of them and brought them to light. Because of Orkney's lack of wood, stone beds were still in use then, 5,000 years later.

I approached the sublime Ring of Brodgar on foot, as one should, first visiting Maes Howe in its meadow off the Stromness-Finstown road. A party of 'Jerusalem-farers' or young Norse crusaders, took shelter in this magnificent corbelled passage-grave, which only admits the mid-winter sunset, and scribbled on its wall such grafitti as: 'Many a proud woman has had to enter here low stooping.' and 'Ingibiorg is the loveliest of the girls'. The chamber was already three and a half thousand years' old when they entered it during the winter of 1151 to say 'we were here' in their feathery runic hand.

Nothing human seems wholly to disappear in Orkney. The dividing line between pre-history and history is faint. Farming and archaeology were going on all the way to Stenness in a sharp wind and great quiet. Stenness is yet another of the county's (any place less like a county it is hard to imagine) natural isthmuses, and its most spectacular. The architects of the ring and its subsidiary circle, the Stones of Stenness, and the ancient people who decided to settle here, must have had an eye to the wonders of the scenery, as well as to its convenience. The twin lochs of Harray and Stenness dominate it. They were glittering when I arrived, with flotillas of swans passing below the monolith, known as the Watch Stone, and banked with what looked like sheet-celandine, so dense were the burnished flowers. Tumuli, larks, the long-dead and the freshly alive, and Hoy and South Ronaldsay closing off the view to Caithness. The Ring of Brodgar is contained within a hand-carved stone ditch. Twenty-seven of the original 60 stones remain where they were set in about 2500 BC. I paced them – six steps between each. One is incised with Victorian graffiti by men with local place-names.

Describing any seaside Orkney kirkyard, George Mackay Brown wrote:

Always, by the shore, kirk and kirkyard.
Legends of men, their carved names
Faced east, into first light, among sea moulds.

Another friend, David Drinkell, an East Anglian come to Orkney to be the organist at St Magnus's Cathedral and to teach music in the village schools, showed me what was, until the Reformation, accepted as the most glorious building in Scandinavia. The immediate impression is of a smaller, warmer Durham in soft red sand-stone, a strange unity of Celtic Catholicism and Presbyterianism. The old mysteries and the later rationalisation appear to have come to terms. The massive fiery columns are a little out of kilter and the walls are lined with enormous tombstones which are lettered all over, and which all end with 'Remember death'. Eric Linklater and Edwin Muir are remembered in Poets' Corner.

I could see Wyre, Muir's home, from my bedroom window in Kirkwall. Just an island smudge, but there it was, the classic country of his *Autobiography*. A shade further lay Egilsay, the island on which Earl Magnus was murdered by his cousin, the co-Earl of Orkney, Hakon. Magnus's nephew, the poet-saint Rognvald, built the cathedral to honour his uncle in the 12th century. There was a long hiatus during the work and the un-roofed interior became weathered and the sharp edges of the carved stone blunted by wind and rain. Hence a great northern Romanesque church which welcomes one like a fire. It is still more Norwegian than Scottish.

St Magnus lies in a pillar a few feet up to the south of the altar, where the rich metrical psalms rise on the sabbath. Higher still, in a loft, lies the Kirkwall hangman's double ladder with 13 rungs. 'Two go up, one comes doon.' St Magnus's role today is to focus Orkney's very considerable art, its literature, painting and music, the latter carried into an international dimension by Peter Maxwell Davies. I clambered along the steep paths above his house to the Old Man of Hoy. His side of the island faces the open Atlantic, and is lined with the dizziest cliff scenery in Britain. St Magnus's Cathedral traps this soaring quality, but doesn't entirely tame it.

For the traveller, Orkney is a very much 'take us as you find us' country. With only some 18,009 inhabitants spread across so many islands, with ordinary tasks and ordinary life going on much as they always did, the visitor feels himself to be the brief sharer of what normally occurs, rather than a holiday-maker on the edge of it. The tedious 'heritage' business is not exploited, the reticence of the capital, Kirkwall, or that of the administration of the pro-historic sites, or the North Hoy nature reserve, for example, being beyond praise. Having no car, I bussed and walked and sailed about, battered by the winds, elated by all these floating fragments of land which had been a unity for those who had inhabited them since the time when the Sphinx was carved from soft rock at Giza. I watched men drying kelp on racks, men digging peat, fishermen mending nets, and men uncovering the Bronze Age. The latest intruders, the oilmen of Flotta, fill the gap between Fara and the Sound of Hoxa.

Confessors

LOST KINGDOMS

(*The New York Times Magazine*, October 4th, 1987)

There are in Britain vanished cities, lost villages, disappeared kingdoms even, some with their names still on the map. Trying to reach them isn't quite as hopeless as reaching the rainbow's end but the point at which their legend and their geography meet is sure to be buried in a thicket of poetry. Digging into both the literature and the earth can produce a few hard facts although one soon comes to accept that the realities of these usually much pined-for places can only exist in the imagination. Hence the centuries of storytelling which keeps them alive when they are no more. Our local vanished city is Dunwich on the Suffolk coast and I have sat on the cliffs there many a time, obediently listening to the bells in drowned churches ringing below the North Sea, for this is what one comes to Dunwich to do. It is precarious to venture to the cliff edge because the soil erosion which tipped this grand medieval city into the waves never stops, but the gentle hour-glass filtering of sand and human bones from the last churchyard to the beach is a sight not to be missed. Such non-places with their resonant names offer a very special attraction. Some travellers find them haunted or sacred; I find them so eloquent that sometimes I can hardly believe what they are saying. The experience is far from new. Think of the eloquence of that bumpy mound called Troy.

My favourite long journey in Britain is from East Anglia to Cornwall and I have made it regularly since I was nineteen. It is a journey from flint to granite, from a hard bright light to opalescent mists, and it is broken at Glastonbury, not at all a vanished town but, for me, a staging-post for Camelot. Camelot is among the most yearned-for lost cities in the world and the modern quest for it has only been surpassed in determination and intensity by its citizen's quest for the Sangreal, the cup used at the Last Supper and then by Joseph of Arimathea to catch the blood of Christ at the Crucifixion. Was Camelot Colchester? ask the historians. Most likely. Could it have been Winchester? Ten years ago a Camelot Research Committee excavated the vast earthworks called Cadbury Castle in order to put King Arthur's lovely capital on the Ordnance Survey, but although there were plenty of archaeological finds, none spelt Camelot and none, I fear, ever will. Tennyson, in the *Idylls of the King* defined Camelot as a symbol of 'the gradual growth of beliefs and institutions, and the spiritual development of Man', a picture of Victorian civic advancement which the great poem tends to refute.

However, it is Glastonbury, the best gathering-place for those hoping to invade Arthur's kingdom, which has now to be credited with a growth of beliefs as, since the Sixties, it has thrived as a shrine for today's transcendelalists. Nourished on the novels of John Cowper Powys, T. H. White and, most influentially, J.R.R. Tolkien, plus the philosophy of John Lennon, they can be seen drifting through the ancient summer country of Somerset to the Tor in search of very different answers to the problems of life than those offered by the hardnosed Eighties. To spell out what Glastonbury has meant to pilgrims over the centuries would be impossible. Mystics say that it is magnetic, folklorists that it is central to the British version of a world-wide legend, and historians say – well, having such a pile of rich tales to work through before they can get anywhere near history proper, they say what they can in the circumstances. Glastonbury is where everybody goes to theorise.

The town is built on an island on a once watery plain and is visible from a great distance due to its famous Tor, a peculiar column-like hill of some 500 feet crowned with a tall church. This Tor dominates all the surrounding countryside like a totem. The countryside is none other than Avalon, the holy 'Vale of Apples', to which not only King Arthur and his knights, but many of England and Ireland's saints made their way, their destination the spot below the Tor where the scanty remains of Glastonbury Abbey now stand, a place of quite enormous sanctity, for it was believed that not only Joseph of Arimathea had walked there, but Jesus himself – 'And did those feet ... ?' as William Blake asked, overwhelmed by the possibility. At the Abbey is Arthur's grave. Here 'the once and future king' waits until it is time to rule a better Britain, and here a thorn blooms at Christmas (a twig goes to the Queen to decorate her dinner table) from a plant struck by St Joseph when he thrust his stick in the Glastonbury soil. The visitor will see the gaping Abbey, the enigmatic Tor, the grave, the thorn and will see with a different eye that a mythology of an heroic nature and size lies spread before him, and could be daunted. For he will also recognise that there are no short cuts to getting at the truth of what happened here. Where local superstitions have taken root and been made to flower in a nation's finest literature they become outside the province of the anthropologist or the sceptic. Here at Glastonbury the visitor embarks on a story which will drag him along in all directions, anywhere and everywhere, from the Garden of the Hesperides to the holy stream in which strong currents of pre-Christian, Celtic-Christian and Roman-Christian enlightenment flow along together. Heady stuff lies before him. So to Tintagel, Lyonnesse, Carbonek, Joyous Gard – and Camelot, of course. Thus his best course before driving a mile is to get the hang of where he hopes to go, even if he cannot manage the full schedule. And who but an Arthurian bookworm could?

Arthur's actual origins were most likely those of a youthful charismatic resistance leader who, during a time of national confusion and despair, rallied his compatriots with a call to extol and fight for the old virtues. Using knighthood as a concept of manly perfection and a round table so that nobody could take precedence, he led his men as one among equals. After his death his character and his exploits became the favourite subject of the hearthside storytellers, gradually becoming a kind of nobly decorated truth. Soon Arthur became Britain's hero-king who had to be given a place in written history. He also became intertwined in the complex main stems of European myth. He was human and he was magic, a devotee of Christ and one who himself would return to usher in an inspired rule. In 1136 a Welshman named Geoffrey of Monmouth wrote his audacious *History of the*

British Kings, the fanciful book from which Shakespeare drew his information for *King Lear* and *Cymbeline*. The heart of this enormously influential invention is the King Arthur story, which now became official, so to speak. This *History* bred Arthur legends and Camelot books in great numbers. Three hundred years after it appeared Sir Thomas Malory re-wrote the story and William Caxton printed it, giving it the title *Le Morte Darthur*. The year was 1485, the moment when Henry VII, a Welsh or Celtic prince, captured the English throne from Richard III. Although Henry's claim was slight, this new and immensely popular version of the Arthurian tales supplied him with a splendidly patriotic ancestor, and he named his first son after the heroic knight-king, and many subsequent Princes of Wales, including the present one, were christened Arthur.

Sir Thomas Malory's *Le Morte Darthur* began to be read again in the early 19th century, with extraordinary consequences. Sir Thomas, who was as unlike the King Arthur ideal as anyone could be, having, it is said, been in and out of prison all his life for cattle rustling, rape and being on the wrong side during the civil wars of the roses, knew everything about real life, and he had turned the emblematic characters of the legend into flesh and blood men and women of fascinating complexity and motive. His account of the Arthur-Guinevere-Launcelot triangle, for instance, is heart-breaking, as is the book's understanding of the emptiness which follows the deaths of lovers. Queen Victoria and her poet laureate Alfred Tennyson had each lost the person they loved most in all the world, she her husband and he his friend Arthur Hallam. Captivated by Malory, Tennyson began his own Arthurian masterpiece, *Idylls of the King*, dedicating it to another lost leader, Prince Albert. From then on throughout Victoria's reign her poets and artists fell under the spell of Arthur and Camelot and William Morris, Thomas Hardy and Matthew Arnold all wrote magnificently on the ancient theme. Abroad, Wagner celebrated the legend in his operas *Parsifal* and *Tristan and Isold*.

The proto-scenery, as it were, of all this national hopefulness, artistry and legend is that of Cornwall. Modern archaeology and literary scholarship aside, to enter Cornwall with a bit of Malory and

Tennyson in one's head is to enter Arthur's world more positively and convincingly than anywhere else in Britain. Joyous Gard, they say, is Bamborough in Northumberland, the Astolat or Shalott is Guildford in Surrey, and so the Arthur-seeker should glimpse him in beautiful or quite ordinary places up and down the land, but to come within real seeing distance of all that clamour and all that passion one must go to Cornwall. The lengthy granite duchy with its incomparable coastline begins at the Tamar and frets into the Atlantic at Land's End. Between these last rocks and the Scillies Lyonnesse lies under the sea. This now submerged country was Tristram's home; Sir Tristram the musician whose love for Isoud, though adulterous, is not his fault.

But better begin at the Devon-Cornwall border and travel by stony and moorland degrees to where the terra firma runs out, though not the story. I like to begin at Morwenstow, the parish high up on the north Cornish coast, where Tennyson used to stay with his old friend Robert Hawker the vicar (who also wrote an Arthur book) and from there make my way down that spectacular cliff-line to Tintagel. This is the country of the local ruler and warrior whom all true Cornishmen acknowledge as an historic founder of their Celtic 'otherness', and who has little to do with the chivalric medieval figure who bestrides English literature. Its centre is Camelford, where Arthur, according to the Cornish version, fought his last battle at the nearby river crossing called Slaughterbridge, and where he lies buried under a vast tombstone. This was the battle of Camlan. Nearby on Bodmin Moor is the freshwater lake called Dozmary Pool where, again according to the Cornish account, Sir Bedivere so reluctantly threw Arthur's glorious sword and witnessed an arm reaching up to catch it. The Moor itself is covered with ancient actualities in the form of Stone Age hut sites, menhirs, strange graves and all the evidence of a long ago occupation. In the middle rises a mountain named Brown Willy from the top of which can be seen the entire geography of the once and future king – of Cornwall. It was from this remote land that the legend-makers stole a brave 6th century general and his men to turn them into national heroes, lovers and suitable ancestors for the British royal line. Or so the Cornish maintain. All that is certain is that after the last battle seven centuries were to pass before the probable defender of Cornwall was to emerge as the enchantingly improbable King of Camelot. This tale, told with such mastery by novelists, poets, composers, painters, not to mention historians, has always reminded me of what Plato called 'the noble lie'. He wrote, 'I wonder if we could contrive some magnificent myth that would in itself carry conviction to our whole community.' Sir Thomas Malory, Lord Tennyson, T. H. White, Wagner and countless unknown singers of folklore certainly have contrived a myth of such glory that, ambiguously, reality itself has come to depend upon it. It is the King Arthur of literature who has moulded the British character, not the local patriot who may be buried on the banks of the River Camel.

But when one is in Cornwall, the fiction and the facts meet as in nowhere else, not even in Glastonbury. The imaginative and the actual come together here in a way which defies scholarly separation. Summer-loads of holidaymakers pour across the open, glittering landscape to the myriad indented beaches which lie below the towering cliffs making no more lasting impression on it than confetti on pavement. Yet Arthur and Queen Guinevere, and all their company, flesh and blood creatures and not members of the monster class, like Cornwall's own regional devil Tregeagle, have left something which is indelible on this harsh and brilliant countryside. The visitor to Tintagel, Camelford and Boscastle is made eerily aware of Arthur's presence, the touristy trivialising of his legend notwithstanding. There is also a definite sense of a lingering holiness due to those marks left by the ancient Celtic Church, the granite preaching crosses which the 'local' Arthur might well have seen, and the spreading across the little fields of the beautiful names of priest-saints, such as Kew, Minver, Issey, Endellion, Tudy, Teath and Breward. It is the territory of an early Christian prince who fought to preserve a culture which still, after all these centuries, manages to show itself – sometimes in the faces of the Cornish people themselves.

The most fascinating way to approach Tintagel Castle, where Malory allowed Arthur to be conceived but which was actually a Celtic monastery when Cornwall's local hero was born, is from Damer Bay on the Camel estuary and taking in a sequence of explorations of Pentire Point, Trelights and Port Isaac on the way. From Port Isaac the hill fort aspect of Tintagel dominates the scene. The present castle was built by Reginald Earl of Cornwall in the 12th century and was a magnificent retreat for recalcitrant Plantagenet princes up to the time when Sir Thomas Malory began to weave his magic tale around it, when it began to tumble into ruin. Both Arthurs exist on this guarded height, the King from Camelot and the Celtic Warrior who prevented the forces of darkness from taking over the West. The two graves, at Glastonbury and by the River Camel, are united by a strange promise – *Hic jacet Arthurus, Rex quondam rexque futuras* (Here lies Arthur, once king, who shall be king again).

At St. Teath, where I stayed so often with a writer friend, the motto of the parish church is 'A straw for a tale bearer'. This was to fortify the locals against gossip, of course. No man or place in Britain has been subjected to such inspired tale-bearing as Camelot and King Arthur, the dream city and the dream ruler.

GEORGE HERBERT AT BEMERTON

(Introduction to *The Country Parson,* Canterbury Press, 2003)

This powerful little 'Rule' for the village clergy was published in 1652, almost twenty years after *The Temple*, George Herbert's collected poems. The latter had been handed to Arthur Woodnoth by the poet as he lay dying in Bemerton Rectory with the instruction to take them to his master Nicholas Ferrar at Little Gidding, who was to burn them if he did not find them worthy to keep. Ferrar recognised a Christian masterpiece and *The Temple* – from Psalm 29 'In his Temple doth every man speak of his honour' – appeared within weeks of Herbert's death on 1 March 1633. But there were other writings. And so there arrived by a now celebrated author, Herbert's *Remains. Or, Sundry Pieces of that Sweet Singer of the Temple, Mr George Herbert*. They included *A Priest to the Temple: or, The Country Parson*, a small book consisting of thirty-seven chapters, some of them hardly more than long paragraphs, but all of them pithy with a kind of commanding advice. All of the chapters except two begin with 'The Countrey Parson...' There follows, not a polite request or a hope, but a requirement. The parson will do this, he will be that. As his Lord's representative in the parish he has no leeway. Since, as we know, George Herbert's experience of being a country clergyman was brief in the extreme, probably no more than two years when he wrote this strict book, we might wonder at his nerve. But as we also know – it is a famous story – his own experience called for protestation. Having given up for ordination so many things to which his aristocratic background entitled him – a grand role at Cambridge, the Court, a seat in Parliament – he had asked for the living of

Fuggleston-cum-Bemerton near Salisbury, only to discover their churches tumbledown and their rectory uninhabitable. Equally ruined was his prebendal church at Leighton Bromswold near Little Gidding. And, we realise, in much the same state as many a country living up and down the land.

Had he not died just before his fortieth birthday from consumption, Herbert's *The Country Parson* would have been his clarion call to the rural Church of England to re-order itself and become worthy of its Lord. Behind its many injunctions lie his pain that things have come to such a state. Buildings apart, and no one more than he was to re-teach the sacredness which existed in church architecture, the country people themselves were unvisited, untaught, even shunned by the clergy, who found them too 'low' to know. By his insistent use of the title 'Parson', Herbert reminds each priest that he is the Person in each little community, the one man to whom all have access for their needs, spiritual and practical, altar and hearth, body and soul. An impossible task, of course, yet none must dodge the attempt. Trying to be Christ-like is what makes many a minister succeed. The twenty-first-century reader of *The Country Parson* will at first be caught up in seventeenth-century prose, though not for long. George Herbert's Rule itself soon becomes quite toughly adaptable to modern parish duties, although, as with the demands of all literary saints, common sense tells us how far we can go in carrying them out. In housekeeping terms – 'who sweeps a room, as for thy laws' – he would be enchanted by the physical state of the average country church today, each one so perfectly kept, flowers and all. But his severe requirements for the clergy still hold up an ideal. They have to do what Christ did. They must aspire to his teachings, to his actions, nothing less. 'Nothing is little in God's service', he tells some priest who senses the trivial nature of much which he is called to do. He has to be full of charity, 'It is his dominant element. His giving is in effect a sermon'. But then in Herbertian terms so is his every action and as we read on we wonder how anyone is able to endure the exposure which a village priest suffers, even now. Although as close to his flock 'as if he had begot the whole parish', he remains an outsider by virtue of his calling. All these years later we are made to recognise an isolation which R. S. Thomas would prove to be indestructible.

George Herbert's short life at Bemerton was an open book to the three hundred or so agriculturists who became his parishioners in April 1630. One might call it a field day for Anglicanism. He had married Jane Danvers his stepfather's cousin a few months earlier and was about to mend not only his 'pittiful little chappell', as John Aubrey called it, but unknown to himself many of the gaps in Anglicanism. He was ill, with tuberculosis 'working like a mole' inside him. He and his wife and their servants walked across the lane twice a day to say their prayers. On Thursdays he walked via the water meadows to Salisbury Cathedral to sing in the choir. The poetry of *The Temple* was being written. He played his lute. Christ accompanied him everywhere and in everything. His happiness and privilege overwhelmed him. And thus it was that he wrote a Rule for those who, like him, sought for what he knew to be the best of all lives, that of a country parson. No one was to tell him that he was a great religious poet or that anyone outside his parish and aristocratic circle would remember him. Where he was concerned his end was a desired simplicity and obscurity. Just his initials on the church wall said G.H. Nothing more.

But then a month or so hence the poems of *The Temple* burst out with that Herbertian cry, 'My God and King!', and with them a new understanding of priesthood in the English Church. Two decades later came a textbook for the clergy, and for us, living so much later, a vivid account of what it was like to run a parish in the post-Reformation years when so much had been changed, destroyed or abandoned, and many priests had lost their confidence, and the old parish churches themselves seemed to have lost their meaning. Tragically by 1652, when *The Country Parson* was published, these ancient buildings were to suffer a further 'cleansing' by having their window imagery smashed. When George Herbert wrote:

A man that looks on glasse,
On it may stay his eye;
Or, if he pleaseth, through it passe,

And then the heav'n espie.

he was describing the iconic purpose of stained glass. Its pictures carried the eye to the divine realities which lay behind them. Or through them. Today, none of his requirements are more carried out to the letter than those in Chapter XIII.

> The Countrey Parson hath a speciall care of his Church, that all things there be decent, and befitting his Name by which it is called [St Andrew at Bemerton]. Therefore first he takes order, that all things be in good repair; as walls plaistered, windows glazed, floore paved, seats whole, firm, and uniform, especially that the Pulpit, and Desk, and Communion Table, and Font be as they ought, for those great duties that are performed in them. Secondly, that the Church be swept, and kept cleane without dust, or Cobwebs, and at great festivalls strawed, and stuck with boughs, and perfumed with incense.

There are to be seemly carpets, fine linen, books and, high up, painted texts. All this we now easily comprehend. Enter any village church and one could not encounter better godly housekeeping. What may have slipped our notice is the status of its incumbent, which is what this little book is all about. We can imagine a young ordinand reading it and finding what is expected of him quite overwhelming. But Herbert says very few things about priestly weakness and inadequacy, and even less about scandal. His purpose is to remind the humblest village clergyman that he is Christ's right-hand man in the parish. Being this, he says, will inevitably set you apart from other men and make your life hard. Yet you must bridge this gulf and come close in Christ's love to every individual in your care.

And then we get – with still a surprising forcefulness from a writer whose background was so patrician and intellectual, who when at Cambridge drew attention to his lineage by wearing fine clothes, whose mother was at the centre of London literary life and whose brothers were at Court – as true and perceptive an account of ordinary country folk as they tilled the land as can be found at that period, accurate vignettes of them which go straight to the heart. If there is anything which proves George Herbert's total transition from what he had been to what he became at Bemerton it is this 'seeing' of his flock. The Country Parson is never to avert his gaze or withold his friendship from the worst who may be sharing his patch. They are his family in Christ and as such must be taught, fed and nursed. The parsonage itself must be a kind of open house, a holy model for the poorest cottage. He must have a knowledge of farming and must actually teach gardening. For Herbert gardens were dispensaries as well as earthly paradises, places of healing and delight. The Parson is to make the 'garden a shop' for 'home-bred medicines' and all Herbert's pleasure in flowers and expertise in herbs makes these pages especially memorable. He was himself a considerable dietitian and he believed that every country clergyman – and his wife – should know about home cures. As he practised what he preached, or wrote, we have to witness revolutionary changes at Bemerton during that short incumbency; changes which, given the popularity of *The Temple* and *The Country Parson* during the seventeenth century, would have travelled across Britain.

> Herbs gladly cure our flesh, because they
> Find their acquaintance there.

As with the Ferrars at Little Gidding, Herbert is keen on literacy and his Country Parson must educate. 'If he finds some one borrowing a Bible he gives him one for his own'. He must catechise, 'building up knowledge until it becomes a spiritual temple', and must be careful when catechising not to have a pupil learning 'by rote, as parrats, without even piercing into the sense of it'. And he the parson-teacher must learn from his parishioners what a plough, hatchet, bushel are, why boys go 'piping and dancing', and why 'country people are much addicted to old customs'. The Parson must love what they love and understand what they understand. And they, in their way, must gain some of his knowledge of religion.

The Country Parson reveals both the routine and the aspiration of a priest's life during the nervous years preceding the Civil War, but which, due to Herbert's genius and personal example, were to make their mark for generations to come. He remains enormously influential. The reader may have to update his sociology and translate his beautiful English, but his spiritual meaning grows brighter by the day. He had a passion for aphorisms and proverbs and in his witty fashion he adds to them, such as when he writes that luxury is 'a very visible sin', and that the priest has to be 'a tracker of God's ways'. Here and there we come across that authoritarianism which caused quarrels to break out between parishioners and priest, 'At Baptism he admits no vain or idle names but such as are usual and accustomed.' But then we have his radical view, 'Evident miseries have a natural privilege and exemption from all Law'. As now, he finds that 'Country people are full of petty injustices'. He has no patience with idleness, 'Even in Paradise man had a calling'. He has the poet's ear for ancient sayings. Every time a candle is brought into a room the Bemerton people say, 'God send us the light of heaven'. *The Country Parson* is part handbook, part village recording and very much part autobiography. It should be read in tandem with Herbert's poems and 'heard' when singing his hymns. These are his thoughts and hopes, his teachings and prayers for the Church of England.

GOOD TO BE ALIVE: THOMAS TRAHERNE

Thomas Traherne's world could not be in greater contrast to that of George Herbert's. But they were one in their gratitude for just being alive, Herbert ill, Traherne we may assume blooming. Death took them off before they were forty; which was thought a good age then. Herbert was a tall aristocrat from the Welsh border and Traherne a shoemaker's son from the English border. Traherne went to Oxford and Herbert to Cambridge. Traherne wrote a masterpiece for a single reader, Susanna Hopton, and Herbert trusted his entire poetry to the judgment of his schoolfriend Nicholas Ferrar. Neither would have had the least notion of their future place in English literature. Traherne called Susanna 'the friend of my best friend' – Christ. Herbert told Nicholas to put a match to his poems if he thought they were no good. No one would have heard of Traherne for hundreds of years. Herbert became famous the year he died. Traherne wrote to Susanna because he had moved from his Herefordshire parish and was no longer able to talk to her. Herbert wrote out of minute Bemerton a personal language for everyone to learn and use.

My copy of Traherne's *Poems, Centuries and Three Thanksgivings* was left to me by the poet James Turner. Like Herbert, he was consumptive, and there are snapshots of us both sitting in deckchairs on the lawn at Beichamp Walter, and later in Cornwall, one of them showing this book in James's hand. And he showing a white face and frailty after an attack. He also left his different sounds in my head, the rattle of his typewriter, which was like that of a tiny concrete mixer, the crash of his spade – he was a constant maker of gardens – and his beautiful voice. We both admired Anne Ridler's Introduction to Traherne and parts of it entered our vocabulary. We very much liked her discovery of his lack of emphasis on sin, I remember. She calls him 'the master of the affirmative way which pursues perfection through delight in the created world'. She goes on, 'Every emphasis in his writings is on inclusive love' and that 'one has only to read the *Centuries* alongside other religious writings of his time to see how unusual he was in the lack of emphasis on sin. The affirmations of the *Centuries* may seem to diverge from the central theme of mysticism, as expressed by St John of the Cross, that the soul must free itself from the love of created beings, for Traherne boldly says, "Never was any thing in this World loved too much". But he continues, "Many things have been loved in a false way and in all too short a Measure".'

Throughout Traherne we catch the voices of earlier and future poets. It is strange and delightful. There is no exactly making him out. Where has he come from? Where is he going? To use a sensuous Herbertian noun he is an enticer. He precedes Wordsworth when he writes, 'A meditationary inward eye/Gazing at quiet did within me lie' and Blake when he says, 'You never enjoy the world aright, till you see how a sand exhibiteth the wisdom and the power of God'.

I find him the supreme poet of childhood. He is at play all his life. Boys and girls run through his theology as they ran through his Hereford. His work is actually a playground for his beliefs. It is tumultuous with Christians bursting from the schools and into the countryside, there to collect anything that nature offered. The first half of the seventeenth century was the time to make a collection. It was the fashion for connoisseurs to turn their rooms into what they called 'cabinets of treasure'. George Herbert, a botanist, was more a collector of 'my stock of natural delights' which included 'Lillies on the Rivers side' (flags on the Nadder below his garden?), 'The crown Imperiall' and the tricky 'Sycomore'. But especially herbs.

Herbs gladly cure our flesh; because that they
  Finde their acquaintance there.
  For us the windes do blow,
The earth doth rest, heav'n move, and fountains flow,
  Nothing we see, but means our good,

As our *delight*, or as our *treasure*:
The whole is, either our cupboard of *food*,
Or cabinet of *pleasure*.

Traherne's *Centuries* is such a cabinet. It contains all creation and everything given and possessed in love. Critics used to prefer his prose-poetry to his poems and even Anne Ridler denies the latter 'a complete formal perfection'. But this to me is their enchantment. She adds that he has 'an honourable place in the line of poets, from Dante to Edwin Muir, who have held and renewed the vision of childhood'. Traherne dislikes to find manufactured objects in his Eden – 'those little, new, invented things which all our happiness destroys' because 'nor Saints, nor little Boys, nor Angels made them, only foolish men'. He himself was a child with very little so he had to fill the spaces with his imagination. 'Once I remember, I think I was about four year old, when I reasoned with myself sitting in a little obscure room in my father's poor house, that if God is the source of infinite riches, and loves me, how comes it that I am so poor?'

Still a boy, he experiences the kind of wretchedness which overcomes us when we are young, the kind which John Bunyan felt when he wrote, 'Another time ... there fell upon me a great cloud of darkness'. 'Another time', says Traherne, 'in a lowering, sad evening, being alone in the field, when all things were dead and quiet, a certain want and horror fell upon me, beyond imagination. The unprofitableness and silence of the place dissatisfied me, its wideness terrified me as from the utmost ends of the earth fears surrounded me ... I was a weak and little child, and had forgotten that there was a man alive in the earth. Yet something also of hope and expectation comforted me from every border. Soon, comfort of houses and friends, and the clear assurance of treasures everywhere, God's care and love, his goodness, wisdom and power, his presence and his watchfulness would be my strength'. Later, Traherne would list his childhood possessions, a drum, a fine coat, a penny, a gilded hook, adding, 'the glass of imagination was my only mirror'. But what an imagination. It is unique among Christian writers. What Traherne saw in the

Herefordshire countryside, in Oxford, in London and finally at Teddington was God with boys and girls, love in the trees and meadows, and beneficence in the universe. His fancifulness halts the learned reader:

If that be all, shine forth and draw me neigher;
Let me behold and die, for my desire
Is phoenix-like to perish in the fire.

Long before either George Herbert or Thomas Traherne had so intensely sought the face of the Lord, a little much-imprisoned Spanish priest had written:

Oh lamps of fiery blaze
To whose refulgent fuel
The deepest caverns of my soul grow bright,
Late blind with gloom and haze.
But in this strange renewal
Giving to the belov'd both heat and light.

What peace, with love enwreathing.
You conjure to my breast
Which only you your dwelling place may call:
While with delicious breathings
In glory, grace and rest,
So daintily in love you make me fall!

It was unlikely that Herbert or Traherne would have heard of St John of the Cross, who died in 1591, but his modern translator Roy Campbell would protest how their contemporary theologians would exclude mysticism, and how many Roman Catholic divines would prefer the practice of virtue than that of searching for Christ as a lover, and to enjoy – a favourite word of Traherne's – everything which told of this love. The Spanish poet had quite extravagantly enjoyed his Christ in the woodlands of Baeza and by the River Guadalimar. George

Herbert wrote many of his poems on the Wiltshire plain and by the River Nadder which flowed through his beloved garden. And Traherne wrote his amazing love-letter to God wherever his brief life took him, famously beginning it with that stunning piece of prose:

> The Corn was Orient and Immortal Wheat, which never should be reaped, nor was ever sown. I thought it had stood from Everlasting to Everlasting. The Dust and Stones of the Street were as Precious as GOLD. The Gates were at first the End of the World, The Green Trees when I saw them first through one of the Gates Transported and Ravished me; their Sweetness and unusual Beauty made my Heart to leap and almost mad with Extasie, they were such strange And Wonderful Things: the Men! O what Venerable and Reverend Creatures did the Aged seem! Immortal Cherubims! And yong Men Glittering and Sparkling Angels and Maids strange Seraphick Pieces of Life and Beauty! Boys and Girles Tumbling in the Street, and Playing, were moving Jewels. I knew not that they were Born or should Die. But all things abided Eternally as they were in their proper Places. Eternity was Manifest in the Light of the Day, and something infinite Behind every thing appeared: which talked with my Expectation and moved my Desire. The Citie [Hereford] seemed to stand in Eden, or to be built in Heaven. The Streets were mine, the Temple [Hereford Cathedral] was mine, the People were mine, their Clothes and Gold and Silver was mine, as much as their Sparkling Eyes fair Skins and ruddy faces. The Skies were mine and so were the Sun and Moon and Stars, and all the World was mine, and I the only Spectator and Enjoyer of it. I knew no Churlish Proprieties, nor Bounds, nor Divisions: but all Proprieties and Divisions were mine; all Treasures and the Possessors of them So that with much more adoe I was corrupted; and made to learn the Dirty Devices of this World. Which now I unlearn, and become as it were a little Child again, that I may enter into the Kingdom of GOD.

All the great mystic writers seem to discover this Kingdom via the enchantments of physical nature. Travelling through the home scenery presents them with the metaphors for what they must eventually come to after mortality. The Church has been scandalised or bewildered by earth-lovers and earth-appreciators, and by a companionable Christ who steps it out with his friends on their way to work or play. The critic

Peter Malekin put it like this:

> Traherne's *Centuries* are a series of meditations turning on the recognition that as God's child he has the access to all the riches of God manifest throughout creation, his conscious enjoyment of these being the fulfilment of their purpose, an expression of the mutual love between him and God, and the key to an unbounded felicity, itself the gift of God ... The *Centuries* are written in a strange and manly but curiously worked prose which conveys a vivid sense of illumination and peace. It deals with the unadulterated joy in the world – which he experienced in childhood and which he has refound in his mature vision of the world as the gleaming manifestation of God.

Traherne in fact has to be read now in tandem with our concern for nature.

Sometimes I walk in a great meadow near the Essex-Suffolk border where many thousands of green-winged orchids are in bloom and are hedged in by may blossom and young oak leaves, and over which the larks sing all day long, and I think of Traherne as well as my old friend Richard Mabey. The two of them join hands here.

Centuries is made up of five meditations on the divine love of all that God has created, on ordinary human love and on the adoration of the natural world. It is today's environmentalist's Book of Psalms. It says what we walkers of the earth cannot or dare not say. Running through them is Traherne's active pleading for leisure. Given a chance he would have done no work at all, life being so brief and nature so enchanting. He would have liked to spend all of it lying under a tree gazing through its leaves at the sky, listening to birdsong, smelling the crushed flowers under his body, spreading his fingers in the surrounding grass and just dreaming. But as we know, as well as writing the strangest holy love letters to Mrs Hopton, he toiled hard as a theologian and as secretary to Sir Orlando Bridgeman, Lord Keeper of the Great Seal. And even when he no longer served as a parish priest he continued to he a 'minister' wherever he went. The swiftly advancing science of astronomy fascinated him and, looking up as he always did, he remarked, 'The world is not this little cottage of heaven and earth'. Rome was at that moment prosecuting scientists for insisting as much.

Traherne detested what we call consumerism, though not for the same reason. He liked to quote Socrates in the market-place at Athens – 'Good gods, ... who would have thought there were so many things in the world which I do not want!' Traherne admired the simplicity of man's first home and objected to its being cluttered. Was not the world but 'a beautiful frontispiece to eternity'? Yet he has his wants and makes long lists of them, like a boy at Christmas. He justifies them because God himself wants. For one thing he wants Thomas Traherne. God wants 'Angels and men, images, companions – all the joys of the Tree of Life'. Therefore, he tells us via Susanna Hopton, you must want like a God. 'Be sensible of your wants, that you may be sensible of your treasures.' He adds, 'It was his wisdom made you need the sun. It was his goodness made you need the sea. Be sensible of what you need ... wants are the bands and cements between God and us'. 'I want, I want', says the Creator, 'I want, I want!' says his child. It is in the first *Century* that Traherne venerates the Cross, man's chief possession, the thing that he must have, must want above all else:

> The Cross is the Abyss of Wonders, the Centre of Desires, the Schole of Virtues, the Hous of Wisdom, the Throne of Lov, the Theatre of Joys and the Place of Sorrows; it is the Root of Happiness, and the Gate of Heaven.

In the second *Century* the poet's imagery runs even more riot as he analyses and catalogues the divine love. 'It is the true Means by which the World is enjoyed. Our Lov to others and others Lov to us. We ought therefore above all Things to get acquainted with the Nature of Lov ... You are as prone to Lov as the Sun is to shine...'

But it is in the third *Century* that Traherne reverts so movingly to his innocence, a little Herefordshire boy who was entertained like an Angel with the Works of God ... [Nature] could not make more Melody to Adam than to me'. And what Rule do you think I walked by? Truly a Strange one, but the Best in the Whole World. I was Guided by an

Implicit Faith in Gods Goodness: and therefore led to the Study of the most Obvious and Common Things ... Air, Light, Heaven and Earth, Water, the Sun, Trees, Men and Women, Cities, Temples, etc.' He writes a poem for the psalmist David, his chief mentor, because he sings nature, and he paraphrases his favourite psalm for Susanna. David's songs were the holy pop of the mid-seventeenth century. Their Middle Eastern imagery was easily translated to the British countryside. The army sang them, the Scots rhymed them and children were made to learn them by heart. They would stream through literature feeding the imagination of Christopher Smart, John Clare, Thomas Hardy and W. H. Auden, as well as becoming a hold-all of words for every occasion. Traherne decided that David 'had a Deep and Perfect Sence', a king-poet-shepherd-warrior who lived in a real place, such as the Welsh border. Traherne had what he modernly called a 'thirst' for news from David's land.

News from a foreign Country came,
As if my Treasure and my Wealth lay there:
So much it did my Heart Enflame!

And it was David who began to bring it to Herefordshire in his poetry. Traherne's own poems, only moderately liked by Anne Ridler but loved by me, are the kind of writing which keeps one on the edge of the seat. My favourite is 'Shadows in the Water', an *Alice Through the Looking-glass* contemplation. Tom stands by a puddle looking down 'Where Skies beneath us shine':

O ye that stand upon the Brink,
Whom I so near me, through the Chink,
With Wonder see: What Faces there,
Whose Feet, whose Bodies, do ye wear?
  I my Companions see In You, another Me.
  They seemed Others, but are We;
Our second Selvs those Shadows be.

About the same time that Traherne was being intrigued by puddles, John Bunyan, a decade or so older, and going through the religious crisis which would produce that masterpiece *Grace Abounding*, was testing God with them:

Wherefore, while I was thus considering [whether he had true faith] and being put to my plunge about it, for you must know, that as yet I had in this matter broken my mind to no man, only did hear and consider, the tempter came in with his delusion, That there was no way for me to know that I had faith, but by trying to work some miracle; urging those Scriptures that seem to look that way, for the enforcing and strengthening his temptation. Nay, one day as I was betwixt Elstow and Bedford, the temptation was hot upon me to try if I had faith, by doing some miracle; which miracle at that time was this, I must say to the puddles that were in the horse pads, Be dry; and to the dry places, Be you the puddles. And truly, one time I was a-going to say so indeed; but just as I was about to speak, this thought came into my mind, But go under yonder hedge and pray first, that God would make you able.

Traherne's God, by contrast, offered a little boy a puddle of delights.

Of all the Play-mates which I knew
That here I do the Image view
In other Selves; what can it mean?
But that below the purling Stream
  Som unknown Joys there be
  Laid up in Store for me;
To which I shall, when that thin Skin
Is broken, be admitted in.

In another childhood poem, 'On Leaping over the Moon', it is Tom's brother Philip who must take care not to 'drop through that thin Element/into a fathomless Descent', he being far above the earth's sky. The brothers have been brought to Hereford from Lugwardine by their prosperous uncle the innkeeper and are comforted to discover that their home moon has come with them.

Brought home from Nurse, going to the door
To do some little thing
He must not do within,
[Philip] With Wonder cries,
As in the Skies
He saw the Moon, *O yonder is the Moon*
Newly come after me to Town,
That shin'd at Lugwardin but yesternight,
Where I enjoy'd the self-same light.

The fourth and fifth *Centuries* are about active happiness and enjoying God. Traherne might be thought prophetic when he writes, 'My love is a spring shut up, a fountain sealed. It is shut up like letter, and concealed, yet in the kingdom of heaven its contents and secrets shall be known'. One has only to alter the address from heaven to a second-hand bookshop in the Farringdon Road where his work had indeed been a fountain sealed, and shut up like a letter for two hundred years. Bertram Dobell 'opened' Thomas Traherne to an amazed literary – and religious – readership in 1903, and the beneficent dictums tumbled from it with more optimism than anyone had dared to imagine, let alone to advise. A question which may well be asked of us when we leave this scene is, 'Why did you not more enjoy the natural world?' At the very least, says Traherne, 'Love is a phoenix that will revive in its own ashes, inherit death, and smell sweetly in the grave'.

RICHARD MABEY AT SELBORNE

I first saw Selborne during a journey to Cornwall. It was usual then to drive from Suffolk to the Lizard and see a friend en-route. So we stayed the night at Sparrow's Hanger with the poet Anthony Rye. Gilbert White had left Sparrow's Hanger with its 'beechen grove' to his brother Benjamin. Our friend's house, built about 1900, leaned from its side and my room seemed to be palely coloured by its association with dense trees. In the morning we went in search of White but as Anthony Rye said:

He is not in the Hanger
 Nor down the Lyth at all,
Nor is he in his garden,
 By the ha-ha wall;
Under the yew he stands not –
 One of a hundred shadows,
Paces now no footpath
 Through familiar meadows,
The churchyard conceals him not –
 Least of all there:
He who is in all things
 Is not anywhere.
Seek him in the contour
 Of the unbroken hill
Find him in the silence,
 The continuant rill;
His the life and habit
 Of the tended place,

And the modest mountain
Tells his eager face.

Years later, after the Great Gale which laid low so many mighty woods, Richard Mabey brought me a log from the yew under which Gilbert White liked to sit. It acts as a bookend in my study, propping up Kilvert's *Diary*. Downstairs in what I grandly call the library – really the old apple-room freshly shelved – stand a little row of White's *Selborne*, including one edited by Richard, and by their side his biography of the naturalist. It is now just over two hundred years since an elderly Hampshire curate took the liberty of 'laying before the public his idea of parochial history'. The idea was novel and the public was that small erudite readership which habitually subscribed to the works of scholarly clergymen. In no circumstance could White or his first readers have imagined that, within a generation, this record of the weather, birds, flowers and creatures generally in his parish would stand in popularity next to the *King James' Bible*, the *Book of Common Prayer* and John Bunyan's *Pilgrim's Progress*.

Gilbert White started to write a journal when he was fifteen but it was not until he was thirty that he began to create *The Garden Kalendar*, the first of his formal accounts of what was happening all around him. It was by no means confined to gardening. Into it there crept every living thing which populated Selborne, including its human beings. He was a collector of all that existed around him, putting his finds together with that odd mixture of artistry, taste and scientific precision which still makes him unique among naturalist-diarists. In 1767 a friend of his brother Benjamin, the Fleet Street bookseller, sent White a beautiful diary which was set out in divisions for recording rainfall and temperature, etc. It had a page for each week and an inviting right-hand column for 'Miscellaneous Observations and Memorandums'. This empty book was the invention of the Hon. Daines Barrington, who gave it to White, having heard of his recording habits. But it was not long before White found its ruling restricting. His diary burst from its bonds and spread to its margins and end-papers – every blank space. Other naturalists were filling-up similar forms at this time and producing useful records. But great diarists and scrupulous form-fillers are opposites and one of the delights of Gilbert White for generations of his readers is to watch him spreading himself – to see him bursting the banks, or covers.

As Richard Mabey says, 'It is possible to read the journals as a simple historical record of natural events, and spanning forty years without a break ... yet it is the lucidity and resonance of the best of his entries that are his most important legacy. Stripping away pastoral allusions, adjectival excess, self-examination, searches for meaning, he distilled a form of spare, literary miniature which had an immediacy not seen in this kind of English prose before ... Yet it is doubtful if White saw his journals as "writing" in any literary sense. For him, I think, they were his intellectual ledger, where he took stock of his understanding of the physical world. They always have this probing, investigative sense about them that lifts them beyond merely passive records: "Thatched roofs smoke in the sun; when this appearance happens rain seldom ensues that day. This morning they sent up vast volumes of reek" (14 November 1777). The tone and structure of this note aren't really those of a casual diary entry. The details are too carefully selected and ordered, as if they were part of the answer to a larger, half-formed question.'

Seeded in the journal is much of *The Natural History of Selborne*. The journal itself lay dormant until 1931, when it was edited and published by Walter Johnson. In 1988 came Francesca Greenoak's entrancing edition, and so we are able to examine the lavish source from which White drew his shining classic. Walking with Richard Mabey in Selborne, joining Anne Mallinson's writers' circle there, starting our lifetime's friendship, were huge diary entries in themselves. I like the way in which Richard 'met' White, brushing Time away and not knowing that he and this old naturalist were linked by a youthful eagerness. He said how he admired White's 'vivid, sensuous attentiveness' although he might have been describing himself. He liked his quick village lad's eye for anything which arrived on his little scene or vanished from it. I have always thought one reason for White's lasting popularity is his ability to reconcile us to death. His rich accounts of Nature's senescence includes human mortality and somehow the latter loses its importance. Being a priest one might have expected him to preach, but he never does. An insect has its hour, its day. Timothy his tortoise has an age which he sleeps away. The parishioners tumble into their churchyard beds and become part of Selborne's compost as their souls rise with the larks. Anthony Rye wrote about the sparrows of Sparrow Hanger, about their 'dullest of voices' although 'How you would miss it if it never recurred'. And, amazing how it would have been to him, we now do miss it.

The Whites had lived in Selborne for generations. Gilbert, born in the Vicarage in 1720, would have succeeded to the living had he not gone to the wrong Oxford college, Oriel instead of Magdalen, which held the patronage. At first it rankled a bit, as did failures in other directions. Known as 'Busser' White when a student because he was always kissing girls, there was nothing at the start which said that here was the man who would revolutionise the study of English natural history. It all began when he started to garden at The Wakes, one of the White's houses and he wrote his first entry in Daines Barrington's *Garden Kalendar*. It was about planting Spanish beans and the date was Jan. 7th 1751. The format of *The Natural History of Selborne* would take a very different line, that of letters which White wrote to Daines Barrington and to another friend Thomas Pennant. An epistolary response was to become an original aspect of eighteenth century literature.

White's main advice to the world was to go outside and look, smell, feel, listen. Some of his readers would liked to have seen more of his neighbours but none can accuse him of neglecting Britain's chief interest, the weather. This, he maintained, was part of a district's natural history and his successors still take a front seat in journalism. Richard Mabey and I have tramped around in all weathers, lightly clad – none of that gear – but in shirt and jeans and with roving eyes and binoculars, halts and discoveries. And this for decades. White was rarely inside and his villagers must have wondered what on earth he was looking for. Mercifully, the clergy were allowed to be strange, even mad. The one thing I envy him for is to see 'my weeding women'.

Selborne was odd enough in White's day and far from being the typical Georgian village. For one thing it had never had a squire. For another its landscape was both deeply sunken and dizzily raised, and thus difficult to enter where coaches were concerned. Nearly everyone lived in a good stone or brick house, and in a kind of seclusion from the rest of Hampshire. Its curate existed in a natural theatre where the entire drama of Nature was staged for him. He could have given us, his future devotees, a tolerable idyll. But Richard, in his biography, sees something very different. He sees a kind of rural freedom which was unknown to the larger English countryside at that date. George Crabbe's Suffolk parishioners rush from their grim toil now and then to botanise with their parson or run after butterflies, and momentarily escape from their 'condition'. But in Crabbe's hard-hitting lines there is none of that commonly-breathed air which seemed to have blown through White's Selborne.

Anthony Rye once descended from Sparrow Hanger to pay homage to Gilbert White's yew when the bough from which Richard gathered my bookend was still leafing:

Time in the circle of these boughs we see
Turned to a monolith or stone-hard tree,
And yet its course upon it seems to be
Molten, like a river's, written free.

YOUNG MR KILVERT

(*The Kilvert Society Journal* 1997)

Perhaps as with so many diaries Kilvert's was a gesture against oblivion. It is certainly an outlet for longings and emotion. V. S. Pritchett saw it as a deliberate work of art – of literature. No scribbled account of the day before the candle was snuffed, the wick turned low. For it holds the kind of information which takes time to select, order and craft. There is a noticeable care in what had to be put in and what must be omitted. Kilvert comes across, often helplessly, not only as a young clergyman with strong pastoral gifts which are modestly handed out to whoever is in need of them, but also with observations and complexities which might better serve a poet or novelist. The fact is that in his diary he intended to be – and succeeded in being – a good writer. Although he wrote for himself alone, and out of the necessity, as with all diarists, to say, 'I was here', one senses an unconfessed hope that other eyes will read him. Even a remarkable literary neighbour of his, Thomas Traherne, though one he did not know existed, wrote a masterpiece for a single reader, his friend Mrs Hopton. Indeed, Francis Kilvert admitted the half hope that, long after he was no more, another would open his private book and wonder about him. What *we* wonder is what the rest of it contained, for his widow destroyed a large part of it and then, as late as 1938 and after William Plomer had made his classic selection from what was left, a Mrs Essex Hope who had inherited the manuscript, 'had done away with it', believing it the right thing to do. William Plomer said, 'he could have strangled her with his own hands'. Mrs Hope, under her maiden name Essex Smith, wrote and published romances. For her the strange romances and real story of Kilvert's short life should never have appeared on the page.

E. M. Forster liked to describe his friend the poet Cavafy as 'A Greek gentleman standing at an angle to the universe'. Francis Kilvert is an English gentleman who is decidedly standing at an angle to his, though without knowing it. His vision of the parish is he believes quite normal and ordinary, and he himself an ordinary country curate, a quite usual member of a race which over-manned the nineteenth century Church of England. Yet how could he not have seen, working so creatively at his diary for hours on end, that he was also an artist? The entries are finely fashioned and the gradual exposure of himself on the page no ordinary self-portrait. He is class-confident yet somehow cut off from the warmth and protection of orthodoxy. Kilvert's close yet unaware near encounters with two great writers, Thomas Traherne and Thomas Hardy, have always intrigued me. One bitterly cold March afternoon we find him in Credenhill church, looking around, and then looking out onto the 'lovely views of the Black Mountains with snow patches, the Golden Fawr and the Skyridd ... Little Brinsop lay peacefully below among the meadows of Brinsop Vale.' It was the view which another young priest saw as he wrote the masterpiece now called *Centuries*, a book which lay hidden for over two hundred years until it was found on a London bookstall in the 1890s. Traherne and Kilvert, waiting-to-be-read geniuses in the same country church one Victorian afternoon! Two hundred years earlier, during the 1650s, Traherne said that being alive in the world was such a beautiful thing that he wished he could lie under a tree all his life and just take it all in, the shade, the sunshine, the God who made it, this earthly paradise, this Herefordshire. And the Reverend Francis Kilvert who, when he left his parish, felt that he must pay homage to it in the local paper, the *Hereford Times*:

Oh, Clyro Water! ceaselessly
For seven sweet years my lullaby;
My life, my love, my footsteps free
For seven sweet years have been by thee

Sweet Clyro Water! Oh let me still

By thy banks remembered be,
And keep yet as thy grasses, green,
The love for me that once has been!

Well, his wish has been amply answered. Traherne died aged thirty-six and Kilvert aged thirty-nine. Their life here lay buried but now spreads before us in dewy freshness in works of literature which must be reckoned among the highest kind of serendipity. Winter or summer, we feel their weather on our faces, their thankfulness for nature.

Kilvert's unaware brush with Thomas Hardy is even more intriguing. During a visit to Dorset the Rector of Fordington, the Reverend Henry Moule, took him to meet William Barnes. It was May-day eve 1874. Kilvert had already written a Traherne-like description of the county:

The pimpernel blazed in the grass with wide open scarlet eyes, and the woods were lighted in their dark green depths by the scarlet bunches of rowan berries. The scent of hay came mixed with the aromatic odour of the fir trees drawn out by the sun ... In a field among the woods the flax sheaves stood in shocks like wheat, the fine-hung bells on their wiry hairy stalks rustling and quaking in the breeze like wag wantons ... In the afternoon I went to pay a visit to the lime avenue. It looked more like a vast church than ever and the strong low sunlight which came up from the green isle seemed to be pouring through a great distant window.

He called Barnes 'the great idyllic poet of England'. We have no idea whether Barnes or Moule told Kilvert of their connection with a neighbour who was exactly the diarist's age, Thomas Hardy. Barnes had taught the young novelist – he had just published *Far from the Madding Crowd* – and so in a different sense had Horace, Mr Moule's son who only a few months previously had committed suicide at Cambridge. Kilvert was profoundly moved when Mr Moule sat at Barnes's piano and sang 'with a sweet melodious voice' a tragic song he had composed for his poor son, 'Lord I love thee'. We don't know if Kilvert had read *Far From the Madding Crowd*, his diary shows little interest in books. We know that he read Keats's *Hyperion* to his mother and Trollope to himself, and that typical of Victorian parsons he was not above doling out moralising slush to the villagers, and even writing embarrassingly about the virtue of honest toil for the working class:

> Honest work is always holy,
> Howsever hard and lowly.
> Envy not the rich, the great,
> Wealthier in your low estate,
> Nobler through your workful days,
> Happier in your simple ways,
> Well beloved of God must be
> Holy men of low degree.

What a distance this is to George Herbert's still acceptable:

> Teach me, my God and King,
> In all things thee to see ...
> A servant with this clause
> Makes drudgery divine;
> Who sweeps a room, as for thy laws
> Makes that and the action fine.

But being a parson, Kilvert was to take every advantage of the entrée he had to this world of ceaseless toil. In his handbook for the country clergy, George Herbert had long ago laid down the laws for visiting even the worst of hovels. Never mind their stink – and aways wear a clean cassock. Kilvert was doubly drawn to this duty to visit the poor, first by a sincere desire to bring what he understood to be heaven into their lives, and by something even more powerful, a writer's keenness to witness what human beings got up to. He was more class-aware than conventionally class-conscious. He was good and kind, physically attractive and helpful, and – welcome. It is the latter quality which shines in the diary, his own welcome to everything he saw or did. His diary is the most open account of the priest as visitor which we have. Kilvert might now and then out of curiosity go in search of a character but usually his mind works best when he is doing his humdrum duty. He invades cottage rooms at some intimate moment, but stays. It is as though their inhabitants need his close attention. If he was now and again bustled out and told to come back in an hour, or tomorrow, he doesn't say so. Whatever it is that is going on when he opens the door – goes on. Poverty and pain as well as private matters go on, as do mad customs. And tall stories. And how at ease he was. 'Mr Kilvert! Mr Kilvert!' shouted the children when they heard his knock. Some of the houses were bursting with health, others stale with misery, and with death hanging about them. Nobody knew that he was saving up what he saw and heard for his quiet study and the lamplight, every precious scrap. The entries are compelling:

> Visited Edward Williams, the man ill of rheumatic fever at the Swan. He said he was better. We talked of the extraordinary wet weather and floods. He said the Wye was a very 'wild river' some years ago and all the valley was frequently flooded in the winter and under water from the Hay up to Llyswen ... Perhaps on account of the cutting of the horseshoe lower down the river at Letton or Stanton ... he recollected the fearful flood at Hay at 8 o'clock in the morning after the waterspout had burst in the night, the furniture whirling down the river with trees, bushes, beams and fragments of the cottage, and the one-armed body of Mrs Lawrence being taken out of the river.

The Swan inn at Clyro was a nuisance, being so near his house, but, 'Last night was very quiet, marvellously quiet and peaceful. No noise, no rowing or fighting whatever and no men, as there sometimes are lying by the roadside all night drunk, cursing, muttering, maundering and vomiting.' We have a tendency to read Kilvert's Diary as an idyll, but it is in many ways a shocking and unsparing description of the Victorian village. There is a slum near his lodgings where sordid women lean from doors and windows and momentarily cease from yelling to listen to a bit of gossip. He sees degradation, ignorance and filth. He calls on Mrs Parker and her 'dwarf' child Emily who is an object of local mockery, telling the little girl 'not to mind' and that she has a beautiful noble spirit caged in a poor deformed stunted body. He walks on to old Layer in his den who is 'unkempt, unshaven, shaggy and grey like a wild beast' and reads to him Father Faber's hymn about the Good Shepherd. Then on to Mrs Thomas 'still on her feet' but in daily expectation. Her children come trooping in from school and are hungry for their tea. Then on to his 'little darling Polly Sackville' to hear news of Mary of Penhan, 'only nineteen last August' but dying from TB. On and on he strides, with Wales rising up before him, energetically passing from wit to horror, from lovely girls to old hags. Girls give him kisses, boys a bit of cheek. 'At Newgate an urchin three feet high was swinging a gate. "Well," said I, "and how are you?" "Pretty well, thank you, how's yourself?"' But painful snubs are too interesting not to be recorded.

During his Cornish holiday in 1870 'the youngest girl, Agatha, I think, planted herself before me and demanded impetuously and imperiously in a loud voice, "What do you want?" "A kiss", said I mischievously, whereat she flung off in high disdain without a word.' Something 'knowing' in the Henry James sense is happening and the thirty year-old Kilvert speculates uncomfortably on what he calls 'young lady affectations, peculiarities, vagaries, &c., &c.' being 'unintelligible'. The Cornish schoolgirls he chats to at the forge whilst the carriage tyre is being mended do not have these affectations 'and reminded me of some of my Clyro pets'. The Cornish holiday itself is the sum of every Cornish holiday starting with the thrilling sight of the cliff-hung railway at Dawlish and continuing with a glimpse of what will be Virginia Woolf's lighthouse at Godrevy, the wretched sea fogs, the terrifying cliffs and the curious feeling of being abroad whilst still in England. Frederick Grice, Kilvert's biographer, lamented a little that Kilvert did not accept the living at Cannes, for then we would have had an account of the Riviera in its British heyday. As it was, his acceptance of Bredwardine and Brobury in 1877 seems to his readers a fatal move towards extinction. He was prophetic about his death at the very start of the Diary, when a parishioner dies instantly from a burst stomach ulcer and he says, 'how absolutely unconscious one may be of carrying one's death warrant about in an unsuspected disease that may bring an end at any moment.'

But two days later Kilvert is all life and vitality as he creates one of his fine set pieces, rural writing which can claim a place beside that of Dorothy Wordsworth, Flora Thompson and John Clare. Such extended essays are frequent in the Diary. It is as if he has put aside the daily task of putting down what happened to him as faithfully as he could, and moved on into the writer's craft proper. Now and then he could be working on a short story. Now and then he dashes off a series of brilliant notes. Here he is on 22 March 1870:

The Clyro women stride about the village like storks. The industrious blacksmith chinks away at his forge night and morning late and early, and the maidens and mothers go up and down the water steps with their pitchers continually. Heavy loads of timber, large long trees on the timber carriages grinding through Clyro village every evening from Cross Ffordd and Cabalva.

It is the setting for some drama, some revelation, but it is left to the reader what to put in it. Here is a passage like the opening of a novel, written when he was thirty:

Faint sunshine on Bryngwyn Hill and a cold cheery gleam of water from the great peat bog below the edge of which stands the grey cluster of buildings and the tall dark yew of Llanshifr. I went down there and waded across the yard to the house through a sea of mud and water. The kitchen was very dark, the bank rising steep in front of the window. Mrs Morgan gave me some tea and cake. On the settle sat a man perfectly still, silent and in such a dark corner that I could not see his face. Morgan showed me the remains of the moat, where the Scotch pedlar was hidden after being murdered for the sake of his pack while lodging in the house and where his skeleton was found when the moat was cleared out. The moat that is left is a broad deep formidable ditch and a rather long pond at one end of the house and full of water. Llanshifr a fearfully wet swampy place, almost under water and I should think very unhealthy. One of the twin yews was lately blown down and cut up into gate posts which will last twice as long as oak. The wood was so hard that Morgan said it turned many of the axes as if they were made of lead. I wonder in which of these yews Gore hid the penknife before his death which made him restless as hidden iron is said to do, and caused his spirit to come back rummaging about the house ... It was getting dusk as I left Llanshifr and after I had plunged about for some time in the swampy Wern up to my ankles in water I lost my bearings and the welcome clank of plough chains on the team came down home and Joe the Llanshifr ploughman directed me up to Holly House. Struck over the top of Vicar's Hill and as I passed Cross Ffordd the frogs were croaking, snoring and bubbling in the pool under the full moon.

Violence, rough farming, ignorance, with just a veneer of church teaching, this is what Kilvert sees. In contrast there is the culture to which he belongs, the rectories and big houses, the parties and the ladies. Where the latter are concerned – and their mothers – curates are two a penny and he may be handsome but he cannot get very far. So what his Diary famously reveals is a strong sexuality without an outlet. Writing it down is a help. And when at long last he does marry, he dies. The Diary reveals him as a conventionally religious person whose work takes him into wild situations. He calls it 'villaging'. He becomes the determined intruder, an adventurer along the footpaths, a watcher of lives which fascinate him but which he instinctively realises are beyond his jurisdiction and outside his experience. He is no reformer and he shows no indignation at the plight of so many of his neighbours, only a tenderness and a pity. The beauty of the young, boys and girls, overwhelms him and he adores their hair and eyes, and shares to an alarming degree their innocence and vulnerability. It makes them easy with him. He could be called a traveller in a barbarous country, a holy man protected by the heavy respect of the parish for the clergy.

V. S. Pritchett says that 'One likes him in the end ... because, entirely without self-importance or self-consciousness, he is serious about himself. That supremely difficult art! It is the special triumph of Kilvert's sincerity that he has conveyed and made credible *his* kind of feeling and whose notions of love are totally alien to those of a bubbling young mid-Victorian curate... We have lost the art of rendering pure sentiment and the feeling for such a tenderness as Kilvert's. When we contrast the note and rhythm of our lives with his we see there is more than a change of fashion between the generations. We perceive with a shock that it is we who are unnatural.'

I quote Pritchett because he, more than any other good writer who has been drawn to comment on Kilvert, and including William Plomer himself, saw that the supreme accomplishment of this diarist was to recognise the quality of his seriousness. What Kilvert seriously tells us, we have trouble in accepting. His being so young yet so complacent about the degradation on his doorstep, his religion which has no intention of moving mountains, his eroticism. Yet the truthfulness of it all! Would all those destroyed notebooks have provided another Kilvert? Those about his marriage to Elizabeth in particular? Almost certainly not. The marriage lasted a little over a month before peritonitis bore him away to a spot he had chosen himself in Bredwardine churchyard. There was no singing at the funeral. It was rainy and dark. Boys and girls dropped flowers into the grave. Robert Francis was thirty-eight. His widow returned home to Oxfordshire in 'overwhelming and inexpressible sorrow'. An anonymous poem appeared in the *Hereford Times*:

> The Marriage feast was spread. With his fair young wife,
> The joyous Bridegroom sat, while each young heart
> Look'd forward to a long and happy life,
> To which true love should fragrant bloom impart.
>
> The Marriage feast was spread in Courts above.
> 'Let him I love be with Me where I am!'
> The Saviour said. He pass'd from human love
> To share the Marriage Supper of the Lamb.

Bredwardine Rectory was filled with wedding presents and the village itself with dismantled triumphant arches.

In the study in its completeness lay a masterly revelation of a curate's soul. Diaries are among the most censored forms of literature. Those who bring the scissors to them leave spaces in which imagination and conjecture thrive. Kilvert's has us peering into his personality but finally into his world, of which he gives as full and satisfying picture as we can desire. It is a diary to read beside old photo albums and nineteenth century memoirs and novels. And the poetry of Gerard Manley Hopkins.

On Tuesday 3 November 1874, after a brilliant entry on the sounds of the countryside as he walked near Langley Burrell, from 'the strange hoarse belling of the buck' to 'the merry voices of the Marquis's children at play', Kilvert wrote, 'Why do I keep this voluminous journal? I can hardly tell. Partly because life appears to me such a curious and wonderful thing that it almost seems a pity that even such a humble and uneventful life as mine should pass altogether away without some record ...'

Once on the Longest Day, whilst on a visit to his birthplace Hardenhuish in Wiltshire, he reflects on his life as he stands by the font for a christening. Outside 'lay the wide fair plain smiling in the summer afternoon sunshine, as I used to see it from my nursery window, looking southward to the tower of Colerne Church on the windy hill, and the long faint blue line of Salisbury Plain. I thought of my own christening on that mid-winter day January 3rd 1841, more than thirty-five years ago. As I left the churchyard and crossed the lane to the stone steps which led up to the little green wicket garden gate between the twin elms there came from the Rectory to meet me a pretty bright-faced, bright-haired girl, the Rector's daughter, sweet Gertrude Headley ... We took no kiss, only she gave me a bright glance ... The "Kiss at the Gate"* is a sweet delicious flower but it is old fashioned now and does not grow by the green wicket. Yet I know a gate by which that flower still blows, and by that gate I once did pluck that flower.'

This is an example of that sentiment which V. S. Pritchett says we have lost – which is beyond us, but which is so surely Kilvertian. Kilvert has been seen as one of those parish-trapped people but he was in fact a constant traveller. Train and carriage journeys, roads and scenery, and walking, keep his Diary always on the move. Compared with today's clergy with their united benefices, his church duties were minimal. He wrote his sermons and they must have been delightful to listen to. He witnessed the effect of the 1870 Education Act and he visited the terrible workhouses. He was officially concerned with the local bank. He was kind and intrigued where vagabonds, gypsies and wanderers were concerned, and we have glimpses of homelessness and Dickensian fates.

* Heartsease = Viola arvensis

PARSON WOODFORDE

(Introduction to *Woodforde's Diaries*, Canterbury Press, 1999)

It was just after World War I that a Hertfordshire doctor persuaded his neighbour John Beresford to take a look at a diary kept by an ancestor who had been the rector of a village near Norwich during the years 1776-1802. The diary actually began on 21 July 1759 when its owner, James Woodforde, heard that he had been accepted as a scholar of New College, Oxford. Beresford was enthralled, as every reader of Parson Woodforde has been to this day, and in 1924 he published the first of his five-volume extract of the diary, complete with notes and a now somewhat bland assessment of its author. Its popularity is now only equalled by that other and quite different clerical masterpiece, *Kilvert's Diary*, which was published a decade or so later. As their authors were the very epitome of the country clergy of their day, the one late Georgian, the other late Victorian, no two journals could be less alike. For they are, amongst so much else, brilliant pictures of traditional English rural society viewed from its orthodox religious base.

Woodforde's is the spiritually comatose base of the Church of England still unawakened by Wesley and the sacramentalists of the Oxford Movement. He himself is a country gentleman occupying a living and doing his duty, a sociable bachelor who is looked after by his niece Nancy and five servants. Strangely it may seem, for he is neither eccentric nor passionate, clever, saintly, nor scandalous, this very ordinary figure for his time is now among the most unforgettable characters of English literature. The reason for this is that in his diary he neither puffs nor censors himself but simply allows his ordinariness to fill its pages – in very beautiful handwriting, as it happens. He has a reverence for small events and the domestic odds and ends of existence: 'This I thought deserving of notice, even in so trifling a book as this is,' he writes on 27 November 1789, as he puts down a cure for the cramp. In his autobiographical *Finding the Gate* V. S. Naipaul remarks, '... as diarists and letter-writers repeatedly prove, any attempt at narration can give value to an experience which might otherwise evaporate away.' The world can only guess at James Woodforde's motive for not letting his very solid life vanish into thin air, although it certainly wasn't vanity.

James Woodforde was born in 1740 at Ansford, Somerset, the second son of the vicar. His father also held the living of nearby Castle Cary. The Woodfordes had been significant priests of the Church of England for three generations and the diarist's grandfather, through his friendship with Izaak Walton and Thomas Ken, had links with the sacred world of George Herbert and Nicholas Ferrar. But all that James inherited from his forebears were the conventions of the country parson's role, plus a modest but unfailing kindness and level-headedness.

He was ordained at twenty-three and spent the next decade as a curate in his father's parishes. It was on Guy Fawkes Day 1774, while working as a proctor at New College, Oxford, that he heard of a vacancy in one of the many livings which were in the gift of his college, '... in Norfolk, by name of Weston Longeville worth it is said £300 per annum'. Five weeks later, '... I was declared and presented with the Presentation of the Rectory.' The immortal days ten miles from Norwich had begun. But there is no rush. This is the Church of England of George III's reign and it takes the new parson a year and a half to take up residence. He does so with his handsome nephew Bill whose effect on the servants makes him 'uneasy'.

The first of a memorable line of male servants, which was to include the Shakespearianly-named Brettingham Scurl and Barnabas Woodcock, also appears. Woodforde always refers to his five servants as 'our folk'. They and he, and everybody in the village, observe rank and are at ease with each other in a way which would be incomprehensible a century later. Pregnancies among the maids are more of an economic than a moral disaster – his neighbour's footman has got two maids with child more or less at the same moment – and willing lads grow up to become 'saucy' young men. It is in his dealings with the staff that we catch rare snatches of emotions and revelation in Woodforde, and also of what it was like to live with six boisterous unmarried people, for as soon as the rectory was in order his niece Miss Woodforde arrived to do the honours, and was never to leave until her uncle died. The more one reads his diary, the more each member of the little household takes on the mystery and interest of a character in a great novel, which is curious, because Woodforde is above all one of those writers who never 'draws' a person. He is artless.

Among so much else, this remarkable diary is one of the most candid statements on the national Church in its doldrums. It is no wonder that another clergyman, the Reverend Charles Wesley, had forsaken snug rectories to re-teach the Gospel throughout Britain. Parson Woodforde disapproved of such 'enthusiasm', as it was called, just as he disapproved of singing in church, and anything which went beyond the formal Christian duties which regulated society: 'I read Prayers and Preached this Afternoon at Weston' sums up his weekly labours. He is very put out when anything occurs which enlarges these duties, such as being required to give a sermon in Norwich Cathedral. Many of his ceremonies are carried out in his best parlour and not in the church, and these include many christenings. Although he has some 360 parishioners, he thinks it quite good to have 'two rails' or thirty communicants at Easter and Christmas. His church is only full for thanksgivings for military victories and recoveries from sickness of members of the royal family. He does no teaching and long before he himself is too ill to take services he pays a curate £30 a year to officiate for him.

Yet, spiritually defunct though his religion is, and unthinking and, to us, deplorable though so many of his ways are, we take to him. He is dully good and yet far from admirable, and the reader intuitively understands his difficulties and his humanity. For one thing, in spite of so much company, he is clearly rather lonely. Not that he ever complains about it, or about his lot generally. Being far more an

English gentleman than a complex priest, his code would not allow it. Parson Woodforde is a stoic.

No day passes without its charity being listed, if it is only a penny to a beggar. The rectory is first port of call in Weston for the destitute who drift through it, little boys, soldiers, pedlars, homeless women. There are many funerals and Woodforde is an authority on how we used to die. He watches executions, once of five young men together at Norwich. He buys smuggled goods. He is a freemason and a pillar of the Establishment. He is discreet and not a gossip. He is a giver of accurate, unadorned information and not a storyteller. But he needs to know what is going on and is always sending Scurl his servant to Norwich for news.

The unfolding in the diary of the English countryside as it was just before the Industrial Revolution and the nineteenth-century Enclosure Acts is magnificent. Woodforde actually says very little about agriculture and its economics, then the nation's chief business activity, but he often provides the nearest thing which we have to a total documentary of a winter or summer day in the 1780s. He and the gentry 'rotate', as they call it, entertaining each other to dinner, backgammon and cards in turn, and again the movement and conservation of some half dozen families, thrown together for the best part of the year due to bad roads and a network of rural dependencies, contain the inner drama of the classic country novel, although one low in dialogue. Woodforde is no Boswell and reports little conversation. He reports what is eaten and what is done, not what is said. His observations are masculine and they lack nuance, insight or even inquisitiveness, though never truthfulness. He ties in human behaviour to the season's food and weather, and, somewhat perfunctorily, to the Church calendar. The diary is one of the most English books ever written.

And here one must say something about what he said so much – meals. The emphasis placed on them is so disproportionate to that placed on anything else that Woodforde has acquired a reputation for gluttony, when he should only have been indicted for conviviality or, as it seems as one reads him into late middle age, for attempted conviviality. The old custom of loading the table with a great many dishes of roasts, fish and game all at once, instead of serving them as courses, now suggests gross appetites, but while Woodforde certainly put eating high on the list of his enjoyments, it would be unfair to say that this is what he lived for. He lived for agreeable company and the intimacy and pleasure it brought to his essentially lonely existence, his niece Nancy notwithstanding. When, last thing before sleeping, he confides the day's menus to his diary it often reminds us of a child's blissful recollections of a party.

Dinner, with dear ones, is the zenith of his day and he never stints himself in the recording of it. The first full appreciation is at Oxford when he is nineteen:

DEC. 25. I received the Sacrament being Xmas Day. The Warden dined in Hall with us. The Bursars give us Scholars 8 Bottles of Port Wine to drink at dinner time. They likewise give us a qutr of a Cheshire Cheese. We have 2 large Grace Cups between courses. We have rabbits for supper, 1 Rabbit between three at the expense of the Domus. Sent a letter to my Father.

Over forty years later come his very last diary words, written ten weeks before his death:

Very weak this Morning, scarce able to put on my Cloaths and with great difficulty, get down Stairs with help. Mr. Dade read Prayers & Preached this Morning at Weston Church – Nancy at Church. Mr. & Mrs. Custance & Lady Bacon at Church. Dinner to day. Rost Beef &c.'

There is no development in Woodforde from teenager to elderly country cleric either as a man or stylist. His diary is extraordinary for the way in which it reveals a person who never changed any of his ideas from beginning to end. He carries within himself the manners, conventions, pleasures, attitudes and hopes of the middle-class man of his age, never decorating, analysing or out-growing them and there are few books which allow us to step so immediately into the rooms and fields of Georgian England. Woodforde even costs his world, for the diary is also a meticulously kept account book, with the price of wages, food, stagecoaches, household necessities, tips, gifts, clothes, theatres, candles, hairdressers, medicines, etc., all carefully entered.

His income was about £400 a year and he lived in some style within it, never grousing about money or trying to get more of it. His conscience and, to a degree, his indifference to wealth earned him a local reputation for generosity, although we, recognizing the tremendous comfort in which he lived, compared with the majority of his parishioners and the citizens of Norwich, might find this easily earned. But Weston Rectory was often very reminiscent of a little medieval hospital in the way it distributed comforts and funds to itinerates, and Woodforde never took fees, although entitled to do so, when he married, buried or in any other way legalized the lives of the poor. Once a year the local farmers bring him their tithes and spend the afternoon with him having a drunken 'tithe frolic', and scarce a week passes without seasonal offerings of fruit, game, fish and other delicacies from the big houses all around.

Not even below the surface, but in plain view of this bounty, is misery and hardship of such chronic proportion and familiarity that it troubles the reader that Woodforde and his circle are able to live with it without guilt. A similar pragmatism applies to his attitude towards hangings and bloodsports. What Woodforde and his civilization could countenance without a qualm, and this might even include their shocking diets, is the most intriguing revelation here. We read things like the following, realizing that we are indeed in a cool era.

> We dined at 3 o'clock and after we had smoked a Pipe etc., we took a ride to the House of Industry about 2 miles West of Dereham, and a very large building at present tho' there wants another Wing. About 380 Poor in it now, but they don't look either healthy or cheerful, a great Number die there, 27 have died since Christmas last [in three months]. We returned from thence to the King's Arms and then we supped and spent the evening together. To Mr. Hall's Clerk of Garveston who came to give him notice of a Burial on Friday, being very poor, gave, 0.1.0.

The other sombre aspect of the diary and part of those dark realities which balance up its enchanting canvas of Gainsborough-like rural society in amiable movement round the respectable figure of a sporting parson, is of illness. Due to Woodforde's honesty and lack of euphemism when it comes to the failings of the flesh – in both senses – we have a record of his health in all its phases. In many ways he was wise about treatment, keen on vaccination and full of practical measures when any of his little household was sick. But we also see how people had to live with all kinds of non-diagnosable complaints, deal with pain and ignorance, especially of what their heavy eating and drinking could do to their bodies. Nor was Woodforde the type of man who thought of a village as a retreat and all through his diary we are ceaselessly aware that we are in one of history's epoch-changing revolutionary periods.

But the overall power of this rich diary stems from its perfect chronicling of the heart of an eighteenth-century clergyman.

GOD'S TRIP TO DORSET

(Introduction to *Mr. Weston's Good Wine*, Hogarth Press, 1984)

Theodore Francis Powys was fifty-two when this, his greatest novel, was published in 1927. He was already thinking of himself as a writer while still in his teens and working a small farm at Swefling, Suffolk. Having been educated at an Aldeburgh school run by family friends, it probably seemed quite a reasonable thing for his parents to do to place this large, strong, seventeen-year-old in such a situation, to give him independence and to see what he would make of it. There were also considerable family associations in the area, for although Theodore's father, the Reverend Charles Powys, was obsessed by what he believed was his descent from Welsh princes, his mother was equally proud of her Norfolk descent from the poet William Cowper. Theodore had often spent holidays at his grandfather's Norfolk rectory, and what with the close companionship of his headmaster's son Louis Wilkinson, a young man who was to play an influential role in the lives of a number of the Powys children, there was a period during his early years when Theodore must have felt himself less West Country than East Anglian. But his brothers John and Llewellyn were never even partially deceived and with that passionate sibling intuition regarding each other's states of mind and emotional need which was to hold them close to the end, they came to regard Theodore in Suffolk as Theodore in exile.

In any case there could not have been a worse time, economically speaking, to be thrown into farming, than this 'coming down time' of the long agricultural depression. Village life was running into poverty and ruin, and a new kind of harshness was beginning to appear in rural society. Added to which, this son of the rectory, brought up in a secure, unquestioning Anglican orthodoxy, was discovering that he was the kind of person who would question everything. Question but not dismiss, not rout or not replace – which is by far the least comforting of all reactions to what one is told one must believe. It was easier for John Cowper Powys, who replaced the Trinity with the thousand divine essences of the universe, and for Llewellyn Powys, who became an atheist and free of all gods. Theodore's difficulty was to retain a mounting admiration for Jesus which was in proportion to his mounting dislike of God. What to do with God became the Powyses' main dilemma, as a moral and imaginative force, that is. John broke him down into sacred facets which caused every hill, stream, rock and plant to illuminate existence, Llewellyn eroticised him (which all three brothers did to a large extent) but Theodore catechised him, and never more brilliantly than in *Mr Weston's Good Wine*. The title comes from the scene in Jane Austen's *Emma* where the young rector Mr Elton, returning with Emma in her carriage when she knew 'he had been drinking too much of Mr Weston's good wine, and felt sure that he would want to be talking nonsense', has the nerve to make love to her. What is it that God gives his creatures? Theodore Powys asks. Is it dutch courage or a blurred vision, or an opiate? Or that bliss which pours from the fruit of the true vine? Men, particularly clergymen of course, having explained God for centuries, he now very respectfully but firmly asks God to explain himself, which he does as well as he can, and certainly without talking nonsense. It is an audacious theme for a novel and perfectly sustained to the last page.

All three Powyses remained profoundly religious men who had, each in his own way, got themselves unchurched. This was in no sense part of the usual post-Darwinian dilemma and loss of faith but the result of their dramatic understanding of the mystical nature of what we call reality. The effect of the rejection of their conventionally imbibed Anglicanism was for all of the brothers one of expansion and release, for Theodore the heretic most of all. They recognised that they had made a collective advance into an exciting creed-less dimension and for the rest of their lives they shared the discoveries made there, including the sexual ones. Yet it remained a sacred dimension and the quandary for the modern reader is how to perceive and comprehend this triple-stranded Powys sacredness. Calling Theodore's novels and short stories 'black comedy', Llewellyn's essays and autobiographies 'erotic' and John's novels Celtic fantasies simply won't do. Powysdom continues to be a rare literary height because it offers some of the eternal views in an inimitable language. Writing of the brothers the poet Peter Redgrove made the point that 'the occult or magical life, the life lived according to "a reality behind the veil", the Romantic or symbolic life, gets an exceedingly bad press in the serious journals of our age. It is the positivistic spirit that has prevailed, which claims that the surface reality apparent to our conscious senses is all that matters, and that there are no "unconscious" senses at all, through which the unseen influences the seen. It has been difficult for scholars to accept that the magical view of life of so great a writer as W. B. Yeats was not just an aberration but his very core; and it is likely that the paganism of the brothers Powys has not helped them towards the wide acceptance which is their right.' This is true. It is fatuous to dismiss the core of a writer's imagination as a weakness or as something which can no longer be taken seriously, when it is clearly the centre of his art and originality. At the heart of all three Powys brothers lay what might be described as a Natural mysticism, that sensuous searching and probing of this life, this earth.

Theodore was the third of the Reverend Charles Powys's eleven children by his wife Mary Cowper Johnson and part of a triumvirate which has no parallel in English literature. Although so individual and so different, John, Theodore and Llewellyn project a unity, a blood vision which continues to synchronise whatever they are writing. They remain curiously undated too, even when, as with *Mr Weston's Good Wine*, nothing is spared to evoke an historic moment in 1923. They were near-contemporaries of Arnold Bennett, H. G. Wells, Virginia Woolf, E. M. Forster and John Galsworthy, but their names do not suggest a similar period connection. It is because by imposing a kind of religious timelessness on their stories and essays, they appear to have severed them from the chronological position in which one would expect to find them. 'The Powys Brothers' do not sound Edwardian, or

Twenties or decadal in any way, they simply sound very old and very new, like a mountain morning. It is still a disturbing business to become involved with them, and with Theodore especially.

He was born in Shirley, Derbyshire on 20 December 1875, where his father was the vicar. Ten years later the family moved to Montacute, Somerset, and into that myth-filled countryside which was to have such a lasting and profound effect on it. Theodore left school when he was fifteen, soon grew a large moustache which, wrote his friend Louis Wilkinson, made him look 'astonishingly like Nietzsche. I remember him as a heavily built young man with grey melancholy eyes. His manners were courteous to the point of what seemed to me an ironic deference. Always he was a countryman ...' Wilkinson added that he also saw in Theodore a mixture of fantasy and cruelty, benevolence and poetic sensitiveness, plus a 'goblin humour'. Already he had begun upon that long dialogue between himself and God which he was to bring to such a brilliant conclusion in *Mr Weston's Good Wine*. He wasn't happy and would rarely ever be. In 1902 he went to write in a cottage at Studland on the Dorset coast. Shortly afterwards he met his future wife, a practical, good-hearted and uneducated village girl named Violet Dodds, telling his brothers, 'I don't want anything intellectual. I want little animals' roguery. I don't like ladies.' It was Violet's famous talkativeness and her entrée to a great range of colourful rural experience which brought him into imaginative contact with a whole new world of rural drama. In 1907 his first book, *An Interpretation of Genesis*, was privately published, after which he turned to fiction, and a long stream of novels and short stories, all of which were rejected. But in 1926 he published an essay called *Soliloquies of a Hermit* in which he sees himself as a 'priest' and a kind of secular mystic, someone who is always on the alert to 'catch God in His own thought', and this too shows him moving towards the darkly witty God-or-man argument of *Mr Weston's Good Wine*. About this time he summed himself up in a caustic thumbnail portrait. 'Mr Thomas is married, and he digs in his garden... [He is] what we call in the polite world, "a crank"... Mr Thomas used... to brood in odd corners and try to hatch a little God out of his eggs – a little God that would save his type, the outcast monk type.' These years of toil and neglect were brought to a halt when a friend introduced him to a writer some eighteen years his junior, and who as yet had had nothing accepted. Her name was Sylvia Townsend Warner. It was she who immediately understood his uniqueness and excellence, and who got the influential David Garnett to bring his work to the attention of Chatto and Windus. The celebrated country stories then began to appear in rapid succession; first *Black Bryony* and then on via *Mockery Gap* and *Mr Tasker's Gods* to his masterpiece.

In his remarkable collective biography *The Brothers Powys*, Richard Perceval Graves quotes Sylvia Townsend Warner on the way in which Theodore worked. His 'books grew like stalactites and stalagmites. He deposited them, secretively and methodically – a process taking place in a cave. After breakfasting, rather late, and leisurely, he went off to the parlour, sat down before a large solid table, read for half an hour (usually in the Bible) and then set to work. He wrote uninterruptedly for three hours or so, put his work back in the table drawer, and began again, where he left off, on the following morning... When I happened to pass the window, I saw the same grave, dispassionate countenance, pen moving over the paper, dipping at regular intervals into the inkpot.'

T. F. Powys's maternal ancestor, William Cowper, could have provided the initial idea for *Mr Weston's Good Wine* when he began a hymn with 'God moves in a mysterious way his wonders to perform' and ending it with, 'God is his own interpreter, and he will make it plain'. The Deity in the guise of a travelling salesman selects an average English village in order to inform himself of the current state of the world. *Has* he made it plain? – that is the recurring question. Life, death, good and evil, time and timelessness? The reader is invited to come to judgment. God, alias Mr Weston, ages past started something which he now needs to take stock of. Not wishing to create too much interest in a country parish, he drives to it in a Ford van labelled 'Mr Weston's Good Wine' but as this is 1923, it creates interest enough. Especially as Mr Weston's assistant is a staggeringly good-looking young man who is clearly the same person as that painted on the sign of the Angel Inn. The date is 20-21 November, a significant one, for it is the week before Advent, and Mr Weston could be thoughtfully getting his visit over before there is another arrival. The Sunday of the week of Mr Weston's visit would have been called 'Stir up Sunday' by the inhabitants of Folly Down, from the first line of the collect, 'Stir up, we beseech thee, O Lord, the wills of thy faithful people,' and stir them up Mr Weston certainly does, but also himself in the process.

What he witnesses, understandingly, forgivingly, and guiltily, is a marred creation, and what he offers is not the possibility of perfection but a palliative. To be human is to be flawed, badly or slightly, but imperfect all the same. His wine cannot, or perhaps must not (or 'what's a heaven for?') mend these flaws but it can make them privately tolerable and publicly less damaging. What Mr Weston offers, in fact, and here lies the essence of the T. F. Powys heresy, is not the wine of salvation but the wine of comfort. Strict to his quirky Christianity, the writer drew comfort from the weekday liturgy in Mappowder Church but refused its chalice on his deathbed.

The novel opens in the market-town of Maidenbridge which serves as the prelude for the main drama of life which, of course, always takes place in a village. Mr Weston's course is to consult his assistant on everybody who walks down the street or emerges from a doorway. The atmosphere is one of ennui and an exquisite provincial dullness wittily observed. What T. F. Powys achieves here is a view of the town as the rustic eye sees it, a community caught up in a broader but not necessarily more dramatic rhythm than that of the countryside. After it has been tantalisingly set in motion for a few brief pages the whole place disappears until the last sentences of the novel when Mr Weston, deputising for the author, says, 'We have forgotten Miss Nancy Gipps.' She is the first of those 'affectionate and forgiving' women who populate Powys's erotic imagination and who he can hardly bear to fall into the clutches of the mainly brute males who either ignore them or pursue them like quarry. Miss Gipps loves Mr Board the Mayor of Maidenbridge, who could scarcely be less worthy of her. The first girl whom Mr Weston and Michael actually encounter is the one they run over on the way to Folly Down, a mere child who, of course, is at once restored to health. But Michael muses on her future:

> 'A human girl-child is a creature set in a dish for time to feed upon. She wears garters, frocks, and petticoats, and later, frills and pink ribbons. She walks out on the seventh day of the week and sighs for a pair of holiday trousers. They meet and embrace, and amuse themselves as best they may for a few short years, and then they fall sick and go down to the dead.'
> 'And what harm is there in that?' asked Mr Weston, guiding the car carefully round a corner.

Before Mr Weston drives down into the hamlet which is to be the representative of all the countless groupings which Christian men have formed on the earth, he stops the car to stretch his legs 'and walk upon this pleasant hill'. Blake's question is answered. Those feet have walked upon England's mountains green. The triumph of *Mr Weston's Good Wine* is achieved by the utmost delicacy of its references, a kind of definite feather touch. This is where it entertains yet is simultaneously profound. Mr Weston-God, who had 'risen, as so many important people do, from nothing', and who 'had once written a prose poem divided into many books', and who can say, 'How often I have to remind you, Michael, that in our trade report the women come last. Ours is the only business, you know, that they do not dominate,' is both Creator and his critique in one. While he puts Folly Down to rights, its people – his creation – are able to tell him a thing or two.

T. F. Powys's English village is far removed from what we have been told by others in fact and fiction. It is his own village-bred sights and deeds and dreams reduced to the common pattern of country life and made to animate an insular community. The characters are all the things he fears or desires. Some are gargoyles, some medieval saints. Class is barely relevant and is kicked around like a piece of meaningless finery. A fiercely protected gullibility reigns. To challenge the general acceptance of what has to be believed would be like cutting short the ramblings and point of some self-satisfying old tale. Everybody knows his or her place, but it is the place in a game.

Nobody stops playing when someone gets hurt. T. F. Powys's most brilliant comic invention is Folly Down's gargantuan ignorance, its meticulously maintained state of unknowing. To possess a vision which went beyond the parochial view of life would be a terrible handicap in Folly Down. Was this the reason why Mr Grobe the rector did not send his daughter Tamar (the height of the author's girl-fantasies) away to school? Or was it simply sloth? Tamar's ignorance of the facts of life did at least allow her to marry an angel unawares, so perhaps her father did right.

Before this apotheosis beneath the oak tree, Michael, now in his role of Recording Angel, presents the local inhabitants, one at a time, to Mr Weston, who lovingly assesses which of them needs the wine of comfort, strength and hope, or the wine of oblivion, who needs a not too clear view of reality and who needs the cup to speed him beneath the waters of Lethe. Except for the rector, who doesn't believe in God and who has a benign notion of his fellow men, Folly Down is roughly divided between those who put all the ills of the world down to the Almighty and those who put them down to human lust, or 'wold Grunter', as they call their gravedigger-sexton. Mr Grunter is the village scapegoat or sin-eater, a role he silently accepts; although quite innocent himself of the debaucheries attributed to him, he carries in his person both the guilt and the gallantry. In a small place, you can't go around blaming everybody for every wronged girl, so you blame only one – 'old Grunter', or human failings personified. The villagers are made to reveal their entire characters through their sexuality alone and, contrary to what the Christian religion insists, Powys's God finds this natural enough. What is hateful to him is male cruelty in the pursuit of sex and the blunting of tenderness in some older women. Mrs Vosper, who procures girls for the layabout sons of the squire, is a heartless, voyeuristic bawd who, it has to be said, also procure's keyhole excitements for the author himself. But they are artistically deliberate excitements and all part of a black comedy in which Powys's creative eroticism has to find literary expression. His unmarried girls drift about the lanes in peril and innocence, his married women are house-bound drudges with sharp tongues in their heads. Jenny Bunce, the landlord's daughter and maid at the Rectory, who is the epitome of all good and lovely village girls, is, by the grace of Mr Weston's wine, brought most joyously to the arms of an untypical man, the rather girlish himself Luke Bird (alias St Francis) who, after losing his job in the brewery by preaching teetotalism, now spends his time bringing bulls and sparrows to Christ.

Having interviewed everybody, taken a look into the church (the first time he has ever been in one), and seen the two extremes of human conduct, plus that large middling section of it which does nothing very good and little that is awful, Mr Weston shakes his head, which, of course, is as white as wool, and asks himself, 'where did I go wrong?' In creating the world and the need for each generation of its living creatures to replenish themselves? In not seeing that all men were given a far greater share of God's finer feelings? Saddened, self-critical, Mr Weston's conclusion is that Man since the Fall having become on the whole incorrigible, his love for him is best expressed in healing, or diverting him from the excesses of his waywardness and instincts, or in drugging him when things become unendurable. And so, in faultless allegorical language, Mr Weston does his Folly Down round while time stands still. A perfect balance is struck between the novel's wit and satire, and its profundity. There is nothing comparable to it. Now over half a century old, it joins the classic tales of the English countryside, as well as being one of the most penetrating statements on the role of the Christian God in the post-Constantinian era.

ALL THIS BLESSEDNESS IS OURS

(The 1995 Julian Lecture)

Delay and anonymity are among the most intriguing forces in religion. Time holds great matters in suspense and ignores signatures. A medieval woman tells us a thousand things about herself but never her name. Evidently she gave it up when she entered her order, for her contemporary Margery Kempe addressed her as 'Dame Jelyan'. The *Revelations of Divine Love* re-surfaced in the 17th century, but only for a few readers, and as a quaint old book. Our own way to it has been cleared by excellent guides, Clifton Wolters in particular. This once Provost of Newcastle not only translated and edited Julian's masterpiece, allowing us easy access, but the mystical writings of Richard Rolle and the anonymous author of *The Cloud of Unknowing*, all three volumes for Penguin Classics, and bestsellers in their way. Most of us know these paths to Christ via Wolters.

The mystics entice us with their holy travels. They say, 'Start moving – you can enter those exciting scenes. All this can be yours.' I was drawn to this spot from which Julian issued her guide because it had suffered a similar fate to an ancient church just up the lane from my old farmhouse. There stood until 21st September 1940 the medieval parish church and priory of St. Peter and St. Paul, when, at 9.40 p.m. it was utterly destroyed by a German landmine. This priory had been founded by a married couple, Robert and Beatrice Godbold. A few days before the bomb a friend of mine, then a girl, had painted the picturesque group of old buildings amidst the late summer trees. Only a few hours before the explosion the last wedding took place, that of an R.A.F. officer and his bride. He would be killed in the air a few months later. So all that remains is a picture. Not long ago I came to Norwich for a wedding and, being rather early, sat here in St Julian's churchyard. I became conscious of something glittering in the flower-bed. it was a fragment of painted glass, a part of a picture from centuries ago.

Dame Julian seems to have been aware that she might attract followers because she several times warns her readers against taking any personal interest in her. 'So I beg you all for God's sake, and advise you for your own, to stop thinking about the poor wretch who has shown you these things, and with all your strength, wisdom and humility look at God'.

She explains, 'The fact that I have had revelation does not mean that I am good'.

She insists, 'There is no doer but He.'

She says, 'So I saw him and sought him. I had him and I wanted him. It seems to me that this is, and should be, an experience common to us all.'

She goes on, 'I could see no difference between God and our substance, it was all God, so to speak.'

And then she adds the reminder which I have taken as the title for this lecture, 'All this blessedness is ours.' Meaning ours just for the taking.

We Christians of the 20th century tend to reel back from such plain language. Let those with clear and holy eyes do such close looking for us. Let these special people advise us in a clear and holy language what we should do, where we should go. But Julian will have none of this. She says, 'My book is not some devotional manual, some pretty book of hours to accompany the stern liturgy, it is a simple textbook for those who wish to study Jesus and to find him, 'So I saw him and I sought him. I had him and I wanted him. It seems to me that this is, and should be, an experience common to us all.'

For all her famous 'poor wretch' put-downs of herself, and for all her cautious references to 'Holy Church', Julian cannot but help give instruction and inspiration with the confidence of a master. Nor was her book intended as a spiritual autobiography and nothing else. It is a collection of lessons. Lesson one for beginners: 'Pray inwardly even if you do not enjoy it.' We are advanced students by the time we reach lesson fifty-nine.

> All this blessedness is ours through mercy and grace. We should never have had it, or known it, if goodness [that is, God] had not been opposed. It is because of this that we enjoy bliss... God is really our Mother as he is our Father. He shows this throughout and particularly when he said that sweet word, 'It is I.' In other words, 'It is I who am the strength and goodness of Fatherhood; I who am light and grace and blessed love. I who am Trinity: I who am Unity: I who am the sovereign goodness over every single thing; I who enable you to love: I who enable you to long; It is I, the eternal satisfaction of every genuine desire.

Julian then proceeds as only she can, logically, revolutionarily, 'So we see that Jesus is the true Mother of our nature, for he made us. He is our Mother too by grace, because he took our created nature upon himself. All the lovely deeds and tender services that beloved motherhood implies are appropriate to him. In him God's will is always safe and sound.'

I began to work on this lecture in Holy Week and one of the things I discovered, as I am sure that you have done, was that large lumps of the Revelations had fallen out of my head. The appallingly naturalistic images of the Crucifixion, for example. Of course I recalled the famous image of the body 'like some cloth hung out to dry.' But I had half-forgotten, probably because it is so dreadful, Julian's clinicism, her merciless descriptions of bruising and discolouration. She never forgot what was going on just up the road from her as the Church exterminated the Lollards. Christ, being man, also decayed under official violence, as did the young heretics in the Norwich pit; as did the myriad innocents in the concentration camps.

> It was after this that Christ showed me something of his passion near the time of his dying. I saw his dear face, dry, bloodless, and pallid with death. It became more pale, deathly and lifeless. Then, dead, it turned a blue colour, gradually changing to a browny blue, as the flesh continued to die. For me his passion was shown primarily through his blessed face, and particularly by his lips. There too I saw these same four colours, though previously they had been... fresh, red and lovely. It was a sorry business to see him change as he progressively died. His nostrils too shrivelled and dried before my eyes, and his dear body became black

and brown as it dried up in death; It was no longer its own fair, living colour.

It is at this point that Julian's description of the death of Jesus reaches consummate heights of literary power. It is as though she has to shake us out of our painless contemplation of the Cross. She goes on, 'For at the same time as our Lord and Saviour was dying on the cross there was, in my picture of it, a strong, dry and piercingly cold wind. Even when the precious blood was drained from that dear body, there still remained a certain moisture in the flesh, as was shown me. The loss of blood and the pain within, the gale and the cold wind without, met together in that dear body... and I thought to myself that the withering of his flesh was the severest part... and his words came to mind, 'I thirst'... She continues quite unbearably. She calls the crown of thorns 'a garland' because 'we are his crown'.

A few years ago I set out on a series of walks from which to write a pilgrimage book. One of these walks was into the country of *Revelations of Divine Love*.

Here is what I found:

Deserts are now often regarded as ecological errors requiring correction. It is a view of them which would have astonished the early Church, for which they were the ultimate places for hearing the voice of God. The desert flower, spiritually speaking, was the hardest to pluck but the prize of all prizes. It thrived in silence and it was this special silence of the wilderness which drew men to it, not its hardships and inhospitality. They, however rough, were mere traveller's difficulties as he the created one, pressed on until, exactly how it was impossible to say for there was no language for such a union, he merged with his creator. People went to deserts because they were voids into which God spoke. Silence, too, is ultimate prayer and those who sought it in deserts felt that they were breathing in and exhaling prayer, that they were nearest to the physical aspect of this world which provided a suitable dwelling for its Maker. 'The silence of the mind is the true religious mind,' said Krishnamurti, 'and the silence of the gods is the silence of the earth. The meditative mind flows in this silence, and love is the way of this mind.' The tradition of deserts being where the divine voice can be listened to is among the most ancient and world-encompassing. Both the Judaic and Christian faiths were struck, as it were, in desert sand, and eremitism, or desert-dwelling, was the way of life of Christ's own cousin John. The eremite, (h)ermite or hermit, was a solitary person who attempted to develop his spiritual nature until, like a spacecraft, it escaped the pull of this earth and took off on a journey to God which transcended description. 'The English Mystics,' wrote Gerald Bullett, 'are those men and women who have enjoyed contact and communion with something more real than is given in everyday human experience, an utterly indubitable quickening power... ' Once in the desert, they besought its message. 'Elected silence, sing to me,' pleaded Gerard Manley Hopkins. St. John of the Cross wrote of 'la soledad sonorra' – of the vibrant sounds which informed solitude. Throughout his ministry Christ continually escaped to secret waste lands to be alone. Once, his desert-listening was shatteringly rewarded with the voice of his enemy, not his beloved Father. Such terrors were to be there for many of his desert-dwelling followers and Martin Luther understood them so well that he warned off Christians from what he regarded as fiend-infested desolate regions. 'The devils are in woods, in waters, in wildernesses, and in dark pooly places, ready to hunt and prejudice people.'

Post-medieval writers are very mixed in their feelings about solitude and its benefits. For them deserts were a treacherous nothingness and solitude itself either a break-down between an individual and society or, worse, a punishment. Although the behaviour of the young contemplatives known as the Essenes in Jesus's time, should have made desert-dwelling a fairly understandable activity, we know from the Jews' reaction to St. John the Baptist, the great proto-eremite, that it had not. St. John insisted that he was nothing more than a voice crying aloud in the wilderness, 'Make way for the Lord' – a herald, no more. His abnormality was to make a loud noise in a landscape where silence was usually practised. Jesus defended this strange kind of eremiticism. If John was mad, as they were calling him (he was near-naked and living on next-to-nothing) then why had they also been drawn to the desert, and in their droves? 'What was the spectacle that drew you to the wilderness? A reed-bed swept by the wind?' You went, he accused them, 'to see a prophet.' The verb in the desert context is startling. They went to stare and not to listen, which is the only reason for resorting to deserts. Later on Christ warned his followers against false prophets who would use deserts to amplify their messages. 'If they tell you, "He is in the wilderness," do not go out; or if they say, "He is there in the inner room" [the hermit's cell], do not believe it.'

It could be said that the early Church was eremitical or desert-dwelling through and through, not only because of the Desert Fathers, who literally lived in wild regions, but because for centuries the Church did its most important work, prayer and evangelisation, from monasteries which had been carefully sited for solitude. Many of the towns in which they now find themselves simply grew up from the settlement which had to provision them, provide labour for their farms or put up their guests. But gradually those who sought the mystic desert flower discovered a way of doing so, either in the community itself or at the very centre of ordinary human activity. After the Reformation even this desert-listening kind of vocation at the heart of things became incomprehensible and the path of solitude and silence became a worrying and questionable one. The wilderness itself ceased to be an empty, untamed terrain and became anywhere where men carried on their-God-ignoring activities. The novelist James Hanley allows a character to say, 'You talk about walking in the wilderness, but what else is the world but that, and besides, aren't we all walking in one wilderness or another since only we can make them?' Hanley was obviously thinking of the opening sentence of Bunyan's *Pilgrim's Progress* in which Christian says, 'As I walked through the wilderness of this world... '

Gradually, desert-dwelling as a way of coming close to the heart-centre of God, as a method of listening to him and catching glimpses of his face, was seen to be a discipline which could be practised in a busy city as advantageously as in an empty tract of waste land. Cities were every bit as parched, stony, dry and howling places as the wildernesses which sprawled between them. Villages too. By the fourteenth century it became almost a civic norm to attract religious solitaries to a town. The hermit was given a cell but was allowed to leave it and walk about, the 'recluse' could not. He or she totally withdrew from the world and were not seen. The anchorites and anchoresses (from the Greek *anachores* = I withdrew) were recluses who lived in rooms attached to churches according to the Ancrene Rule. They could not leave their anchorages but, having a window on to the world as well as one on to the altar, they combined their intensive prayer life with that of community advisor, and in many cases were the wisest of psychologists, welfare officers and confidants.

How and why Norwich became the eremitical centre of Britain remains mysterious in itself. Certainly as a city of metropolitan standing by the Middle Ages, the evidence of whose cultural, religious and political splendour can be seen to this day, and near enough to Europe's northern ports to receive every fresh idea and discovery, it could well have attracted the kind of intellectual men and women for whom reclusion presented an ideal existence. But the slowly emerging fact seems to be that there was something special about this tear-shaped Eastern capital in its many-towered flint walls lying on the south bank of the Wensum which paradoxically, drew together hundreds of solitaries, making it at one time as peopled a 'desert' as certain actual deserts were in the fourth century, when hermits lived in them in crowds. Norwich's role in this mystic journey would have been little more than a few scratchings in the local Records Office were it not for the fact that one of its many recluses, an anchoress named Julian after the little church to which her anchorhold was attached, wrote a book, the very first book, indeed to be written in English by a woman. It is called *Revelations of Divine Love* and because it has come down to us in two contemporary versions it is thought that the author wrote a short first account of the visions or 'showings' that are the subject soon after they happened, and then, twenty or so years later, a longer version which reflected the spiritual and intellectual growth which has occurred as a result of them, and also as a result of her highly developed prayer-life as a recluse. There is no proof that her fellow solitaries, or anyone else in Norwich or elsewhere either read it, or even knew of its existence, during her lifetime. Margery Kempe, the first English woman to write her autobiography, and who came to Julian for advice, and who spent 'many days' with her, makes no mention of it. Or it would be correct to say that Margery Kempe had her astonishing autobiography written down by a scribe, as she herself was illiterate, but such is its individuality, vigour and raciness that it cannot be said to be 'ghosted' in the modern sense. She was a solid well-to-do matron from Bishop's (King's) Lynn with a passion for God and travel who, after bearing fourteen children made a pact with her husband that they should have no more sex, and began to travel the world. Her adventures on the way to Canterbury, Jerusalem, Compostella and Rome, her troubled pursuit of holiness, and most overwhelmingly her candid portrait of herself as a noisy, tiresome female lacking in restraint, makes the *Book of Margery Kempe* one of the most revealing of all personal documentations of the late Middle Ages. In effect, Margery was the antithesis of Julian, yet the careers of both women witness to a degree of feminine freedom and power which can also be counted as fruits of the desert. Margery's description of her coming to Julian for advice over 'many days', written in what might be called as the self-despising third person, which was Margery's way of humility, is the only one we have of the great mystic. It is one of those treasured eyewitness statements which fall into the 'and did you once see Shelley plain' categories.

Then she was bidden by Our Lord to go to an anchoress in the same city, named Dame Jelyan, and so she did, and showed her the grace that God put into her soul, of compunction, contrition, sweetness and devotion, compassion with holy meditation and high contemplation, and fully many holy speeches and dalliance that Our Lord spoke to her soul; and many wonderful revelations, which she showed to the anchoress to find out it there were any deceit in them, for the anchoress was expert in such things, and good counsel could give. The anchoress, hearing the marvellous goodness of Our Lord, highly thanked God with all her heart for his visitation, counselling this creature to be obedient to the will of Our Lord and to fulfil with all her might whatever he put into her soul... I pray God, [said Julian] grant you perseverance. Set all your trust in God and fear not the language of the world, for the more despite, shame an reproof that you have in the world, [Margery's explosive behaviour and her loud weeping during worship in a Norwich church had brought her much abuse and criticism, as had her often challengely original theological views brought her near to accusations of heresy.] the more is your merit in the sight of God. Patience is necessary for you, for in that shall ye keep your soul.

The two women, Julian over seventy and Margery born the very year of Julian's 'showings' in 1373, would have stood on either side of the parlour window, learned ladies in their way, their profoundly different desert routes having brought them far along the path leading to the same goal. In her thumbnail sketch, Margery dictates a sentence from Julian which might be a quote from her *Revelations of Divine Love*. Margery has said in effect that the Holy Spirit sometimes inspires her to react unlovingly towards church services and those taking part in them, to which Julian replies, 'The Holy Spirit moveth ne'er a thing against love, for if he did, he would be contrary to his own self for he is all love.'

The most striking contract between Julian and Margery was that brought on their outlooks by a minimal and maximum sight, respectively, of the physical world. Margery had seen what few women of her time had seen, virtually the entire world as it was known to the medieval Christian. With her own restless Norfolk eyes. Julian had seen, perhaps, no more than a single city from the east and, after her enclosure, that same city from the south. Yet Margery the world-traveller came to her because she knew that the cell had provided Julian with a view of God that far surpassed anything she had seen in spite of all her experiences of Europe and the Middle East.

On the eighth of May 1373, the third Sunday after Easter, at four in the morning – the timing has a precision which seems at odds with a medieval century – the future 'Recluse atte Norwyche' had among other revelations a 'showing', as she preferred to call it, of God and his Son as a lord and his gardener. Julian was then thirty and would have been known to those surrounding what was very nearly her death-bed by her real name, which is now lost. Julian she probably came to be because the Benedictine Community at Carrow gave her leave to anchor herself to a little thatched church within its jurisdiction and dedicated to Julian the first Bishop of Mans, patron saint of hospitality, and to St. Edward. The church stood just above the Wensum ford which since Roman times had provided entrance to Norwich, and was convenient for anyone hoping to be well-received in it. From her world-window, Julian would have seen a constant procession of travellers seeking such divine favours as they climbed the hill to the church, also the new, crisp, flint walls and towers of the city, the new spire on the cathedral, the crowded King's Street running into it and the wild marshes and heathland beyond the river. It was there, in the desert, or on an uncared-for 'earth', as she called it, that her lord and his gardener expressed their 'two-fold truth.'

It is only scholastically human that when a six hundred-year old literary masterpiece is re-discovered that it should be combed for information other than that to do with its subject. One doesn't have to read very far into Julian's *Revelations of Divine Love* not to realise that its author, who lived a long life in this world, saw everything in it with a delight and comprehension which are unparalleled in devotional literature. So might there not be in its pages, unconsciously crept in below the figurative landscape of prayer, just a handful of plain views of fourteenth century Norfolk? There are, but only a few, and they catch the musing eye like the shadows cast by trees in an old photograph. Everybody who is momentarily captured by this kind of reality finds himself breaking Julian's God-bound narrative to stare at the actual mile or two of medieval scenery which is passing. These now famous distractions include an allusion to 'the seaground, with its hills and dales green seeming as it were most begrowing with wrake (seaweed) and gravel', a reference to the celebrated shrine of St. John of Beverley in the East Riding, which has made some historians wonder if she was a Yorkshire woman, particularly as the *Revelations* contain certain northern phrases, and touchingly homely things such as the blood from the crown of thorns spreading out across Christ's forehead 'like the scales of a herring', also, in its abundance falling 'like the drops of water that fall from the eaves after a heavy shower' and in an overwhelmingly realistic picture of the crucifixion, 'his hanging in the air, like some cloth hung out to dry'. What we have too is the great mass of eleventh to fourteenth century buildings of Norwich, and their decorative furnishings, which Julian would have seen before she was enclosed and which she would have heard about long after the door had been shut on the world, and the pattern of the city still virtually the same as the pattern of it which she held in mind.

As well as being full of mystics and solitaries of all kinds, Norwich was filled too with unprecedented disasters. The Lollard suppression, the Black Death, the Hundred Years' War and the Peasants' Revolt fall across its highly-developed religious life like the plagues of Egypt.

Julian saw its six thousand population cut by a third – she who had written 'Since I was still young I thought it a great pity to die' but yet able to write 'all shall be well.' Held at the centre of things by her vocation, Julian's felt words gain in authority when it is realised that she was able to say them when so much surrounding her was seething in violence, epidemics and annihilation. 'The ultimate philosophy of mysticism, as I understand it,' wrote Gerald Bullett, 'makes the world in which we find ourselves not less but more real: not a figment of fancy, not a solipsist dream, but an indubitable and significant experience in which we all share.' Julian's genius was her ability to show others how to share the highest reality that there is. Most mystics can do little more than point to a path. She found words to describe every inch of the sacred territory which prayer had opened-up to her. She remained in one spot and wrote one of the most tremendous of travel-books.

Naturally she would depict God and his Son (the Lord and his gardener) where she had come closest to them, in the desert, or on 'the bare, deserted earth', as she called it. There God sits until each individual finds him, when he makes 'man's soul to be his own city and his home.' Aware as she is that what was revealed during her sixteen 'showings' is, like the nature of God himself, inexpressible, Julian has no option but to resort to metaphor and to her own consummate use of English. 'Concrete imagery is the life of language; that which by its nature eludes exact expression can only be suggested, or hinted at, by resort to symbolism', says Gerald Bullet. 'Something is lost as well as gained by the process; but it is an inevitable one, and we can no more be surprised that the mystic expresses himself in terms of his own religious tradition than that he uses his own language... Mysticism is essentially empirical, not theoretical. Any theories built upon it can be, and should be, judged in the light of pure reason.' Julian's journey to God through Christ is that of a mystic of her day, but her ability to record it is such a dazzling one that its effect has been to make it a journey of all time. *Revelations of Divine Love* has become, six hundred years later, one of the most alluring of all spiritual progresses. Who, caught up in its optimism, rationality and verve, would not take his soul into the wilderness as a city for the Love dwelling there?

Julian, like her contemporary desert-guides, Walter Hilton, Richard Rolle and the anonymous author of *The Cloud of Unknowing* were one in their wish not to keep the delights of their spiritual path-findings to themselves. Quite the reverse, their books are charts which are purposely designed to lead anyone who reads them along the road to God. Julian, in her analogy of God and his Son to a rural lord and his obedient gardener, tells her readers, in effect, not to worry. She has a teaching, she says, which is 'like the beginning of the ABC'. Although she, like the other mystic guidebook authors, is writing for fellow solitaries, there is nothing cabalistic about her *Revelations of Divine Love*. It exists to channel the love of Christ into the universe. In the gardener revelation she explains about deserts and cities in the spiritual sense in which she experiences them. But before she arrives at this scene of Christ's matchless cultivation of love in a barren place, she provides the reader with her celebrated image of a hazelnut as God's perfectly finished, perfectly love-encompassed creation. It was the second thing she saw during the long sequence of her showings on that May morning as death receded from her, and when all her pain and weakness suddenly disappeared and 'I was as fit and well as I had ever been'. The first showing had been of the cruelly garlanded head of the dying Jesus, and of the Virgin looking like an ordinary simple girl, literally 'the handmaid of the Lord', instead of the Mother of God. After describing it Julian moves into one of the most inspired written concepts of the divine love since St. Paul. Nothing is lost or distractingly added if we fleetingly glimpse the spinneys and copses just beyond the walls of Norwich as we read it. Julian is only following her Master in her supremely effective use of plants as metaphors.

'And he showed me more, a little thing, the size of a hazelnut, on the palm of my hand, round like a ball. I looked at it thoughtfully and wondered, "What is this?" And the answer came, "It is all that is made." I marvelled that it continued to exist and did not suddenly disintegrate; it was so small. And again my mind supplied the answer, "It exists, both now and forever, because God loves it." In short, everything owes its existence to the love of God. In this little thing I saw three truths, the first that God made it; the second is that God loves it; and the third is that God sustains it... We have got to realize the littleness of creation and to see it for the nothing that it is before we can love and possess God who is uncreated.'

However reticent Julian is on the beauties and wonders of what has been created, it is impossible to read her without recognising that her joy, vitality, her sanity and spiritual energy were partly a response to the physical world. Like most recluses, she would have treasured its minutiae, the latticed sunshine, the tendrils of bindweed finding their way into the cell, the ways of her cat, the contrasting scents of the winter and summer fields blowing across the city, the single view of the outside which, due to the seasons and her own brilliantly trained gaze, did indeed become 'all that is made'.

When, in the fourteenth showing of God's love towards what he had made, Julian sees him as a lord who delights in the earthly treasure which he owns, it becomes clear that she is not at all the type of mystic who suppresses the splendours of this life for the life to come. As 'all that is made' was made out of love, and as love is infinite, the whole of Creation, according to her sensible thinking, was threaded through with what was deathless and eternal. Else, why should God have shown himself to her in the guise of a conscientious landowner who sent his only servant off to, 'do work that was the hardest and most exhausting possible'? The servant was to be 'a gardener, digging and banking, toiling and setting, turning and trenching the ground, watering the plants the while. And by keeping at this work he would, make sweet streams to flow, fine abundant fruits to grow... ' and that the treasure of the earth 'had its being in the wonderful depth of his eternal love. But its worth to him depended on the servant's careful preparation of it, and his setting it before him, personally. All around the master was nothing but wilderness'. Gradually, via agonising labour, the servant and his master are to be discovered neither in deserts nor in nature but at rest and peace in [their] own 'city'! Cities, not the countryside, however well-cultivated, being where one would expect to find all that was worthy, all that was powerful and sublime. A thousand years before Julian St Augustine had seen the Church as 'The City of God', and St. John had seen heaven as a new Jerusalem. Unlike those three other hermit geniuses of her day, the author of the incomparable *Cloud of Unknowing*, Richard Rolle and Walter Hilton, whose desert-dwelling seems to have been entirely developed in rural surroundings, Julian's appears to have been the far more difficult task of listening to God in a city which, during her lifetime, was the very antithesis of 'rest and peace'. How, for example, did she manage to exclude the spiritual hubbub set up by those other desert-dwellers cooped-up in Norwich's new walls? But how most of all did that amazing comprehension of love which she discovered, and (almost as amazing) found a language for, not become distracted and distorted by what was occurring around her? How was she able to say that, 'Sin is behovely [necessary] but all shall be well', when her city, fashioned in so many architectural ways according to heavenly principles, was black with the deaths of the plague-stricken, rebels against the feudal system, spiritual enquirers, not unlike herself, who came to grief with orthodoxy, and those engaged in what must have struck everybody as an everlasting war? It is salutary for the modern pilgrim to the site of Julian's cell to realize that today's Norwich, with all its traffic and a population swollen from six to a hundred and nineteen thousand, to remind himself that this city is probably quieter now than when she lived in it. And ironical to discover that St. Julian's, the tiny church to which she clung for her quiet life, itself ended up in the uproar of a direct hit by a German bomb in 1942. Fragments of the stones she saw have been incorporated in the new St. Julian's. But the building itself, in East Anglian terms, could never have been much and, like Bemerton and Little Gidding, and like the Baptist himself, one should visit it to listen, not to look. Julian grew old in the cell here, just one of a succession of listening women who dwelt by the chancel wall, and whose existence would now be as remote and elusive as theirs are had she not written or talked down her book.

The history of *Revelations of Divine* Love is not unlike the history of one of those ancient seeds which lie around for centuries in dry corners until some propitious combination of circumstances makes them germinate. And not only this, but its philosophical origins, too, had taken their time before managing to arrive at such an enchanting flowering. Where did Julian's astounding ideas come from? What is the point of her declaring that her visions were shown to 'a simple and uneducated creature' when she is clearly neither? Because of the conventions of her times, say some. Yet she clearly has a right to take her place with the supreme writers of her age, including Chaucer and Langland.

Apart from the Vulgate, Julian's main influence were the writings of a mystic named Dionysius whom she and all her contemporaries believed to be the Dionysius whom St. Paul converted at Athens, but who was actually a sixth century Syrian monk whose name is now lost. Neither of these feeders of her imagination were able to restrain her originality. She deflates the widely-held notion of her day that pursuing God was the specialised activity of a few good people. 'There is nothing very special about seeking. It is a thing that every soul can do with God's grace... So I saw him and sought him; I had him and wanted him. It seems to me that this is and should be an experience common to us all'. God is not only our Father but our Mother. Because we are for ever being born of him, Jesus too is our ever-loving Mother. 'This fine and lovely word Mother is so sweet and so much its own that it cannot properly be used of any but him.' Towards the end of her book she sums up the common experience of Adam-Everyman, as she calls him, or each human being. It is her Compline.

'Our faith is a light, coming to us naturally from him who is our everlasting Day, our Father and our God. By this light Christ, our Mother, and the Holy

Spirit, our Good Lord, lead us through these passing years. The light is measured to our individual needs as we face our night. Because of the light we live: because of the night we suffer and grieve. Through this grief we earn reward and thanks from God! With the help of mercy and grace, we know and trust our light quite deliberately and with it we go forward intelligently and firmly... ' Later she adds, wittily, 'In God's sight we do not fall; in our own we do not stand'.

Mother Julian is an upsetting and dangerous writer. It could never have been her intention to destabilise orthodox Christianity, yet she does. She draws her readers away from the comforts of accepted religious practices by which she herself must have been sustained to a great extent, and leaves them somewhat stranded in a brightness which at first puts them at a loss. While being a marvellous gazetteer to the spiritual rewards of the desert, every individual who succumbs to her guidance is finally left with a, 'Where do I go from here?' For reading about a journey is not the same as having made it. Mother Julian's readers are taken to where a sun-like love which permeates every fraction of the universe pours down on them, and are then expected to journey on in this glorious climate. Somebody said that the words 'Theodidacta, profunda, ecstatica' should be carved on her tomb. Taught of God, profound, ecstatic. But where is her tomb? Beneath the little car-park? Beneath long-settled bomb-dust from 1942? At Carrow Abbey with those of many other clever ladies? Where ever it is, or was, for her it would have been of no consequence. There is something distinctly anti-relic about her and she might well have appreciated those Arabian customs which decree that even the bodies of kings should lie in unmarked sand. As Britain's increasingly powerful desert-trained religious voice, Mother Julian speaks only from where life is. Her mysticism incorporates all things physical and all things spiritual. 'I had in part, received a touch of God – and it was fundamentally natural. For the foundation of our reason is in God, who is the substance of everything natural... We have our life and our being in nature... '